THE

BLESSING

THE BLESSING

God's Plan for Mankind

ROTIMI KALEB

Word Alive
International

WHAT LEADERS ARE SAYING ABOUT THE BLESSING: GOD'S PLAN FOR MANKIND

Rotimi Kaleb has seen the greatness of God first hand. He comes from a family of powerful influences. His gifting is to tell the next generation about the praiseworthy deeds of the Lord. Rotimi in this book teaches us not only our identity in God but on how to have a supernatural mentality. This book can inspire all of us to live a life at an Utmost Level.

- DR. TIM STOREY
> Life coach, Inspirational and Motivational speaker
> Senior Pastor of The Congregation
> Los Angeles, California

This is a great and inspiring book by Rotimi Kaleb. Rotimi has masterfully expressed revelational truth with such depth and brilliance that is profound. The book that you hold in your hands is not only informative but scripturally sound. In this book, you will discover how to enter into the fullness of God's Blessing.

- DR. PETER GAMMONS
> Bible Scholar and International Evangelist

With the skill of a wordsmith and the clarity of a teacher, Rotimi Kaleb uncovers truth regarding what it means to be blessed by God and how our live our lives in the Fullness of The Blessing of God. This book is a masterpiece that gives precise understanding of this subject. He has made his mark with this exceptional work. Everyone should read this one.

- BISHOP WAYNE MALCOLM
        Senior Pastor ICAN Community Church
        London, England

Our world is dominated by materialism and, for many believers, our Christian worldview and understanding of God's blessing is coloured by this popular perspective. Rotimi Kaleb helps us to refocus on what the Blessing really is. You will be refreshingly satisfied when you drop what you thought you knew of the Blessing and replace it with this timely revelation of God's point-of-view of the blessing through scripture. I already feel empowered!

- MUYIWA OLAREWAJU
        Radio and TV Presenter, Premier Radio and
        Turning Point International
        Recording Artiste
        London, England

The Word "BLESSING" is one of the most used among believers, yet it is one of the least understood. Having a thorough understanding of THE BLESSING is through revelation. Revelation is a reality that cannot always be seen, but can be discovered. In this book "THE BLESSING: GOD'S PLAN FOR MANKIND", Rev Rotimi Kaleb has unfolded a deep revelation that is capable of transforming your life if you can catch it.

The revelation begins from the introduction of the book; it is made clear that "THE BLESSING IS ALL THAT GOD HAS, RELEASED UNTO YOU." What a Blessing! No wonder Psalms 115:15 says "Ye are BLESSED of the Lord which made Heaven and Earth." No man can fully comprehend all that God has made in the Heaven and Earth that tell you about the quantum of THE BLESSING. But as far as you can see, you can get. Hallelujah!

Rev Rotimi clearly unfolded the revelation of the Root of the Word "To Bless" in another dimension that will revolutionize your life. The "Anatomy of THE BLESSING" is another portion of the Book that will change your entire life.

The book is loaded from the beginning to the end with incredible spiritual nourishment that will avail you with THE BLESSING. I highly recommend it for every believer. It is indeed THE BLESSING.

When Revelation comes, sorrow ceases and THE BLESSING is inevitable. If you read this Book carefully, you will say without any doubt that you have THE BLESSING indeed.

- REV. DR. JANE ONAOLAPO
> Author and Senior Pastor, Abundant Life Gospel Church
> Lagos, Nigeria

There have been many books penned in regards to blessings or the blessing of the Lord. However in his book, Rotimi Kaleb exposes hidden and powerful keys that will unlock the door to power living on the earth. After reading this expository treatise, I am once again challenged to dig deeper in the Scripture. The revelations of this book will jump off the pages and have great impact upon your life. It is a must read!

- DR. GLENN AREKION
> International Bible Teacher and Conference Speaker
> Louisville, Kentucky

Rotimi Kaleb has provided us with some powerful insights into the important subject of God's blessing. This is one of those topics, which properly understood, has the power to change our lives. I do pray that all who read Rotimi's book will find that it contributes to a truly life changing experience.

- DR. HUGH OSGOOD
> President, Churches in Communities
> International and Moderator, Free Churches in England
> London, England

Rotimi Kaleb has written a brilliant book that both encourages and challenges us with a fresh, vibrant and educating perspective on The Blessing. This book, The Blessing: God's Plan for mankind is a gourmet meal of spiritual and intelligent thought. If you are looking for God's Blessing on your life, I would encourage you to prayerfully read this, and receive the divine revelations that this book contains. I know you will be blessed!

- DAVID and CHENNELLE PALMER
        Senior Pastors, Harvest Time Ministry
        Vallejo, California

Rotimi Kaleb's book "The Blessing" is a blessed book, and certainly lives up to its name! Rotimi systematically unpackages an understanding of what the Blessing of God really is in an easy to read, yet profound book. I believe his writing is timely for our generation, and the contents of this book are necessary for the hour in which we are living. As the title states, "The Blessing" is "God's Plan for Mankind." I encourage everyone to read this book and embrace the blessing that God has for you!

- DEREK SCHNEIDER
        President of History Makers Academy
        and Founder of History Makers Society

Rev Rotimi is a dear friend who possesses the Spirit of excellence and inspires me every time I get around him. His passion to see every believer walk in the true image of God is unequivocal. That same passion shines through in this book and can be felt as you read it. There are books that encourage and inform and there are life-changing books. Read this one carefully and prayerfully; there is change between the pages! Congratulations to all those who will be privileged to read this book. It is my prayer that you will be transformed by the truth that is clearly set forth in this work.

- PASTOR ANTHONY AISIEN
        Anthony Aisien Ministries
        Manchester, England

ACKNOWLEDGEMENTS

Firstly, I would like to give all glory, honour, thanks and praise to my Lord and God from whom The Blessing flows; especially, for the awesome privilege to have been used to birth this book. Words cannot adequately acknowledge all that you have done for me. I love You more than I will ever be able to express or articulate. I am forever Yours.

I would also want to give profound thanks to my parents, Pastor Ayo and Mrs Helen Oritsejafor. Arguably the best parents anyone could ask for. Thank you for my great spiritual heritage. I would especially like to thank my dad for the example of godliness, faith and excellence. Thank you for stirring up a deep love for the Word of God (and the study of it) in me. Only eternity can compute your immense contribution to Nigeria, Africa and the rest of world. Thank you for your phenomenal legacy of Faith.

Dr Lawrence and Mrs Barbara Tetteh, for the opportunity to serve with you in your ministries and the privilege to do life with you, I am eternally grateful. Also to Dr Peter Gammons for the unique opportunity to serve with you in the Gospel of our Lord and Saviour Jesus Christ.

For many ideas and discussions that inspired me during the writing process, Pastor Tony Aisien, Pastors David and Chennelle Palmer, Pastor Bright Onoka, Pastor Julian Melfi and Pastor Yinka Akintunde, thank you! Also, special thanks go to Dr Jane Onaolapo for your kind heart and support.

Many thanks to Rabbi Jason Holtz of the Bromley Reform Synagogue, for helping me gain some insight into the meanings of some Hebrew words and concepts.

A special thanks goes to my mother in-law Ms Adelaide Atiemo, for your unwavering love and support during the process of writing this book; you are one in a million. Thank you to Ms. Florence Ehinmoti, a mother indeed.

Thanks to AKANSON Media Group LLC for editing and design. Special thanks to the über talented Mrs. LaRonda Koffi, for editing, praying and for many other things that I know about and have no clue about. Thank you for practically taking ownership this work. You, my friend, are a star!

I would like to especially thank big brother Bayo Adewoye for his support. Thanks to my copy editor Ola Aboderin for his brilliant contribution. To Kunle Falodun, Elizabeth Martins, Dabo Davies, Wilfred Boafo, Jacqueline Malcolm and Dozie David Atueyi, thank you for your feedback, prayers and encouragement.

To my best friend, my lover and my wife; the amazing Yvonne; what more can I say? I am grateful to God for the privilege to do life with this amazing woman. For the remarkable sacrifices and for letting me make notes on my phone at 3am in the morning as the many ideas kept flowing, thereby giving you many sleepless nights. You are more special than you know. I love you dearly!

Finally, to the many spiritual leaders who have shaped my life through writing, teaching and preaching, thank you!

The Blessing
God's Plan for Mankind

Copyright © 2016, Rotimi Kaleb

Take note that the name satan and other related names are not capitalised. We choose not to acknowledge him, even to the point of violating grammatical rules.

Editor: LaRonda Koffi, www.akansonpr.com

Copyright © 2016, Rotimi Kaleb
First Edition: 2016
ISBN: 978-0-692-62034-2

Publisher: Word Alive International

www.rotimikaleb.com

CONTENTS

FOREWORD

As Christians, we have words and phrases that we use that are unique to our faith. And there's usually nothing wrong with those words. But oftentimes, we fail to explain what they mean to others, especially those just coming into Christianity. Or even worse, we use them ourselves without ever learning what they actually mean. A supreme example of this is that of the antonymous words: Blessing and Curse.

In this beautifully written book, Rotimi Kaleb provides a life-transforming, spiritual insight into the concept of the Blessing. This book unfolds the truth and beauty of the biblical concept of blessing and what it means to live under God's blessing in our everyday lives. Having been in the ministry for over forty years, I can affirm that there are few more delightful or richer subjects than God's Blessing; this book gives it the attention it deserves. The book is insightful, fresh, inspirational, and thought-provoking.

The truth exposed in this book will transform your life for the better, bringing you guaranteed spiritual and material results. In fact, it will change every area of your life; marriage, family, health, career, relationship and much more. When you know what *The Blessing* is, and how to maximize its benefits, every part of your journey is affected.

If all believers operate in the fullness of the Blessing, every life will be fulfilled, every church will be built, and every nation would have abundance. More importantly, we would know that we are on God's side and, at the end of time, where we will be standing.

I believe in the Blessing, because God always keeps His promises. He always does.

The author Rotimi Kaleb is my son. I have had the privilege of nurturing, supervising and watching over his growth from his little beginning as a child. That is why I am so excited, not only about this book being published, but more so about the powerful spiritual truths set forth in it.

This book is truly a wonderful blessing that I would like to recommend to everyone. Rotimi can be confident that there will be many grateful readers who will have gained a broader, deeper perspective and understanding of the Blessing as a result of this book. May you find a rich resource of the Life of God in Christ as you prayerfully read the pages of this well-written treatise.

PASTOR AYO ORITSEJAFOR (OFR)
> President, Christian Association of Nigeria (CAN)
> Pastor and Founder, Word of Life Bible Church
> Warri, Nigeria

Also author of several books, including the bestselling book, *Breaking the Power of Yesterday.*

INTRODUCTION

Abraham took another wife, whose name was Keturah. She bore him Zimran, Jokshan, Medan, Midian, Ishbak, and Shuah. Jokshan fathered Sheba and Dedan. The sons of Dedan were Asshurim, Letushim, and Leummim. The sons of Midian were Ephah, Epher, Hanoch, Abida, and Eldaah. All these were the children of Keturah. **Abraham gave all he had to Isaac.** *But to the sons of his concubines Abraham gave gifts,* and while he was still living he sent them away from his son Isaac, eastward to the east country. (Genesis 25:1-6, ESV)

Abraham is one of the most revered figures in the Judeo-Christian Faith, as well as other Abrahamic systems of belief. Our introductory text presents him in the later stages of his life. He was about 140 years of age and Sarah had passed on. Though he was well advanced in age, he was still productive. As the Psalmist says about the righteous, "they shall still bring forth fruit in their old age" (Psalm 92:14), I do believe that it is God's plan for us to still be productive even as the clock winds down on our lives. Old age should not be a barrier to our productivity.

A closer look at the above text from Genesis presents a little mystery. In verse 5, we see Abraham bequeathing all he has to Isaac, yet in verse 6 he gives gifts to the sons from his other wives and concubines. It makes neither arithmetical nor logical sense for Abraham to give gifts to his other children if he had already given all that he had to Isaac.

I strongly believe that what Abraham gave to Isaac was not something material. What he gave to Isaac was something more transcendent; this is the *transference of the Blessing that Abraham received as a result of his walk with God.*

The Blessing was what Abraham walked in. The Blessing was what he gave to Isaac, and The Blessing was what made Isaac mighty in his time. It was the same blessing that Isaac transferred onto Jacob. It was what Jacob gave to Joseph and the other patriarchs.

The Blessing was what the nation of Israel enjoyed as they moved from victory to victory, until they were established as a nation in their Promised Land. During His earthly ministry, Jesus operated in The Blessing and He has now bestowed it upon us (The Church) – who are the continuation of His earthly ministry.

There are two opposing forces at work on earth today that determine the course of a person's life: The Blessing and the Curse. The Blessing is a summons on all the elements on earth, in the heavens and the universe to assist a person, while the curse is a release of the elements in the universe to counteract a person.

This book is an attempt to unveil and convey what I believe The Blessing is and how to maximise its benefits. I pray that the Lord grants unto you a spirit of revelation to see even beyond what is written in this book, so you can walk in the *Fullness of The Blessing*.

THE BLESSING OF THE LORD

The Blessing of the LORD makes rich, and he adds no sorrow with it.

Proverbs 10:22

In all my years of living on earth, I have never met a person who deliberately wanted to be disadvantaged. Every man or woman from every race, culture or creed would rather live in advantage and some form of comfort instead of being in a state of destitution. Still, let me quickly say here that *The Blessing* is not about money or financial wherewithal.
The revelation about *The Blessing* is one of the truths that the Church of Jesus Christ needs to embrace, so that we can fully enjoy the possibilities that lay within it.

In the very first chapter of the Bible, the word "Blessed" is introduced to us in Genesis 1:28. As God began His work of creation, He blessed every living creature that He created - "And God blessed them, saying, "Be fruitful and multiply and fill the waters in the seas, and let birds multiply on the earth."

When mankind, the pinnacle of His creation, entered the scene, He blessed them:

Then God said, "Let us make man in our image, after our likeness. And let them have dominion over the fish of the sea and over the birds of the heavens and over the livestock and over all the earth and over every creeping thing that creeps on the earth." So God created man in his own image, in the image of God he created him; male and female he created them. **And God blessed them.** And God said to them, "Be fruitful and multiply and fill the earth and subdue it, and have dominion over the fish of the sea and over the birds of the heavens and over every living thing that moves on the earth." And God said, "Behold, I have given you every plant yielding seed that is on the face of all the earth, and every tree with seed in its fruit. You shall have them for food

Genesis 1:26-29 (Emphasis mine)

The English expression "to Bless" is rooted in an old English tradition. It means "from blood." It also carries the idea of having blood from an animal sacrifice smeared on a person. It was mostly used for warriors as they were about to go into battle. This "blessing" ritual was to ensure that they were safe in battle and that they overcame whatever enemy they faced. This "blessing" was a guarantee of victory over sometimes seemingly insurmountable opposition.

There is no gainsaying that every human being is in a battle. The Old Testament sage, Job, said that all the days of man were full of trouble (Job 14:1) or battles. He also asserted that his days on earth were "warfare" (Job 14:14 AMP). As believers in Jesus Christ, His Blood was shed for us and thus we can figuratively say that the Blood of the Eternal Covenant has been "smeared" on us. The blood of Jesus is our assurance for victory in the everyday battles of life.

The Bible says in Psalms 5:12, that "the Lord will bless the righteous and surround him with favour as with a shield." I have observed that in Christian circles, the word "righteous" is commonly misunderstood. So, I will proceed to provide a brief demystification of the concept because of its connection with our subject of consideration.

Righteousness

God has three dimensions of moral purity, one of which is righteousness. The other two are holiness and justice.[1] When we say that God is righteous it means that God is perfect. The concept of someone being righteous in the Old Testament means that such person has been declared by a judge to be free of guilt, where the task of a judge is to condemn the guilty and free the innocent.

4

With God as the judge of all human beings (primarily, their actions and intentions); those who are acquitted in His sight have been adjudged to stand in right relationship to Him. Therefore, from an Old Testament perspective, righteousness or justification involves the ruling that a person is innocent, and declaring that this judgement is indeed true that he or she is righteous. That is, to say, he or she has fulfilled the law.

The word "righteous" transliterated from the Hebrew word *Tsaddiyq* means Just. It signifies a person that is lawful and upright in character and conduct; someone who has been justified and vindicated by God. When a person is tried in the court of law and found not guilty, they are declared righteous. Therefore, *righteousness* is a legal term.

Righteousness means to have right standing with God. It is the ability to stand before God without any sense of guilt or shame. In his epistle to the Romans, Paul the Apostle shows us a clear description of righteousness in Chapter 4:

> Even as David also describeth the blessedness of the man, unto whom God imputeth righteousness without works Saying, Blessed are they whose iniquities are forgiven, and whose sins are covered Blessed is the man to whom the Lord will not impute sin.
>
> Romans 4:6-8

According to the aforementioned text from Romans, within the context of the New Covenant, righteousness is God "forgiving our lawless acts and covering our sins." It is God "not counting our sins against us." In this regard, it is a legal term that implies that we are not guilty of the charges that were brought before us in the heavenly court of law. This was only made possible by the eternal sacrifice of Jesus Christ on the cross of Calvary.

The New Testament, on the other hand, takes this view to another dimension. Justice, as we understand, places certain demands on the guilty and allows the acquitted to go free without penalty. If a judge allows the guilty to go free without penalty, the judge is now deemed unrighteous. For God to declare us righteous while being righteous Himself, justice had to be served.

For all have sinned and fall short of the glory of God. They are justified freely by His grace through the redemption that is in Christ

Jesus. God presented Him as a propitiation through faith in His blood, to demonstrate His righteousness, because in His restraint God passed over the sins previously committed. God presented Him to demonstrate His righteousness at the present time, so that He would be righteous and declare righteous the one who has faith in Jesus.

Romans 3:23-26

The Christian, by the Blood of Jesus, has been declared righteous. By Jesus dying in our place as the sacrificial lamb, God acted righteously and declared righteous the people who would accept that sacrifice. Justification is God's declarative act by which, on the basis of the sufficiency of Christ's atoning death, He pronounces believers to have fulfilled all of the requirements of the law that pertain to them. Justification is therefore a forensic act imputing the righteousness of Christ to the believer.[2] We must understand that the vehicle by which God declares us righteous is by imputing the righteousness of Jesus Christ on us.

We see an impressive juxtaposition of Adam and Christ in Romans 5. The Apostle Paul asserts that, as a result of Adam's sin, both natural and spiritual death came into the world; and, as a result of Jesus' life and His act of righteousness, we receive life. If we received Adam's condemnation and guilt without necessarily participating in his sin, we can hence receive the imputation of Christ's righteousness without having died His death.

What is even more impressive is that as our original spiritual father, we were all involved in Adam's sin, and thus received the corrupted nature that became his after the fall, and the resultant guilt and condemnation. Consequent to Christ's passion on the cross of Calvary, we have also received His righteousness, access to God's presence and His divine nature as a part of the transaction.

> For he hath made him to be sin for us, who knew no sin; that we might be made the righteousness of God in him.
>
> 2 Corinthians 5:21

Jesus Christ was made a sin offering for us so that we might become the righteousness of God. Righteousness in a broader sense means *Divine Rectification*. Rectification, in this regard, is to be set right and purified by God's divine power.

That which God does in the human spirit, He ultimately accomplishes in our souls and bodies. By the same operation that the Lord is able to subdue all things unto Himself, He will fashion our bodies like His own glorious body (Philippians 3:21). At its culmination, *Divine Rectification* is the goal of the New Creation. When New Heavens and New Earth are come into existence, the work of rectification and righteousness becomes complete. *Divine Love* that was seen on the cross rectifies everything seen and unseen.

The work of the Righteousness of God culminates in all of creation entering the Glorious Liberty of the sons of God (Romans 8:18). The Agency of *Divine Rectification* in man and the universe is the regenerative work of the Spirit of God.

One of God's Covenant names is *Jehovah Tsidkenu* (Pronounced sid-kay-nu). This means "the Lord, our Righteousness". *Jehovah Tsidkenu* will eventually make it all brand new. Thank You, Lord, for the rectifying work of your righteousness, not only beheld in man, but to be seen throughout the universe.

For our present discussion, the basis on which we are blessed is that God "blesses the righteous" (Psalm 5:12). Therefore, if you have been declared righteous by the blood of Jesus, by default, you are automatically blessed. It is like someone who falls into a pool of water; they must get wet. You cannot get in the water without getting wet; and you cannot have the Righteousness of Christ Jesus, without the Blessing coming on you.

The Crux of the Story

When we read the Bible as an entire narrative, we get to see the truths it presents more clearly. Many Bible teachers say that a careful study of the Word of God shows us various themes in the Bible. Covenant is a theme that is seen throughout the Bible. Redemption is another theme that can be traced throughout the Bible. As I studied the Bible in a season of my life, I began to clearly see and understand that The Blessing stands out as a major theme, if not the major theme of the Bible.

In the very first chapter of the Bible—in the book of beginnings—we see that, as God created mankind, the first thing that mankind heard God say to them was when He blessed them (Genesis 1:28). Adam committed high treason and stepped into the curse. The opposite of the word "blessed" is the word "cursed." Adam and his generation were plunged into the curse—not because God cursed him—but because any place outside of God is riddled with the curse.

In the very last chapter of the Bible, we see John narrating his final vision, and in verse 3, we see this phrase, "and there was no more curse" (Revelation 3:22a). What we see at the end of the age is that the curse is eradicated and replaced by The Blessing. "The final vision in Revelation is, of course, about heaven and its holiness, or better said, about the invasion of earth by heaven; thereby entirely sanctifying the earthly realm."[3] This heavenly invasion of *The Blessing* can be experienced in the here and now to a great degree and that is what this book is all about.

In the book of Hebrews, the writer talks about a people "who have tasted of the powers of the world to come" (Hebrews 6:5). The world to come is the New Heavens and the New Earth, where *The Blessing* finally encompasses every nook and cranny of the earth. Until that time comes, we can begin to live beyond the curse by partaking in this 'future power' that has been made available to us; and that power is called *The Blessing*.

I began to see from Genesis to Revelation, in the Law and in the Prophets that the Bible was all about *The Blessing*. Even what we call the Holy Communion or the covenant meal is called the cup of the *Blessing*. (1 Corinthians 10:16). The Bible is the story of how man received the *Blessing*, lost the *Blessing* and regained the *Blessing*; and how to live in the *Blessing*.

In the very popular blessing and cursing chapter in Deuteronomy (Chapter 28), we see sickness as one of the manifestations of the curse. The Lord Jesus in His earth walk healed people of sicknesses and various types of spiritual oppression. Logically speaking, if sickness was a manifestation of the curse, and Jesus healed the sick, we can deduce that Jesus healed the sick by the power of the Blessing.

In Acts 3:26, Peter said that *"Unto you first God, having raised up his Son Jesus, sent him to bless you, in turning away every one of you from his iniquities"*. What we see here is the fact that Jesus was raised and sent to us that we might receive the Blessing. What a glorious plan!

Identity

Before God spoke over man the famous first words of Blessing, we see that he created man "in His image and in His likeness" (Genesis 1:26). Before the empowerment came, there was identity. Possibly, the most important question you will ever need to ask yourself is *"Who am I?"*

Identity is defined as the fact of what a person or thing is. When satan confronted the Lord during His period of fasting, he asked Him about His identity: *"If you are the Son of God…"* We live in a world today where many people are looking for self-definition. They are chasing an identity. The search for identity has become the Holy Grail of the 21st century.[4]

The word "image," as used in Genesis 1:26, means resemblance or what you look like; whilst "likeness" means the quality (what you are made of) or state of being similar to something. When God wanted to make the other creatures, He spoke to the elements He had already created; when He wanted to make man He spoke to Himself. There was a heavenly council within the Triune God when He said "Let us make man." In the Godhead, Christ is the only person that is said to possess an image; He was declared as the "image" of the Godhead (2 Corinthians 4:4). This reveals that our identities as people can only be found in Christ in God.

In 1943, the renowned psychologist, Abraham Maslow, postulated what is popularly known as "Maslow's hierarchy of needs." At the bottom of Maslow's hierarchy, is our very basic human need to eat and survive. At the top is self-actualisation. Self-actualisation refers to what a person's full potential is and the realisation of that potential. Maslow describes this level as the desire to accomplish everything that one can, to become the most that one can be.

Self-actualisation is similar to other ego-focused concepts, such as self-discovery, self-reflection, self-realisation and self-exploration. We have gone to various lengths in our quest to *self-actualise* through our work and achievements in life. While I do not in any way have anything against our need to work and gain pride in our work, I believe that all true believers have *self-actualised* in Christ, because we are *complete* in Him (Colossians 2:9).

Our first parents, Adam and Eve, had their identity questioned. When the enemy came into the garden and approached them, he said:

For God doth know that in the day ye eat thereof, then your eyes shall be opened, *and ye shall be as gods*, knowing good and evil.

Genesis 3:5

Satan told them that they would be like God. Falling for the deception of the enemy, they failed to realize that they were made in the image of God, so they were already like God: made in the similitude and likeness of God. They did not know what God had made them—that they were made a little lower than God. They became convinced that they needed a new identity. Paradise was lost because they did not know who they were. When you don't know who you are, you will most likely lose what you have.

As a man walking on earth, Jesus knew who He was. When the devil met Jesus in the wilderness, he questioned His identity:

> And when the tempter came to him, he said, ***If thou be the Son of God***, command that these stones be made bread. And saith unto him, ***If thou be the Son of God***, cast thyself down: for it is written, He shall give his angels charge concerning thee: and in their hands they shall bear thee up, lest at any time thou dash thy foot against a stone.
>
> Matthew 4:3,6

When John the Baptist came on the scene, people began to ask him about his identity, to know if he was the Christ.

> And this is the record of John, when the Jews sent priests and Levites from Jerusalem to ask him, who art thou? And he confessed, and denied not; but confessed, I am not the Christ. And they asked him, what then? Art thou Elias? And he saith I am not. Art thou that prophet? And he answered, No.
>
> John 1:19-21

John answered their query that he was neither the Christ nor the prophet. Then they asked him what he said about himself:

> Then said they unto him, who art thou? that we may give an answer to them that sent us. What sayest thou of thyself? He said, I am the voice of one crying in the wilderness, Make straight the way of the Lord, as said the prophet Esaias.
>
> John 1:22-23

John was conscious of who he wasn't, but he was very aware of who he was. He found himself in the book of the Prophet Isaiah. You must become conscious of who you are not. You have to know that you are not the negative things people have labelled you. You are not the things that have happened to you. Your identity is not rooted in the shameful or even pride-worthy things you've done.

When I mention the great things you've done, I'm not downplaying achievement; I'm highlighting the fact that your identity is in Christ. As believers, the knowledge of who we are is of paramount importance. We must find ourselves in the Word of God, because it speaks about us and to us.

The question is: *Do you know who you are?* There are many unnatural lifestyle choices that have become acceptable ways of life in certain parts of the world today. Many people call it "finding their truth." They believed a lie because of an identity issue; therefore, the lie they believed became their truth. Jesus called the Word of God "The Truth" (John 17:17). It is in that Word that we find our truth.

This is the truth that the Bible says about us:

> But ye are a chosen generation, a royal priesthood, an holy nation, a peculiar people; that ye should shew forth the praises of him who hath called you out of darkness into his marvellous light
>
> 1 Peter 2:9

One day, the Lord asked His disciples who men said that He was. They responded that people called Him a re-emergence of various Old Testament prophets. Then He asked His disciples who they said that He was (Matthew 16:13-15). Not because He didn't know who He was, but because without knowing who He is, we can't know who we are. When we see Him, we see ourselves because it is "In Him we live and move and have our being" (Acts 17:28).

There is more to you than you've ever imagined. You are more than what has been revealed to you about yourself. You are not the negative comments you've heard about yourself. Regardless of where you are or what you've done, you were created in the image of God. As you plug into a living dynamic relationship with Jesus Christ, you will see what He has made you to be.

By the working of God's grace, we have been given an identity of righteousness. God has already accepted us to be His own. If you are a born-again believer, you have the nature of God within you: the righteous nature. It is in you. It is on you. You are not trying to be righteous, you are already righteous. As we become secure in our identity as the righteousness of God in Christ Jesus, we will be free to walk in the Blessing that God has bestowed on us in Christ.

In the next chapter, we will examine some Hebrew and Greek terms that are translated to mean *Blessed* and *Blessing*.

Chapter 2

BLESSED

In the Genesis 1 account of man's creation, we see that when God made man He blessed him and spoke certain words over him:

> "And God blessed them. And God said to them, "Be *fruitful* and *multiply* and *replenish* the earth and *subdue* it, and *have dominion* over the fish of the sea and over the birds of the heavens and over every living thing that moves on the earth."
>
> Genesis 1:28

From the above, we can assert that to bless someone means to empower them by means of a word spoken to bring good fortune into their lives. The Lord spoke to mankind and declared over them to be fruitful, multiply, replenish, subdue and have dominion. The Blessing is the divine ability or empowerment to be fruitful, productive, to increase, to replenish, to win and to dominate. It is the empowerment to prosper and succeed. The five words that the original blessing included are:

Fruitful: To bear fruit, to increase with offspring. We are created to be fruitful and productive. The *Blessing of God* empowers us to be just that in every sphere of our lives. When a tree is no longer fruitful, it has outlived its usefulness. As human beings, we are most useful when we are most fruitful. The importance of a tree is tied to its use. Our usefulness in life is tied to our fruitfulness. God designed that we be fruitful in life, on our jobs, in our careers, in ministry, in marriage, in our academics and in pretty much anything in which we are involved.

Multiply: To be or become great, many, much, or numerous; to increase greatly or exceedingly. It means to make large, enlarge, increase, multiply (of people, animals, things) and to grow great. Whatever you have may begin small, but it will become great because of the *Blessing*.

Replenish: This literally means *bring to fullness again*; to make abundant or refill. Replenish can also be defined as restoration. The idea of the word replenish in this passage, indicates that the earth was once full and then became empty, but God gave mankind the mandate to restock the earth; to fill it up again.

The Blessing gives us the ability to have our lives refilled again. You may have lost some things in life, but by the power and operation of the *Blessing*, there shall be replenishment. God, by the Blessing, has made you a "replenisher"; a rebuilder of once broken and destroyed foundations. We are called to re-establish things that have been broken down. We are called to be rebuilders of lives, families and communities by the power of the Blessing.

Subdue: To subject, subdue, force, keep under, and bring into bondage; to tread with the feet; to trample underfoot. That the Lord blessed Adam and Eve to subdue would mean that there was something or someone to be subdued. Lucifer and his horde of renegade angels had been cast out of heaven; so they were naturally man's enemies. They were interested in occupying the land that belonged to man.

The *Blessing*, including the ability to subdue, means that we have power to put in bondage every force that wants to keep us in bondage. By subduing the negative multitude against us, we are putting our feet on the necks of our enemies and defeating them in every battle that we face. By the *Blessing*, we have been empowered to win, to subjugate every intending subjugator and be victorious in every battle of life.

Dominion. Dominion is the Hebrew word *Radah*. It means to rule, to dominate, to tread down to take possession to rule over. It also means to have mastery over everything we face in life. We have been given mastery over sickness, mastery over poverty, failure and every negative thing that could try to limit our progress.

In the same way that God rules and reigns in Heaven, His desire for us is to rule and reign on earth. We have the right to reign in life as co-regents with the Lord on His earth:

> The heavens, even the heavens, are the LORD'S: but the earth hath he given to the children of men.
>
> Psalms 116:15

We need to be a people of dominion to be all God has designed us to be. It is impossible for us to experience the fullness of the *Blessed Life* without exercising our God-given dominion. When Adam sinned, man lost his dominion, but the Lord Jesus died and rose again that we might regain our lost dominion.

> If, because of the one man's trespass, death exercised dominion through that one, much more surely will those who receive the abundance of grace and the free gift of righteousness exercise dominion in life through the one man, Jesus Christ.
>
> Romans 5:17 ESV

As we walk in our understanding that we are righteous people, we will exercise dominion. We will gain the mastery in the sphere of life that God has designed us to occupy.

The word "dominion" is also replaced with rule or reign as kings in certain versions of the Bible. We've been made kings and priests by our God, and where the word of a king is, there is power (Ecclesiastes 8:4). As a royal priesthood, we have received kingly powers and privileges to exercise dominion through our words and actions.

The word dominion also connotes that we have a domain. A domain is indicative of a field or endeavour. We have been given the right and privilege to reign in certain sectors in life. As you discover the field that God has ordained for you, you shall shine in Jesus' name.

Blessed/Blessing
(Words and Meanings)

We often read words in the Bible without knowing their real meanings or significance. As I studied the Hebrew and Greek words for our English word *Bless,* I discovered that, more often than not, the Greek and English deal in abstract terms, while the ancient Hebrews were concrete thinkers who related all things to concrete ideas.

The Hebrew word for "bless" is the word *"Barak",* which literally means "to kneel". The Hebrew that is interpreted Blessing is the word *Berakah.* It also means the source of prosperity. The Blessing is the source of prosperity. It is that which empowers the root to produce fruit. In the Septuagint (Greek Old Testament), the word *Barak* and *Berakah* are the same Greek words used for Blessed and Blessing in Ephesians 1:3.

> Blessed be the God and Father of our Lord the Christ, who has blessed us with every spiritual blessing in the heavenly places in Christ.
> Ephesians 1:3, NASB

From the above verse, the words "blessed" and blessing are repeated, and appear to be similar; however, they don't mean the same thing. These words are all built on the same root from which we get our word "eulogy" in common use. Eulogy is something that we would usually recite at a funeral, and means "to speak well of someone."

The first "blessed" in Ephesians 1:3, is the Greek word, *eulogetos,* which is only used of God, and ascribes praise to Him. The second "blessed" is the Greek verb, *eulogeo.* It has the connotation of acting graciously towards someone. The word "blessing", as used here, is the Greek word, *eulogia;* and has the idea of "a gift." This word is the Greek equivalent for the Hebrew word *berakah.* A *berakah* is a "blessing" but more literally, the bringing of a gift to another on a bended "knee." The image that comes to mind is that when we "bless" God or others, we are bringing a gift on "bended knee." The language and posture of the covenant is really one of service.

So what we have in verse 3 of our text in Ephesians 1:3 is this: God, who alone is to be *Blessed* with praise and adoration, is the One who *Blesses* us with His graciousness in bestowing to us *The Blessing* in Christ. We are to bless God, because He has blessed us!

Though the New Testament was written in Greek, the writer of Ephesians was the Apostle Paul, who being a Jew would have written from the Hebrew perspective of a *Berakah* (Praise to God). To get a clearer insight, let me repeat that the word "blessed" from a Hebrew perspective is *Barak*. The English word *blessed*, or the Greek word *eulogetos*, are purely abstract words. As already stated, the Hebrews did not think in purely abstract terms, but in concrete terms; therefore, we must seek out the original concrete meaning of this word.

The phrase "to kneel down" is the action used to describe the Hebrew word *Barak*, or *blessed* in English. We see a concrete use of the word *Barak* when Abraham sent his servant Eleazar to get a wife for his son, Isaac:

> He made the camels kneel down outside the city by the well of water at evening time, the time when women go out to draw water.
>
> Genesis 24:11

When the word 'bless' is used in the Bible, it is the intensive form of the verb *Barak*. In the Hebrew, it means: "to drop to the knees in respect to another person as if to present them a gift." This can be literal or figurative. For example, the English expression, "I'm on my knees" does not always mean the person saying it is on their knees literally. It is a figurative expression that could be used when making a plea.

The question is often asked, how can we, as mortal beings *bless (Barak)* The Most High God, the One who created everything? I have had to explain this concept to a few people. When we present a *berakah* (gift) to God, we are not blessing the Lord in the sense of adding to His worth, but are expressing how *Blessed* He is. When we give our blessings to God, we give Him our gifts (our sacrifice of praise) by kneeling down in awe and adoration. Therefore, from the Greek perspective, blessings are just words; whereas from the Hebrew perspective, blessings are actions. That's why the Hebrew words for praise and worship are action words.

Our scripture from Ephesians 1:3 says, "Who has blessed us." The word for "blessed" in the Greek, is the same as the Greek translation of the Hebrew word *Barak* in the Septuagint.[1] Now, remember that in the Hebrew it means "to drop to the knees in respect to another person as if to present them a gift." Does God drop to His knees to present us a gift?

It sounds quite irreverent, but I believe that in the person of Jesus Christ, on the cross of Calvary, God humbled Himself to give us Himself. What awe-inspiring thought! That's why the Bible says in the sharing of God's Grace the Lord "became poor that through His poverty we might become rich" (2 Corinthians 8:9). The Lord took upon Himself our curse that we might become blessed.

When we think about these things we have no other choice than to bow the knee and give Him our very best *Berakah* (Gift of Praise), because His ways are past finding out.

Covenant

After another encounter with God where He reiterated His promise to him, Abraham asked for some type of surety by which he could be fully certain that God would keep His promise. Abraham at this time was still childless and found it difficult to accept the promise of the *Blessing* outliving him. To bring him to a place of full conviction, God used an act that Abraham understood from his tradition and experience:

> And he said unto him, I am the LORD that brought thee out of Ur of the Chaldees, to give thee this land to inherit it. And he said, Lord GOD, whereby shall I know that I shall inherit it? And he said unto him, Take me an heifer of three years old, and a she goat of three years old, and a ram of three years old, and a turtledove, and a young pigeon. And he took unto him all these, and divided them in the midst, and laid each piece one against another: but the birds divided he not.
>
> Genesis 15:8-10

God always wants us to grasp what He is trying to get across to us. He is not vague with what He reveals to us. Anytime the message seems vague, He always helps us to get to a place of full comprehension. In helping Abraham trust and comprehend the validity of His promise, God entered into a covenant with him.

According to Vine's Expository Dictionary, "the Hebrew word translates the word covenant as *berith*. It means "to divide or cut in two". It can also be compared to the verb dividing the parts of the victim mentioned in Genesis 15:9, 10, and 17 where the verb used is *bathar*. From the arrangement of the dividing of the parts of the victims came the expression "to cut a covenant."

In the ancient Hebrew culture, entering a covenant was a sacred ceremony that included several steps. The parties involved in the covenant ceremony exchanged their robes, symbolically demonstrating that they were all that they were to each other. They exchanged their belts—the belt held their armour together—illustrating that whenever any one of them was attacked, the other one would fight for him. Then they cut the covenant.

Usually, the act of cutting a covenant involved two parties dividing an animal, say a bull (referred to as the victim), through its middle. Both halves of the animal were placed opposite each other with a narrow walkway in-between. Then they walked from the outside of the animal with their backs facing each other, and proceeded on to walk through the middle of the "victim." In this covenant, each half of the animal represented the two parties entering into the covenant. They swore to each other that they would not deal falsely with each other and that if anyone reneged on the oath, the lot of the "victim animal" would become theirs by God.

They cut each other's palms, raised their arms and mixed blood, declaring that their lives had become intermingled. They took each other's last names as part of their names. They made a scar as a reminder of their covenant responsibilities to each other. If anyone tried to harm them, all they had to do was raise their hands up to present the scar saying, "don't mess with me or my covenant partner will come for you." As believers, we bear the invisible marks of the eternal covenant. I am quite convinced that demonic entities in the spirit realm are able to recognise our "invisible" mark, so they know not to cross the line.

In conclusion of the covenant rituals, the ancient Hebrews gave the covenant terms, after which they would eat a memorial meal that included a celebration. Finally, they planted a memorial that stood as a reminder of their covenant.

A covenant, in the sense of an agreement on the part of two contracting parties, cannot apply to a covenant between God and man. His covenant is essentially a matter of grace on His part. When God cut the covenant with Abraham, he didn't particularly qualify to enter into covenant with the Holy God; therefore, Christ entered the covenant with God on His and our behalf.

And this I say, that the covenant, *that was confirmed before of God in Christ*, the law, which was four hundred and thirty years after, cannot disannul, that it should make the promise of none effect.

Galatians 3:17

In Genesis 15, when Abraham had cut the victims as instructed, as the evening approached, a deep sleep fell upon him (similar to Adam's sleep) and great darkness fell upon him. God then told him about the slavery that was to come upon his generation for four hundred years and the great wealth that would be included in their deliverance. The Lord also promised him peace in his old age and death. God foretold the sojourn of Abraham's descendants into a strange land and thee harsh treatment to follow, but with the dismal foretelling came the promise of ultimate victory.

When it became dark, we see an amazing picture in Genesis 15:17:

And it came to pass, that, when the sun went down, and it was dark, behold *a smoking furnace*, and *a burning lamp* that passed between those pieces. (Emphasis mine)

While there are differing viewpoints, I am convinced that the smoking furnace that passed through the sacrifice is the Lord God. The Bible calls Him a consuming fire (Hebrews 12:29). The burning lamp is the Lord Jesus. In His appearance in Revelation Chapter 1, Jesus is fire from His loins down and to His loins up.

The Book of Hebrews says that, because there was no one greater than God, He swore by Himself (Hebrews 6:13). The Father and Son in the Godhead entered a covenant, and we have been included in this covenant in Christ. What a glorious truth!

In Christ, we've entered a covenant with the Godhead that is based on better promises. As a partaker of Abraham's blessing, imagine God in Christ swearing to you that "In *Blessing*, I will bless you and in multiplying, I will multiply you"! (Hebrews 6:14)

On the cross of Calvary, the Lord Jesus, with His blood, inaugurated a new covenant. What God has given us in the New Covenant, is what Israel had and more. The *Blessing* is not just a good idea, it is something that has been bestowed on you and confirmed by a blood covenant. You are blessed whether you know it or not; you are blessed even when you don't feel like it. Our *Blessing* is a done deal. It is a complete transaction; no unfinished business here. Our partnership with God has been ratified by the blood of the eternal covenant.

The Blessing Makes Rich

When you look at the list of the richest people on earth, made up of billionaires in Forbes Magazine, in the column for the source of wealth, their attribution of wealth is identified as either "by inheritance" or "self-made." There are many other people, millionaires and billionaires, who self-identify as "self-made." But God wants us to be a people who are *Blessing*-made. Made rich by the *Blessing*, wealthy by the *Blessing*, and, made abundant by the *Blessing*. The Bible says that *Blessed* Abraham was rich:

> And Abram went up out of Egypt, he, and his wife, and all that he had, and Lot with him, into the south. And **Abram was very rich** in cattle, in silver, and in gold.
>
> Genesis 13:1-2, Emphasis mine

The *Blessing* has the capacity to make you enjoy God's abundance. The *Blessing* may meet you small, but if you stay with it, it will make you great and a force to be reckoned with in your chosen field. The *Blessing* doesn't empower us or make us rich without purpose. The divine supply is for the establishment of God's kingdom on earth.

In line with the concrete perspective of Hebrew words, God's promise to bless Abraham meant that He was going to give him land, children and wealth. Abraham indeed received land, children and wealth, as a result of the *Blessing*.

Although the Bible states that the *Blessing* makes rich and Abraham was financially wealthy, we must also understand, once again, that the *Blessing* is not primarily about money or financial prosperity. The *Blessing* of the Lord gives us access to "the unsearchable riches of Christ" (Ephesians 3:8). It opens the door to "the riches of His glory" (Ephesians 3:16). It is about having God's manifest abundance to meet the needs of the people around us. It is an empowerment for destiny. It is an intangible, ethereal force that works in our spirits empowering us with the ability to influence the world for the kingdom of God.

The Blessing vs a blessing(s)

More often than not, when the word blessing is used, especially among Christians, the image it conjures up is that of someone receiving something good, and yes *The Blessing* is definitely something good. For example, if someone buys a new car or gets a fabulous job offer we say they have been blessed.

I would want to differ slightly with popular convention at the risk of appearing tad pedantic. A positive addition to our lives like a car, a house, a business contract, a wonderful job and even a fabulous wife is not *The Blessing* but more often than not could be the product of *The Blessing*. We can term these things "blessings".

The Blessing is not something we can touch or feel but we can definitely see the effect of its work. The Blessing is an intangible substance that has the ability to produce things that we can see. Its effect can be financial, physical and material. The good things that we receive could be classified as blessings, but the Power that produces these things is *The Blessing*. That's why in speaking about it, I use the definite article 'The' to differentiate between *The Blessing* and a blessing.

Throughout this book, when we speak about *The Blessing*, I am speaking about an intangible, immaterial Divine Force that has the ability to impact every aspect of our lives.

In the Genesis 1:26 account of God's creation of man, He made us in His image. In other words, He put us on earth to be imagers of Him. Two verses later, He gives us what theologians call "The Dominion Mandate"; to be fruitful, increase, subdue and rule on His planet. *The Blessing* is the enablement from God that gives us the ability to be fruitful, productive and prosperous, and live our lives in total mastery over everything that we encounter in life. *The Blessing* is the Power given to us by God to enable us to carry out this "Dominion Mandate", and thereby be able representatives of Him; stewarding the earth and harnessing its resources.

The Powerful Potential of the Blessing

The man who carries the *Blessing* is as powerful as they come. One of my favourite pictures in the Bible is in Genesis 47. After Joseph had revealed himself to his brothers, and had his family migrate to Egypt, his father Jacob met with Pharaoh and something transpired:

And Joseph brought in Jacob his father, and set him before Pharaoh: and Jacob blessed Pharaoh. And Jacob blessed Pharaoh, and went out from before Pharaoh.

Genesis 47:7; 10

Jacob blessed Pharaoh; we discover later in the Bible, that the less is blessed by the better (Hebrews 7:7). As the monarch of Egypt, Pharaoh at that time in history was the most powerful man in the world. By implication, Jacob blessing Pharaoh meant that Jacob was the most powerful man in the world. Of course, there is no room for argument about who the wealthier of these two men was, at least financially. However, one of them definitely carried the *Blessing*, and he is referred to as the better; hence, the greater.

We are yet to see the full dimensions of possibilities that are locked within the *Blessing* in our day. The *Blessing* is the most powerful force on earth. We don't know how powerful we are. If we did, we would speak differently, act differently, and face life from a place of power, no matter our circumstance.

I see a day coming when the church will rise by the power of the *Blessing*, all over the world, and political leaders will seek the Church, because they will recognise that we carry something that cannot only propel the destinies of men and women, but change the course of nations.

Chapter 3

THE ANATOMY OF THE BLESSING

About ten generations after the fall of Adam, God found a man through whom the world was going to be blessed again. He commissioned Noah to build an ark; He was sending a flood to destroy the world because it was consumed by wickedness. Over a period of 100 years, Noah built the ark while preaching to the people about the coming flood, but his warning was ignored. The Bible records that everyone in Noah's generation was destroyed by the flood, save Noah and his family. After the water of the flood had receded, God spoke words that are similar to the original blessing in Genesis 1:28 to Noah:

> And God blessed Noah and his sons, and said unto them, be *fruitful*, and *multiply*, and *replenish* the earth. And *the fear of you and the dread of you shall be upon every beast of the earth*, and upon every fowl of the air, upon all that moveth upon the earth, and upon all the fishes of the sea; *into your hand are they delivered*. And you, be ye fruitful, and multiply; bring forth abundantly in the earth, and multiply therein.
>
> Genesis 9:1-2; 7

God is not trying to do something essentially new; His purpose has always been for man will live in the *Blessing* and walk in total dominion on earth. When God met Abraham, He reiterated the same thing in similar words - His desire to bless mankind. We first encounter God's covenant promises to Abraham in Genesis 12. But that episode is not the beginning of God's dealing with Abraham. In Genesis 11, we see that Abraham had begun a journey with his family (including his father, Terah) after God had appeared to him in Mesopotamia (Acts 7:2-4).

They came to a place called Haran, which incidentally bears the same name as Terah's son (who died before they left for Canaan), and they settled there. The word Haran means "a mountainous land." Mountains are often indicative of obstacles. This is the place where they chose to 'settle'. In the journey of life, we can go through challenges that sometimes make us wonder if God is still with us. Sometimes, it is easier for us to 'settle' for average than to pursue our God-given purpose.

I don't know what may have caused you to settle in any area of your life, but I pray for you to receive strength, encouragement and courage from God wherever you are, so that you can continue on the journey that the Lord has earmarked for you. God does not want us to settle. The *Blessing* is on the other side of the mountain. As you overcome your struggles by the help of God, you will discover and encounter that purpose which the Lord has prepared for you from before the foundation of the world.

Once again, God spoke to Abraham and asked him to leave where he had settled and begin a journey that would end with him receiving the *Blessing* (Genesis 12:1-3). The promises for Abraham's obedience to God included the following declarations:

"I will make you a great nation"

It is God's desire that we become great men and women. The potential to become great is locked within the *Blessing*. Of Isaac it was said that "He waxed great." (Genesis 26:13) Another word for *great*, as used in this verse, is *prospering*.

"I will Bless you"

Abraham being blessed by the Lord was guaranteed as long as he followed God on this journey. The *Blessing* is a consequence of our walk with God.

Staying with the concrete idea of the word "Bless", which is to kneel down, the idea in this particular declaration also carries the image of service. We can interpret this to mean God telling Abraham that He would come down to his level and help him. This is God coming down to meet us where we are, to do life with us, to help us with what we are involved in.

Just before He was crucified, the Lord in His earthly ministry modelled this by kneeling down to wash the feet of His disciples. One of the disciples, Peter, refused to let Him. Having received the revelation that Jesus was the Christ, he couldn't imagine the Christ kneeling down to wash His feet as a servant. The Lord's response to him was, "if you don't let me do this, we are not in partnership".

Similarly, the declaration, "I will bless you", was God telling Abraham that I have now become your partner to help you. As inheritors of the Blessing, God is telling us the same thing that He is coming down to help us, to do life with us.

The declaration also included the phrase, *"I will make your name great."* God wants to make us acclaimed in our sphere of interaction, and thus cause our influence to spread beyond our surroundings. God wants to make us known as solution providers.

"You shall be a Blessing"

Again, going by the meaning of the Hebrew for blessing, *Berakah,* which means gift, we can conclude that you are a gift to your family, friends and your community, because you are a Blessing-carrier; therefore, you have become the solution to people's problems. The blessing is not only for our benefit - it gives us the ability to positively affect and influence the lives of those around us. When you wake up in the morning, look yourself in the mirror and say "I am a gift to my world." You are the answer to questions that people are facing in life.

"I will bless those that bless you"

What a privilege for us! Your life becomes not just a *Blessing* magnet but a *Blessing* deflector; when people bless you and are kind, they too receive the *Blessing.* Helping a Blessed man provokes Divine help also. As Jesus said, "whoever welcomes a righteous person as a righteous person will receive a righteous person's reward" (Matthew 10:41 NIV).

There is another side to the *Blessing.* When someone curses a blessed man, God says, *"I will curse those that curse you."* When the Pharaoh took Abraham's wife during his sojourn to Egypt, God became involved in the matter, because He and Abraham had become partners in life (Genesis 12:10-20). There is a default setting in the spirit of the born-again believer that rejects and repels the curse, and it goes back to where it came from. You can live rest assured that any spell or voodoo that is sent to attack you will return to the sender by default.

This must be what the prophet Isaiah meant when he said, "No weapon formed against you shall prosper, and every tongue that rises against you in judgement you shall condemn." Why? Because "this is the heritage of the servants of the Lord, and their righteousness is from Me says the Lord". (Isaiah 54:17 NKJV)

"In you shall all families of the earth be Blessed"

We already know that the word Barak means to kneel down, to serve and empower. What Jehovah was saying to Abram can be paraphrased as "I'm not only kneeling down to serve you but your obedience will create an avenue for me to serve every family in the world". This part of the promise was fulfilled when Jesus who is called the seed of Abraham (Galatians 3:16) came to earth as God in human flesh and died for our sins.

Through His sacrifice, every family on earth has been given The Blessing on a silver platter. The Blessing is like serving golden apples on a platter of silver. The Blessing is God's offer of help and empowerment to every person that has been born into this world.

Five Things about *The Blessing*

At the time of writing this, the *Blessing* had become the major theme that I spoke about in most of my meetings as I travelled across the world. Before one of my meetings, as I was taking a shower, the Lord began to download some key revelations about the *Blessing* into my spirit. God speaks to me, and many others I know, in the shower; it must be the reason for the popular phrase, "Cleanliness is next to Godliness."

The Blessing is in a Place

Often times God's power is manifested through us more effectively as we find our roots in certain places. God told Abraham to go to "a place I will show you." In that place, God said "I will bless you." God promised to empower Abraham to succeed in a certain place. Places are very important to God. God made places before He made people, and He made certain people for certain places.

When you find your place, you will fit. When you find your place, you will manifest your God-given power and destiny more effectively. In Genesis 26, Isaac was about to leave where he was because of a famine, but God instructed him to stay there and in that place God blessed him.

After Elijah had prophesied a famine, he was led to a brook in Cherith, where God sent ravens to feed him. After a while, the brook dried up and God sent him to a widow in Zarephath. Our God is truly a God of specificity. There was a place for Elijah to be where he could be fed and not suffer the consequences of the famine that was being experienced by everyone. Because God is not particularly static, He calls us to certain places at various points in time. I believe that God can keep us in plenty, even when most are experiencing the impact of famine in a dry season.

When Jesus was about to ascend into heaven, He commanded the disciples to wait for the baptism of the Holy Spirit. He instructed them to go to a specific place - the Upper Room—where they would eventually be filled with the Spirit. It was in this particular place that they were first baptised with the Spirit.

This is one of the reasons God wants us to have a dynamic relationship with His Spirit. Without Him, we can go around in circles when we could have been fed in a drought. There is a certain location where God has set aside your portion. It is my sincere prayer that as you read this book and seek the Lord, you will find it.

The Blessing is a Path

If the *Blessing* is in a place, then there must be a path that leads to its location. There are certain paths that lead us to certain places. The Book of Proverbs discusses the path of the just (Proverbs 4:18). There is a path that the man who has been justified must walk in. David calls it the path of righteousness (Psalm 23:3).

> For we are God's [own] handiwork (His workmanship), recreated in Christ Jesus, [born anew] that we may do those good works which God predestined (planned beforehand) for us [**TAKING PATHS WHICH HE PREPARED AHEAD OF TIME**], that we should walk in them [living the good life which He prearranged and made ready for us to live]
> Ephesians 2:10 AMP (Emphasis mine)

The *good* life is the *Blessed* life, but for us to experience this *good* life, we must take the paths that God has prepared for us. Not every place is our blessed place and not every path leads to the blessed place.

Job talks about "a path which no fowl knows." In the parable of the sower, Jesus describes the devil and his demons as fowls that steal the seed (the Word of God). The uncommon path of the *Blessing* that the Lord has laid out for us, is undiscernible to the eyes of the evil one. God has paths that the devil has no access to. This path is so hidden that it is oblivious to the keenest observer and the "vulture's eye hath not seen" (Job 28:7).

Vultures normally feed on the carcass of dead animals. If the vultures cannot see this path, then it is because there is no death in the *Blessed* path. The Psalmist once declared to the Lord that "He will show him the path of life" (Psalm 16:11).

The path that Job talks about is the path that is only accessed by the wisdom of God. The pathway of wisdom leads to life (Proverbs 15:24). We have been given the Spirit of God to know and find this path. We can truly say with Paul the Apostle, that "eyes have not seen, ears have not heard, neither has it entered into the hearts of man (or the devil for that matter) the things that have been freely given to us, but we can know them by the Spirit" (1 Corinthians 2:9).

The Blessing is the Presence of a Person

As simple as it sounds, one of the most profound things that God dropped in my spirit is that the *Blessing* is found in His presence. The *Blessing* has been defined as an empowerment to succeed, and we see in the life of Joseph that he was successful in a strange land. We see one of the secrets of his success in Genesis 39:2:

> The LORD was with Joseph, and he became a successful man, and he was in the house of his Egyptian master.

What made Joseph successful was not his good looks, even though he looked good. What made Joseph successful was not his intelligence or natural bent and talents. He became a success in slavery by the presence of God. God was with Him. Throughout His sojourn in life we see that his success was always attributed to the fact that God was with him.

The warden did not bother with anything under Joseph's authority, because the LORD was with him, and the LORD made everything that he did successful

Genesis 39:23 HSCB

If we walk in the *Blessing*, we must be a people who are carriers of God's divine *Presence*.

The Blessing is a Principle

A principle is the law or essence that operates in an organism that makes it act the way it does. There is a principle in the fish that makes it swim. There is a life in the frog that makes it comfortable in both land and water. There is a principle in the cheetah that gives it its ability to run at 70 miles per hour. There is a law working in the dog that makes it bark.

If you ever saw a goat barking instead of bleating, I am thoroughly convinced that it would be one of the weirdest scenes you've ever witnessed. The principle that is at work in a living organism is a result of the life that is in that organism. The *Blessing* is the manifestation of the Life of God in Christ for our experience and enjoyment.

There is a certain principle that is at work in every believer; that principle is called the *Blessing*. It is failure proof; it is sickness proof; it is defeat proof. If you are a born again child of God, there is within the very essence of your being, a result-producing ability. It will make you shine in your academics. It will make you outstanding at work. It will make you successful in business. If you stay with the Blessing, this life principle will put you over in life.

After Jacob had supplanted Esau out of his birth right and blessing, he ran away to live with his uncle, Laban. After a while, Laban became aware of the increase in output achieved after he had appointed Jacob to oversee his business; that led him to have a discussion with Jacob:

And Laban said unto him, I pray thee, if I have found favour in thine eyes, tarry: *for I have learned by experience that* **the Lord hath blessed me for thy sake.**

Genesis 30:27 (Emphasis mine)

There was something that was at work in Jacob that he received from his father, Isaac. It affected his work so much that his boss begged him to not to leave. That is the power of the *Blessing* at work. It is a strong principle that can have a significant impact on every area of our lives.

The Blessing is for a Purpose

Though this wasn't expressly spoken to me directly on that day, I believe it is just as important. Our God is a God of purpose and design. There is always a reason behind what He does. We've already seen that the *Blessing* is the empowerment to prosper. The Prophet Zechariah by a divine declaration reveals the reason God prospers us:

> Cry yet, saying, thus saith the LORD of hosts; My cities through prosperity shall yet be spread abroad; and the LORD shall yet comfort Zion, and shall yet choose Jerusalem
>
> Zechariah 1:17

The Lord wants us as the Body of Christ to prosper so that we can cause 'His city' to "be spread abroad on earth." The gospel is free, but it is very costly to spread it across the world.

When Alexander the Great conquered the world, one of the things he did was to impose the culture of Greece across the world. To accomplish this, the Grecian Kingdom had to have men who were tasked with the responsibility of colonising the known world on behalf of their emperor. They were to immerse the world into the Greek language and culture. Our purpose as church men and church women is to win the lost, and disciple them in the culture of heaven where we hold our citizenship; hence colonising the world for the King of our kingdom, our Lord Jesus Christ. We can only achieve this by the working and full operation of the *Blessing* of God in our lives.

All the wealth of Egypt was taken by the children of Israel, for the purpose of building the tabernacle of God. David was a very wealthy king, but laid aside his wealth and ambition for the building of God's kingdom, so much so that he became the standard by which the other kings of Israel were measured.

Therein lies the purpose of the blessing: that we may be empowered to fulfil that which God wants accomplished on the earth. Every manifestation of the *Blessing*, whether physical, material, financial or spiritual, is given to the end that the kingdom of God is established on earth, and for God's will to be done on earth as it is in Heaven (Matthew 6:10)

The Generational Blessing

From my limited experience in this area, I have noticed many in the body of Christ who focus on the generational curse or curses, in general. I will not in my right mind deny the existence of the curse, but I will rather major on the power of the *Blessing* and its ability that transcends the curse and its effects. The *Blessing* reverses the curse and puts us on the stream of fruitfulness.

The concept of the generational curse is seen in the Old Testament. The Lord, in giving the Law to the nation of Israel, through Moses said that a curse that would last for three or four generations would come on idolaters. Many Christians attend seminars and special deliverance sessions trying to break generational and ancestral curses, sometimes without result. If we rightly divide the *Word of Truth*, we will realise that those scriptures about generational curses were primarily directed towards the nation of Israel and, above all, those who are in Christ have been redeemed from the curse of the Law.

Even in the Old Testament period, people who broke the cycle of idolatry in their families were considered free from the punishment that came with the sin and were once again reprogrammed into the cycle of generational blessing.

As born-again believers, we can stand on the authority of God's Word and, by intercessory prayer, release ourselves from the grip of the enemy on the basis of the finished work of Jesus. We can do this because he stripped principalities and powers of their authority and made an open show of them in His passion.

Solomon asserted that "the Lord's curse is on the house of the wicked, but he blesses the home of the just" (Proverbs 3:33). By the 'wicked' he is referring a person who is totally at dissonance with God. If you are born again, you are Abraham's seed and an heir of the promise. Even if you sin, God does not consider you *wicked*; forgiveness is available for you.

But God commendeth his love toward us, in that, while we were yet sinners, Christ died for us, much more then, being now justified by his blood, we shall be saved from wrath through him. For if, when we were enemies, we were reconciled to God And not only so, but we also joy in

God through our Lord Jesus Christ, by whom we have now received the atonement.by the death of his Son, much more, being reconciled, we shall be saved by his life.

Romans 5:8-11

God went the length of the universe; He sent His Son to die for us. If, when you were a heathen, God loved you enough for Christ to die for you, imagine how far He will go for and with you, now that you are a member of the family. Think about it!

"...He blesses the home of the just." He blesses the house of the righteous. If you are born again, you are a just man whose spirit has been made perfect by the blood of Jesus. The Psalmist said that "the generation of the upright is blessed." As I mentioned earlier, the righteous man is the man who has been accepted as the *Beloved* by the sacrifice of Jesus on the Cross of Calvary.

When man was created, God's idea was that man would continually reproduce a blessed generation. The *Blessing* ought to continue from one generation to another. Seth, being born in Adam's image (without the divine image being skewed and corrupted), was what the original divine plan of God was. For one generation to create another generation in their image, to continue His plan of filling the earth with His Glory.

From studying the Bible, I have come to realise that God thinks generationally. When God blesses a man, He is thinking about affecting many generations to come. That's why He told Abraham that through him the world would be blessed. It wasn't just about Abraham; it was about his children after him. As a result of Abraham's obedience, the nation of Israel was born and the man, Jesus, came on earth through his lineage. Through Christ's death, burial, resurrection and life, the Blessing of God is increasingly gaining an entrance into families across the earth through the Church.

Because Abraham walked with God, he thought generationally. When you walk with someone, you will definitely pick up some things from them. That is why God testified of him that he would command his children to follow after him (Genesis 18:19). I believe Abraham passed down the same generational thinking to his son and grandsons. In the Book of Genesis, Isaac blessed Jacob, who then blessed his sons, speaking prophetically or generationally into their lives. Jacob even prophesied about the coming of our Lord: "until Shiloh comes."

Abraham had Isaac at the age of 100 and lived until he was 175 years old. Isaac had his sons at the age of 60; therefore, Abraham spent 15 years with Esau and Jacob, teaching them generational systems.

Joseph, who was Abraham's great-grandson, also thought generationally. Before he died, he knew that Israel would leave Egypt. He had plans for his bones to be buried in the *Promised Land*. I pray that we become men and women of vision and prophecy, who see and think in generational terms.

God, through Moses, taught Israel to think generationally. He commanded them to teach their children who would in turn teach generations about His wondrous works. Oral tradition wasn't just to pass down culture, but to give another generation the spirituality of a generation they never encountered: about how Israel became a nation, and how that Yahweh is a God that guards, heals, delivers and guides.

The devil, the great counterfeiter, also thinks generationally. When prayer was taken out of schools in many Western countries, it wasn't necessarily for the day it was done; it was for the next generation and many generations later to become unchurched. At the time of writing this book, less than 5% of the population in the United Kingdom attend church. The devil was already at work many generations ago.

If, as church men and women, we 'play church' in our generation, we will fail generations yet unborn, should Jesus tarry. As the body of Christ worldwide, we must also begin to think generationally. If Jesus tarries, do we have systems in place that will make the Church relevant 100 years from today?

> And the LORD said, Shall I hide from Abraham that thing which I do; seeing that Abraham shall surely become a great and mighty nation, and all the nations of the earth shall be blessed in him? For I know him, that he will command his children and his household after him, and they shall keep the way of the LORD, to do justice and judgment; that the LORD may bring upon Abraham that which he hath spoken of him.
>
> Genesis 18:16-19

There is a special place in the heart of God for a man or woman who will think generationally. The Lord shared the plans of His heart with Abraham, because it was certain that he would direct his household to keep the way of the Lord.

We must realise that we have to contend with forces that would rather truncate the increase of the Blessing in a family and one generation passing it down to the next. Prayer being taken out of schools in the West, and parental authority being reduced is all geared towards preventing the coming generations from partaking in the *Blessing*. But the devil is a liar. In the midst of satanic onslaught and opposition, God will give us strategies and insights into raising strong Christian families, where the *Blessing* is passed down to generations until Jesus returns.

One of the most remarkable facts that have stuck with me for almost 20 years (at the time of this writing) after leaving Bible School, is that The Welsh Revival of 1905 that was led by Evan Roberts, died a natural death because it was not transferred to the next generation.[1] Now, it may not have been seen in that way at the time, but God's strategy remains "train up a child...."

In his first epistle to Timothy, Paul talks about the unfeigned generational faith that Timothy seemed to inherit from his grandmother (Lois) and his mother (Eunice) respectively (2 Timothy 1:5). If faith can be generational, then the *Blessing* can be generational. In his diatribe against the Jews, Stephen called their resisting the Holy Ghost a generational problem (Acts 7:51). If resisting the Holy Ghost can be inherited, addiction to the Holy Ghost can also be inherited.

According to the Old Testament Prophet Malachi, the Lord cannot send his revival and restoration without the hearts of the fathers and that of the children coming together (Malachi 4:5-6). It is a tragedy that sometimes fathers, both spiritual and natural, expect their children to learn and pick up their own experiences. We see farther because we stand on the shoulders of giants. Experience and spirituality must be passed down generationally.

When we see the richest people in the world enlisted in Forbes magazine, we realise that a lot of them inherited their wealth. Wealth has been in certain families for five generations. As it is in the natural, so it is in the realm of the spirit; spiritual heritage should be passed down. Yes, the new generation must be willing to learn and receive, but the older generation must be willing to bequeath and to share that which they received from the *Presence of God* in their walk with Him.

Fathers have the experience, while children have strength and the ability to fit into new systems. If the current generation doesn't train, equip, share experience and command the next generation, the next generation will labour greater than they ought, to experience the fullness of God. As the parents command their household after them, and as we collaborate generationally, I see us operating in a wave of trans-generational blessing.

David and Hezekiah

When you study the books of First and Second Kings, you see that David's dedication to God averted God's judgement a number of times. When the Kings were good, they were said to live after David's order. The Blessing that they enjoyed was always traced back to David's walk with God.

> For I will defend this city to save it, for mine own sake, and for my servant David's sake.
>
> 2 Kings 19:24

God promised David that he would not lack a man on the throne. Even when the Israelites came out of captivity, Zerubbabel, one of David's descendants, was the one that governed the nation. Little wonder that when Jesus walked the earth, He was called the son of David!

Because of God's goodness and kindness to David, he came up with an amazing dream; to build God a house. David already had a tabernacle where worship went on throughout the day to the Lord. I can imagine that David caught a revelation of God's grandeur, and concluded that what he had was not close to being good enough for the God of the glory that he had seen.

God was impressed with the idea, but decided against David doing it because his hands were stained with blood from wars. God instructed the Prophet Nathan to tell David that Solomon would build the temple in his stead. David was actually humbled that God would want to keep this assignment in his family.

God called David a man after His own heart, basically saying, "I really love this guy's attitude." Why do we think that God chooses certain people or families? Why does God invoke so much favour on particular people? While I understand the concept of *grace*, without trying to sound derogatory, I know that God does not cast His pearls before swine (Mathew 7:6).

In other words, God will not use certain believers to accomplish greatness for His kingdom. God has given us equal-opportunity favour, and our response to His opportunity determines the level of access we have with Him. What we do with this initial favour determines what we receive from Him.

David put together the materials and relationships required for the building of this temple. He made preparation for the temple:

> Now, behold, in my trouble I have prepared for the house of the LORD an hundred thousand talents of gold, and a thousand thousand talents of silver; and of brass and iron without weight; for it is in abundance: timber also and stone have I prepared; and thou mayest add thereto. Moreover, there are workmen with thee in abundance, hewers and workers of stone and timber, and all manner of cunning men for every manner of work. Of the gold, the silver, and the brass, and the iron, there is no number. Arise therefore, and be doing, and the LORD be with thee.
>
> 1 Chronicles 22:14-16

According to theological historians, the equivalent of what David put together in today's value was over two hundred billion U.S. dollars! *(You don't need to be a mathematician or a finance expert to know that's a whole lot of money.)* When the temple was finished, it was called Solomon's Temple; but it was as much Solomon's as it was David's.

David could have been content to pass the baton to Solomon without breaking a sweat, but he was not that type of guy; he was fully committed and he gave God his all. May we be a people with a heart like David, whose priority was God, His Kingdom and His work. Not only in our generation, but in the next generation and in generations yet unborn!

Now contrast David's character with that of King Hezekiah. While I do not deny the fact that King Hezekiah was a great man, he had a serious failure towards the end of his life. Hezekiah took ill and the Prophet Isaiah went to see him with a word from the Lord. God told him to "set your house in order, for you shall die and not live" as a result of the sickness he had. The message was pretty much, "get ready to die."

The Bible says Hezekiah responded by praying and recounting what he had done for God (Isaiah 38:2-3). He prayed to God and his prayer was answered. God sent Isaiah back to Hezekiah, saying that he would be healed from his ailment and that he would live for another fifteen years. Therefore, what God did was to give Hezekiah fifteen years to put his house in order, but all he did was give birth to and create a monster king, Manasseh, and expose the next generation.

Instead of following God's instruction to prepare his house by getting the next generation ready to continue from where he had stopped, he didn't. When he received his healing, he invited the Babylonians to come and see the gold and precious things of the temple (Isaiah 39:1-2).

The Lord sent His prophet, Isaiah, to Hezekiah because of his error:

Then came Isaiah the prophet unto King Hezekiah, and said unto him, what said these men? And from whence came they unto thee? And Hezekiah said, they are come from a far country unto me, even from Babylon. Then said he, what have they seen in thine house? And Hezekiah answered, All that is in mine house have they seen: there is nothing among my treasures that I have not shewed them. Then said Isaiah to Hezekiah, Hear the word of the LORD of hosts: Behold, the days come, that all that is in thine house, and that which thy fathers have laid up in store until this day, shall be carried to Babylon: nothing shall be left, saith the LORD. And of thy sons that shall issue from thee, which thou shalt beget, shall they take away; and they shall be eunuchs in the palace of the king of Babylon.

Isaiah 39:4-7

Hezekiah's response is quite telling:

Then said Hezekiah to Isaiah, Good is the word of the LORD which thou hast spoken. He said moreover, for there shall be peace and truth in my days.

Isaiah 39:8

He said it was good if that's what God had decided. When he received notice of impending death from God, he went on his face before God and cried till he had an answer. However, when the consequences of his action did not involve direct harm to him, he did not really bother much. Strangely enough, Hezekiah's greatest deeds after his fifteen-year life extension were to father Manasseh (he killed Isaiah according to tradition) and cause the Babylonian siege.

When David invoked God's wrath, when he sinned against God by counting the men of war in Israel and not giving the required sacrifice, he atoned for the disaster by making a costly sacrifice. Could Hezekiah have turned things around? Our best answer will still be a conjecture; however, I am convinced that he could have.

When you juxtapose the focus of these two men, it is easy to see why David was as dear to God as he was. Conversely, while he is seen as a great king in the Bible, Hezekiah cared more for himself and his present than for his kids and their generations.

May God raise up men like David in every generation till Jesus returns.

The Fullness of *The Blessing*

The moment we get born again, we enter into the Blessing of Jesus Christ. What we receive is a measure of it, but we can experience the Blessing in its fullness.

> And I am sure that, when I come unto you, I shall come in the fullness of the blessing of the gospel of Christ
>
> Romans 15:29

The word "fullness" is from the Greek word *Pleroma*. It means that which has been filled or the thing with which it is filled with. It also means completeness and abundance. It denotes the picture of a ship being filled with freight and merchandise, sailors, oarsmen and soldiers.[2]

If there is the full measure of the *Blessing* then there must also be measures of the *Blessing* that do not represent living in it to its fullness. I believe that it is God's plan for us as individual believers, that we experience the fullness of the blessing.

I define the *Blessing* as the manifestation of the life of God in Christ for our experience and enjoyment. In the first chapter of this book, we established that Jesus came that we might be blessed. With this thought in our minds, let us look at a popular scripture:

> The thief cometh not, but for to steal, and to kill, and to destroy: I am come that they might have life, and that they might have it more abundantly.
>
> John 10:10

I like to paraphrase the 'b' part of John 10:10 as "I have come that you might experience and enjoy the *Blessing* and have this *Blessing* in its full manifestation." It is my desire that as the Body of Christ, we will all walk in the full manifestation of the *Blessing*, and see lives transformed by God's power.

In the Old Testament, we can agree that Israel definitely walked in a measure of the Blessing but they did not have the fullness of the Blessing to the degree that God's Word to Abraham conveyed it. It is only in Christ that the fullness of the Blessing is made possible and that, in the dispensation of the Church. As we proceed further in this book, we will look at what I call *Seven Pillars of the Blessing.*

Wisdom hath builded her house, she hath hewn out her seven pillars:
Proverbs 9:1

Seven is the number of perfection in the Bible. I believe by adhering to these seven pillars, we will come to a place of full experience of God's blessing. As you read and practise the principles set out in this book, it is my prayer that you will experience the *Fullness* of the *Blessing.*

Chapter 4

CURSES AND CAUSES

Before we go into detail about how we can become established in the *Blessing*, I want to explore a subject that could be viewed *controversial* in certain streams of the church.

In my elementary school English class, I was taught words and their opposites. In every English Language dictionary, the word that is used as the antonym for *Blessing*, is the word *curse*. We can't delve into the meaning of the *Blessing* without understanding its direct opposite- the *curse*. In this chapter, we are going to discuss curses: what they are, and whether they can legitimately affect the believer.

What is a Curse?

A curse is an expression of a wish, that misfortune, evil or doom will befall a person or group of people. It is a formula or charm intended to cause such misfortune to another. It is an incantation of magical words that are said to cause trouble or bad luck for someone, or the condition that results when such words are said. It is a prayer or invocation for harm or injury to come upon one.[1]

A curse can be defined as an invocation (a calling down) of harm or injury upon a person or people, either immediately or contingent upon particular circumstances. It is an utterance of a deity or a person invoking a deity consigning person(s) or thing(s) to destruction, or divine vengeance.

It is a malediction—the opposite of benediction—or imprecation: an evil inflicted on another.[2]

The first time the word *curse* is used in the Bible in relation to man is in Genesis Chapter 3, after man had committed high treason against God.

> And unto Adam he said, because thou hast hearkened unto the voice of thy wife, and hast eaten of the tree, of which I commanded thee, saying, Thou shalt not eat of it: cursed is the ground for thy sake; in sorrow shalt thou eat of it all the days of thy life;
>
> Genesis 3:17

When God made the earth He called it good; when He made mankind He called them good. God placed man in the garden of His pleasure and gave him a commandment. He said every tree was good for food except the tree of the knowledge of good and evil.

God told him that the day he eats from the tree, he will die or like the original Hebrew says it, "in dying you shall die." As the story goes, man disobeyed and ate the fruit of the tree from which God instructed him not to eat. God announced to man the effect of his disobedience. He said the ground was cursed for man's sake; therefore, man will have to suffer to make ends meet.

Though God said Adam will die in the eating of the fruit, Adam ate the fruit and was still alive. It is obvious that the type of death God meant was not a physical death, but a spiritual death. Death, in this sense, is the separation from one's life source or, in this case, separation from God. Adam was separated from God, who is both *Light* and *Life*, and was therefore plunged into darkness.

God did not curse Adam; He only told Adam of the consequences of his disobedience, and that was that the ground was now cursed because of him. Therefore, he was now plunged into an unfavourable environment. By being in darkness, Adam was cut off from God's *Light*, and His *Light* is the *Life* of men (John 1:4). By his action, Adam was now in darkness and spiritual death reigned in this darkness. The curse finds its strength in the place of darkness. What God was saying to Adam in Genesis 3:17, was that since he was cut off from light and now in darkness, the *Blessing* was no longer applied to his life, because God's *Blessing* cannot operate in darkness. Instead he was going to have to struggle against the force that holds sway in darkness: the *curse*.

Hebrew and Greek words for *Curse*

The word cursed in Genesis 3:17 is from the Hebrew word *arar*, which means to abhor or to bitterly curse. It is the direct opposite of the word for blessed, *Barak*. *Barak* means divine favour that empowers a person, while *arar* refers to a spiritual bondage that renders one powerless. Because of the curse, Adam was now subject to bondage.

Another Hebrew word that is translated curse in the Old Testament is the word *qalal*. It was first used in Genesis 8:21

> And the LORD smelled a sweet savour; and the LORD said in his heart, I will not again **curse** the ground any more for man's sake; for the imagination of man's heart is evil from his youth; neither will I again smite any more everything living, as I have done.

This word was used after Noah came out of the ark and made a sacrifice to God. God promised that He would no longer curse (*qalal*) the ground for man's sake. *Qalal* means to "make light or small." It carries the idea of causing something to become small or smaller than they originally were.

There are other Hebrew words that are also translated to mean curse in the Bible. They are:

Qabab: to scoop out or to stab with words
Naqab: to puncture or to perforate or sabotage
Herem: to shut in (i.e. in a net); to appoint to destruction
Ala: imprecation
Meera: Execrate

The Greek words used for curse in the New Testament are *katara* and *kataraomai*, respectively. They both mean imprecation, execration, malediction, to swear, to cast a spell to cause doom or disaster. It also means to intensely invoke a spiritual force to cause a person's downfall or misfortune. Therefore, a curse or the effect of a curse is to empower someone to fail. It is sent to make things difficult for a person or a family. It is meant to prevent people's progress, or make things difficult or impossible for them.

As mentioned earlier, the consequence of Adam's treason was spiritual death. Adam could still talk, think and feel, but he was now separated from his source and evicted from Eden. I'm sure Adam must have been very

45

depressed. The scenario from Genesis 3 shows us how the curse entered into the world. About two generations after the fall of the first Adam, his wife gave birth to a son name Seth. Seth had his son whom he named Enos, and at that time, men started calling on the name of the Lord (Genesis 4:26).

The name Enos means *frail*.[3] I am convinced that at this time they began to realise that they were frail; that they were subject to the forces of nature. That sickness, disease and weakness could overwhelm them. So, they began to call on God. They had no choice but to pray.

Because of Adam's sin, he lost the *Blessing* and came under spiritual death, and the curse that came with this death. His spiritual death greatly diminished his ability to be fruitful. He knew the difference. Spiritual death had produced an *empowerment* to fail. God has always been on the side of the *Blessing*. He wanted to restore man to his *Blessed* state. He found him a man, Abraham, and blessed him. The *Blessing* stayed with Abraham and his descendants. Through Abraham's descendants he founded the nation of Israel.

He gave the people of Israel laws, where if they obeyed, they would live in the blessing; if, however, they violated the laws, they would live outside of the blessing and under the curse. In Deuteronomy 28, the Israelites are told in detail what the *Blessing* of obeying the Covenant included. They were also warned of the consequence of not keeping the commandments that the Lord had given them:

> But it shall come to pass, if thou wilt not hearken unto the voice of the LORD thy God, to observe to do all his commandments and his statutes which I command thee this day; that all these curses shall come upon thee, and overtake thee:
>
> Deuteronomy 28:15

There were different classes of curses that were to come on them if they were not diligent to follow all His commands and statutes. These curses were a reversal of the *Blessings* that God said would come upon them in verses 1-14 of Deuteronomy 28. They would be cursed by disease, drought, defeat, deportation, military siege and, eventually, the termination of the covenant.

In the King James version of the Bible, the words *curse, cursed, cursing, accursed* and *curseth*, appear 227 times, while the words *bless, blessed, blessing, blessings* and *blesseth*, appear 1,061 times. The *curse* appears more times in the Old Testament than in the New Testament. This proves to us that God is more interested in *Blessing* than in the *curse*. In fact, God does not curse anybody. The Christian believer has entered into a Covenant of blessings, not curses. Our Covenant brings with it a new dispensation of blessings. The New Covenant has a sign that reads "only *The Blessing* allowed here." It is all about the *Blessing!*

Three Laws, Two curses

In the third chapter of the book of Galatians, we see that for the *Blessing* to actually come upon us, Jesus had to bear the *curse*. He had to become the embodiment of the *curse* that the *Blessing* of Abraham should come upon the Gentiles (Galatians 3:13-14).

As I study the Bible, I see three basic laws and two curses in general in operation. When God made man, He blessed him, but after man sinned, a system was released on the earth that was diametrically opposed to the *Blessing.* The earth became cursed, because of Adam's sin. With the curse, a law was enacted by default; this law is known as the *law of sin and death.* Since sin was the cause of both death and the curse, Adam's disobedience set in motion the law of sin and death, and its resultant curse.

When God finally raised a nation unto Himself, He gave them a law through the man Moses. This law had a basic purpose: to differentiate them as a people on earth. They were a peculiar people and a holy nation; a kingdom of priests. The law was also given to them to keep them in a place where they could function in the *Blessing.*

Breaking this law would result in their being placed under a curse, sometimes in the form of a generational curse. The curse was called the *curse of the law.* Let me state here that it is never God's intention to curse a man, woman, family or nation. God is on the side of the *Blessing.* God is on the side of your empowerment, progress and prosperity; however, because of Adam's sin, negative forces have been set in motion where only by a dynamic relationship in obedience to God, can we transcend the *curse.*

This brings me to the final law: the *Law of the Spirit of Life.* The *Law of the Spirit of Life* is the law that we, as church men and church women, live under. The minute we get born again, we come under the jurisdiction of the *Law of Life.* The *Law of Life* finds its strength in our union with Christ Jesus. The *Law of the Spirit of life* in Christ Jesus sets us free from the dominion law of *sin and death* (Romans 8:1). When we are under the leadership of the *Law of Life*, the *curse of the law*, and *the curse of sin and death* are without power to truncate our destinies and purpose.

The *curse of the law* is a subset of the *law of sin and death*. When Jesus died on Calvary, He fulfilled the law, thus abolishing it, and its effect and effectiveness. The curse of the law was against the Jew and the curse of sin and death was against the Gentile. In His death on the cross He abolished both laws and robbed them of their power to limit both the Jew and the Gentile.

> Blotting out the handwriting of the ordinances that was against us, which was contrary to us, and took it out the way, nailing it to the cross;
>
> Colossians 2:11

Analogous to the laws in Ancient Rome in relation to the crucifixion of Jesus Christ, when a man was sentenced to death because he committed a crime, or was thrown in jail because a debt that he could not pay, his offence was written on a legal document and nailed to the cross. If he was in jail, by his jail cell was a document nailed to the wall that decreed the offence for which the man was in jail.

What Jesus did on the cross as our substitute, was to take every ordinance that was written against us, and every edict that declared our crime, and nail them with Him to the Cross. He died in our place. He suffered in our place. He became sin on our behalf. He became the curse in our place.

What happened on the cross of Calvary was a legal transaction, to take our verdict of guilt and replace it with His status as *Righteous*. By doing so, He took our identity as *cursed* and replaced it with His identity as *Blessed*. Our being placed in the blessing is a legal transaction in the spirit realm. You are legally blessed if you are in Christ. The curse has been broken. We don't have to be cursed anymore. We don't have to be broke anymore. We don't have to be defeated anymore. We don't have to be sick anymore. Jesus took our place. We are *blessed*! We are victorious! We are wealthy! Praise the Lord!

Can a Christian be Cursed?

This is a very controversial issue. But let us take a look at the scriptural evidence before we come to a conclusion. The Bible is accepted by

Christians as the self-revelation of God. In scripture, God reveals Himself in the arena of human affairs, events and history. As a literary work, it is a written witness to God's Revelation of Himself, inspired by the Holy Spirit, to tell us a message about God and His interaction with humanity.

For us to understand the Bible, we must realise the fact that the Bible is a narrative. When you read a novel or a story book, every scene leads from one plot to the other, until we reach a climax. To gain clear insight into God's Word, it must also be read in context. Most teachings we term as heresies or errors in the Body of Christ today, are doctrines which were derived from the Bible, but within the wrong context. The right context to study to derive the precise knowledge of the truth that the Bible presents is one from the context of redemption.

For the narrative and truth of the Old Testament to profit me, I will have to study it in the light of the New Covenant; in the light of *Redemption*. To grasp the truth of God's Word, we must see it in the person of Jesus Christ.

> Christ hath redeemed us from the curse of the law, being made a curse for us: for it is written, Cursed is every one that hangeth on a tree: That the blessing of Abraham might come on the Gentiles through Jesus Christ; that we might receive the promise of the Spirit through faith.
>
> Galatians 3:13-14

The word *redeemed* is the Greek word *exagorazo*, which means to buy back; it denotes to buy out, particularly a slave, to secure his freedom. It is used metaphorically of the deliverance by Christ of Christian Jews from the *Law* and its curse.[4] One of the things we must first realise is that the Gentile believer was never under the curse of the *Law* (the *Law of Moses*).

If the outcome of Christ becoming a curse meant that the *Blessing* extended to the Gentiles, we can then assert that He also became a curse for the non-Jews and bore in His body whatever penalty might have been due to them. One of the great mysteries that Paul received from God, was that the Gentiles were now fellow participators of the same promise that God gave to Abraham and his seed (Ephesians 3:6). Christ went to the Cross of Calvary as the representative *Man* for all mankind. He became sin on our behalf (2 Cor. 5:21), and became a curse on our behalf that we might now become recipients of the *Blessing of Abraham*.

The curse found its way into the world by Adam's disobedience, and this disobedience brought death.

> Wherefore, as by one man sin entered into the world, and death by sin; and so death passed upon all men, for that all have sinned (For until the law sin was in the world: but sin is not imputed when there is no law. Nevertheless death reigned from Adam to Moses, even over them that had not sinned after the similitude of Adam's transgression, who is the figure of him that was to come.
>
> Romans 5:12-14

Though the *curse* came through Adam, Christ came to deliver us from the *curse* and break every satanic yoke of oppression.

> Forasmuch then as the children are partakers of flesh and blood, he also himself likewise took part of the same; that through death he might destroy him that had the power of death, that is, the devil; And deliver them who through fear of death were all their lifetime subject to bondage.
>
> Hebrews 2:14-15

The Lord Jesus became a man that He might confront, conquer, destroy and obliterate the power of darkness, death and the devil. The sacrifice of Jesus on the Cross of Cavalry broke satan's dominion over man forever. He achieved all this once and for all by one sacrifice. The *curse* works in the arena of death, and Jesus died, rose and ascended to deliver us from death, so that we can live in and through His Life.

The Church in the Wilderness

The nation of Israel was in bondage for just over 400 years in Egypt. The Lord by His mighty hand delivered them from their slavery. They crossed through the red sea and camped in the wilderness. As they embarked on their journey to the Promised Land, they encountered a few enemies in battle and defeated them.

A king of one of the nations that Israel passed by, a man named Balak, hired a prophet, Balaam, to curse Israel; that is to prevent them from making progress. Balaam was so powerful that the Bible says that anyone he cursed was cursed, and anyone he blessed was blessed.

Balaam climbed seven mountains to try to curse God's people; however, he couldn't, because they were the nation that had been blessed by God. When he tried to curse them, he uttered blessings instead, like this one:

> God is not a man, that he should lie; neither the son of man, that he should repent: hath he said, and shall he not do it? or hath he spoken, and shall he not make it good? *Behold, I have received commandment to bless: and he hath blessed; and I cannot reverse it. He hath not beheld iniquity in Jacob, neither hath he seen perverseness in Israel.* **the LORD his God is with him, and the shout of a king is among them.** *Surely there is no enchantment against Jacob, neither is there any divination against Israel:* according to this time it shall be said of Jacob and of Israel, What hath God wrought!
>
> Numbers 23:19-21; 23 NKJV (Emphasis mine)

God is on the side of the believer, to keep her from any harm that is sent by the enemy. It doesn't matter who it is that has been assigned to release a curse upon your life, God is on your side and the curse will become a *Blessing.* Though the nation of Israel couldn't see what was happening, God all the while was fighting for them. It is reminiscent of what happened when the Syrian army tried to capture Elisha from his home. In 2 Kings 6:16, Elisha explained to his servant that, "there is more fighting for us than those that are against us." More often than not, we are preoccupied with who and what is against us.

We must always remember that God is with and for us, and "If God be for us, who can be against us" (Romans 8:31). We may not always see what is happening in the spirit realm, but we must be rest assured that God is fighting for us. Whenever the people of Israel were about to move, they asked that God arise for them. When He arises on our behalf, all His enemies scatter. Because God arose for them, no curse from the evil one was able to prevent or overtake them; instead, it became a blessing.

If under the Old Covenant, Israel could not be cursed, how can a believer under the New Covenant--that has better promises and has been ratified by the blood of Jesus come under the effect of a curse?

When David encountered Goliath at the valley of Elah, Goliath cursed him with his gods (1 Samuel 17:43). Goliath wasn't only a warrior, he was a man versed in the dark side.

David reiterated his trust in the Lord and the Covenant, and spoke in the midst of grave danger; and David killed Goliath. If Goliath's curses could not affect David (an Old Covenant saint) then the believer under the New Covenant is free from the influence of curses.

We cannot emphasise enough the fact that we have been given a New Covenant that is based on better promises. Moses, David, Samuel and the other Old Testament giants don't have it as good as us. For those of us who have believed and firmly propagated the message that believers are cursed or under a generational curse, you may want to rethink your stance on curses and generational curses as far as the believer is concerned.

Saints in the Light

The Word of God says that we have been delivered. We are not trying to be delivered, we have already been delivered. We have left dominion of darkness and we now enjoy the inheritance as *Saints in the Light.* One of the inheritances of the *Saints in Light* is the *Blessing.*

> Giving thanks unto the Father, which hath made us meet to be partakers of the inheritance of the saints in light: Who hath delivered us from the power of darkness, and hath translated us into the kingdom of his dear Son:
>
> Colossians 1:12-13

To take this thought a little bit further, the believer is not just a *Saint* that now has his spiritual living in the *Light;* the believer is actually called *light.* The Lord is described as "the Father of lights with whom is no variableness, neither shadow of turning" (James 1:17). If He is the father, and we are His children, then we must be the ones that are being referred to as *lights.* As a born-again believer, you have not just been called to dwell in *Light,* you are *light.* In the same way that the Father is *Light,* we have the same essence as our Father in our spirits. In his epistle, John said, "as He is so are we in this world" (1 John 4:17). Our life in this world is the same as Christ's. If He is *Light,* then we are *lights.*

> Be ye not unequally yoked together with unbelievers: for what fellowship hath righteousness with unrighteousness? and what communion hath **light** with darkness?
>
> 2 Corinthians 6:14

Paul, in admonishing us about our relational connections, calls the believer *light*:

> For ye were sometimes darkness, ***but now are ye light in the Lord***: walk as children of light.
>
> Ephesians 5:8

Jesus is the *Light* of the world. As He was, so are we in this world. The only time He exhibited His *Light Essence* was on the mount of transfiguration (Matthew 17). The believer is the same. Though our cloak of flesh keeps it from the natural eye, this is what we really are in the spirit. Like begets like; therefore, if God is *Light*, then *Light* begets *light*.

The only way a Christian can come under the influence of a curse, is if he, by his own doing, turns off his light and steps into darkness. The devil or a warlock cannot whimsically throw a curse on the believer just because he can or wants to. The believer can easily step out of the curse. All he has to do is to turn on his light and step back into the arena of light. In the arena of light, darkness becomes totally non-existent. In the arena of light, the believer will whip the enemy once every day and twice on Sunday!

When Balaam saw that he could not curse Israel, he gave Balak insight on how to get them to curse themselves, because "Like a fluttering sparrow or a darting swallow, an undeserved curse will not land on its intended victim" (Proverbs 26:2). We must be clear on this fact, that any consequence that a believer suffers is not God punishing them, but the enemy taking advantage of an open door. As the Bible says, "whoever breaks a hedge, a serpent shall bite him."[5] That is a result of lifestyle choices. How we live our lives can protect us from or expose us to the weapons of the enemy, which includes a curse.

The Bible says that we should "Give no place to the devil" (Ephesians 4:27). That means does not give him a foothold from where he can wreak havoc. We have been given the ability to stay curse-free and live in victory over the evil one and his demons. The responsibility lies with you, not God. It is our obligation to "walk as children of light" (Ephesians 5:8).

Outside of outright rebellion, ignorance, passivity and complacency are the doors through which a believer can come under the influence of a curse. Jesus talked about the danger of passivity. About a man who owned a farm; He told a story that when the man was asleep, the enemy came and sowed tares to contaminate the outcome of his harvest (Matthew 13:24-

25). The enemy wants you sleeping. He wants you passive. In the state of sleepiness, the enemy can easily usurp you. Every attempt of the enemy to make you increasingly inactive spiritually is geared towards lulling you to sleep, so that any hex or curse that is sent against you can prevail.

That is why Paul admonished to sleepers to "wake up so that Christ can give them light" (Ephesians 5:14). So a man who is legally not supposed to be under a curse can come under the influence of a curse by not living right. Not living right doesn't necessarily mean that he lives a life of sin. It just means that he's not living the Christian life that he ought to live. There is only one kind of effective Christianity and that is the "Hot Christianity" or the one on fire for God. Any other form of faith practice is ineffective at best.

The real reason for the enemy bringing a believer or anybody under the influence of a curse, is not because he wants the believer to become broke, barren or unfruitful; it is so that that the believer does not fulfil their God-given destiny. There are certain assignments that God has pre-planned for us to do for the Kingdom, and the purpose of the curse is to prevent us from to carrying them out. Breaking the curse is not so that you can now live "the good life;" it is so that you can be free to live in the fullness of the *Blessing*, and do what God has called you to do.

Growing up in church, I heard this statement in the early 1990s and it has stuck with me ever since. Jesus called the devil Beelzebub. Beelzebub means "lord of the flies." The devil is not lord over anything except demons and the demonic world system. So the flies are demons. You will never see a fly perch on a hot stove. No sir! It is never going to happen. The devil will attempt to put things on believers, but when we are hot and stay hot, the flies have enough sense to go to the lukewarm and cold places.

In the second chapter of this book, I mentioned the fact that our *Blessing* is secured by a covenant. Every covenant has terms and conditions. Beyond obeying a number of rules, as New Covenant believers, it is a walk of the Spirit, which keeps us on the path of the *Blessing*. So therefore, anyone who lives the lifestyle of righteousness cannot abide in sin. It is foreign to them to stay in it. If they fall into it, they will always be quick to repent. By so doing, they are in constant Divine covering; both of the *Blessing* and mercy of God.

Generational Curse

Something else that is also popular in certain Christian circles is the concept of the generational curse. A generational curse, as the name implies, is a curse that starts with one person and moves from that generation to subsequent generations. It is a negative force that is set in motion in a family, and is propagated by a principality in that family for generations until someone in the family becomes born again and puts a stop to it.

The generational curse teaching gains its strength from God's command to the children of Israel to abstain from idolatry. God said that the families of idolaters will have their iniquity visited upon the children to the third and fourth generation, thereby inheriting a curse; while those who love Him and keep His commandments will experience His mercy to the thousandth generation, if they stay true to Him (Exodus 20:3-5).

From my experience in attending clinics to see a Medical Doctor for routine check-ups, they ask about the sicknesses in your family to determine what could go wrong, or if the ailment from which you are suffering is hereditary. As it is in the natural, so it is in spiritual matters. Nevertheless, as regenerated new creation people, we've been given a new bloodline. We are connected to this new family by blood. We share the *Bloodline of the King of kings.*

For people who deal in the market of racehorses, they usually have to find out if the horse that they are buying is from a bloodline of champion horses. A horse with the right bloodline is a lot more expensive than a horse that is not from a champion bloodline. By the New Covenant, we have been plugged into a family with the bloodline of the *Blessed.*

When someone gets born again, he is supernaturally severed from his or her natural family and they become a child of God; this is what regeneration is. You have been re-generated. The word regeneration means *new birth.* That means the old person died and a new person was born.

> Therefore if any man be in Christ, he is a new creature: old things are passed away; behold, all things are become new
>
> 2 Corinthians 5:17

As far as the born-again person is concerned they have been created anew, born anew. The old creation no longer exists again. Your old spiritual self has been obliterated and you are a brand new person in your spirit.

You were once generated, but you have now been given another life; a different type of life from that which you received from your natural parents.

> But as many as received him, to them gave He power to become the sons of God, even to them that believe on his name: Which were born, not of blood, nor of the will of the flesh, nor of the will of man, but of God.
>
> John 1:12-13

Though this is true, there is the legal side of our redemption and the experiential side to walking in the truth of God's Word. Because you still have biological life from your family tree, the enemy may try to sneak up on you. If you do not know your rights as a believer, you will fall prey to his tricks. We have been regenerated, but the oppressions of the old creation can still linger if the believer doesn't know their rights and who they are in Christ.

It reminds me of the Emancipation Proclamation of January 1, 1863, issued by President Abraham Lincoln after the end of the American Civil War. Slavery was abolished in America, but it is on record that there were many ex-slaves who still lived in slavery 10 years after their freedom. They were ignorant of their rights as free men and women. So it is with the believer, though he is free, he can still come under the limitation of a generational curse. Ignorance is the devil's biggest weapon.

> Therefore my people are gone into captivity, because they have no knowledge: and their honourable men are famished, and their multitude dried up with thirst. Therefore hell hath enlarged herself, and opened her mouth without measure: and their glory, and their multitude, and their pomp, and he that rejoiceth, shall descend into it.
>
> Isaiah 5:13-14

God said that His people had become captives, because of their lack of knowledge. A captive is a person who is enslaved or dominated. A captive is one who has been held or made prisoner by someone with more power than they have. A captive is usually kept in confinement and restraint. If that is your situation today, this is good news tailor-made for you. It does not matter what a believer is held captive by, he can walk out of captivity once he gains the knowledge of his freedom is Christ.

Shall the prey be taken from the mighty, or the lawful captive delivered? But thus saith the LORD, Even the captives of the mighty shall be taken away, and the prey of the terrible shall be delivered: for I will contend with him that contendeth with thee, and I will save thy children.

Isaiah 49:24-25

The Bible says that God even delivers the lawful captive. Whether the captivity you are in is lawful or not, by the power of the mercy of God, deliverance is made available to you. Jesus said that "you shall know the truth, and the truth will make you free" (John 8:32). Once you have revelation about your redemptive rights, get ready, because it is freedom time.

In the next scripture we see the matter of ignorance taken even further:

My people are destroyed for lack of knowledge: because thou hast rejected knowledge, I will also reject thee, that thou shalt be no priest to me: seeing thou hast forgotten the law of thy God, I will also forget thy children.

Hosea 4:6

The word *destroyed* from the verse above, is the Hebrew word *Damah,* which means to cut off or cause to cease. The opposite of destroyed is to create or built up. Knowledge will build you up and keep you in freedom. The Bible says that "by knowledge shall be the just be delivered" (Proverbs 11:9). Your walking in vital deliverance is tied to your revelation knowledge of the redemptive benefits in Christ.

Light is also an allegory of the revelation of God's Word. It's direct opposite, *darkness*, is a lack of revelation of God's Word or an ignorance of your redemptive rights as a believer. When we have *light*, we can pierce the enemy's darkness and live in dominion. John, in one of his epistles, linked our all-round prosperity to walking in the light (3 John 2-3).

It is easier for the believer to walk out of curse than it is for her to come under the influence of a curse. The believer cannot be cursed. He can be influenced by a curse because of ignorance, but he cannot be cursed. You don't have to be in bondage to any curse or satanic oppression anymore. Your freedom was purchased. This very moment, by the truth of God's Word, you can begin to experience the *Blessing* and live above every generational curse.

I know a family in Nigeria where everyone begins to suffer with high blood pressure as they reach the age of 35. There is a history of high blood pressure on the father's side of the family. This is an example of a generational curse. The only person in the family who is exempt from this sickness, is the only member of the family that is born again. When they reach a certain age they all begin to suffer from this malaise, but when she got to the age it couldn't come upon her. It is no coincidence that she doesn't have it; she has changed families. She has moved from death to life; from the generational curse of high blood pressure to good health.

Your old Inherited Self

Abraham, who is called our father today, was a heathen. This man walked away from his family and his past, and entered into a generational blessing. We must remove our focus from where we originated biologically and begin to focus our eyes on our spiritual heritage. *We must focus on Jesus!* He has delivered us from the power of darkness by His sacrifice on the Cross of Calvary. We are now members of the family of God, and our heavenly Father's condition has become our condition.

> ***Knowing this, that our old man is crucified with him,*** that the body of sin might be destroyed, that henceforth we should not serve sin… Likewise reckon ye also yourselves to be dead indeed…
>
> Romans 6:6, 11(Emphasis mine)

Our "old man" is also translated to mean "our old inherited self." We must know that our old inherited self was crucified with Christ on the cross and died with Christ. Knowing is not enough, as a result of this knowledge, we must now reckon ourselves as dead with the old man, and now alive unto God. The word, *reckon* is an accounting term. It means "establish by calculation," "to compute," "to consider," or have the opinion that something is as "stated." We must now reckon ourselves as no longer spiritually connected to our natural families, but now bonded with the family of God.

What happened to your father should not happen to you; the afflictions that bedevilled your mother should not be part of your condition. This is because you have now been plugged in to a new family, and the life that flows from this family dissolves anything that you could have inherited or otherwise. By the power of the new life, sickness dissolves from your body; the negative conditions in your family have been separated from you by the power of the *Life* of God that now flows in you.

To take this thought further, as much as God recognises natural parental heritage, God sees us in one of two people: Adam or Christ. The pertinent question is: *Are you in Christ or are you in Adam?* If you are born again, then you are in Christ, and if you are in Christ, you must continue reckoning your current condition as true. Keep on reckoning the death of your old inherited self. This is the beginning of our expedition into complete freedom in Christ.

> And so it is written, "the first man Adam was made a living soul; the last Adam was made a quickening spirit."
>
> 1 Corinthians 15:45

You are no longer a member of the first Adam's family. You are now connected to the family of the second Adam. You now bare the image of the last Adam, Jesus Christ. The last Adam became a life-giving *Spirit*. The *Blessing* is the *Zoe Life* of God in manifestation. Christ in you is a *Blessing*-giving *Spirit*. You are too blessed to be cursed. You are too full of *Life* for death to hold court in your matter. You are *light* in the Lord. When you show up darkness flees.

Destroying Altars and Covenants

There are many people who have ancestors from pagan cultures who were also involved in demon worship. Sometimes the devil tries to rear his ugly head to bring up limitations in their lives by reason of the covenant with which their parents were involved. The devil is a legalist, and he will try to use any trick in the book that he can find to overwhelm the believer if he can. This is often confused and misconstrued as a generational curse, but this is ought not to be so.

In the Book of Judges, we see a man, Gideon. At this time, the nation of Israel was again in bondage, because they had practically turned their backs on God and were now involved in idolatry. As the terms of their covenant with the Lord dictated, they became victims of a military siege for years and could not enjoy their harvest.

Then The Lord sent an angel to Gideon:

> And there came an angel of the LORD, and sat under an oak which was in Ophrah, that pertained unto Joash the Abiezrite: and his son Gideon

threshed wheat by the winepress, to hide it from the Midianites. And the angel of the LORD appeared unto him, and said unto him, The LORD is with thee, thou mighty man of valour.

Judges 6:11-12

By this supernatural encounter, Gideon was called and commissioned to become Israel's deliverer and Judge. One of the things Gideon had to do, as directed by the Lord on the night he had the visitation, was to raise a new altar unto God in his family and to destroy the idol in his father's house that was dedicated to Baal. Though Gideon was a *mighty man of valour,* he still had to destroy the altar in his father's house.

And build an altar unto the LORD thy God upon the top of this rock, in the ordered place, and take the second bullock, and offer a burnt sacrifice with the wood of the grove which thou shalt cut down. Then Gideon took ten men of his servants, and did as the LORD had said unto him: and so it was, because he feared his father's household, and the men of the city, that he could not do it by day, that he did it by night.

Judges 6:26-27

Sometimes, people come to Christ who have been involved in the occult, and are entangled in their souls. As new Christians, they may need to be ministered to, in order to destroy every entanglement of the enemy. Then the believers must stand their ground in faith on the finished work of Jesus, should the enemy come against them by reason of their past affiliations.

We see a similar scenario in the book of Acts in the city of Ephesus, when the people who gave their lives to Christ burned their charms and occult materials:

And this was known to all the Jews and Greeks also dwelling at Ephesus; and fear fell on them all, and the name of the Lord Jesus was magnified. And many that believed came, and confessed, and shewed their deeds. *Many of them also which used curious arts brought their books together, and burned them before all men:* and they counted the price of them, and found it fifty thousand pieces of silver. *So mightily grew the word of God and prevailed.*

Acts 19:17-20 (Emphasis mine)

We see the impact of the cleansing that God's Word gained in their lives, as they kept themselves from idols. We see something similar in the first Book of Genesis, after Jacob had left Laban's house and was now returning back to his father's house:

> And God said unto Jacob, Arise, go up to Bethel, and dwell there: and make there an altar unto God, that appeared unto thee when thou fleddest from the face of Esau thy brother. **Then Jacob said unto his household, and to all that were with him, Put away the strange gods that are among you, and be clean, and change your garments.** *And let us arise, and go up to Bethel; and I will make there an altar* unto God, who answered me in the day of my distress, and was with me in the way which I went. *And they gave unto Jacob all the strange gods which were in their hand, and all their earrings which were in their ears; and Jacob hid them under the oak which was by Shechem.* And they journeyed: **and the terror of God was upon the cities that were round about them, and they did not pursue after the sons of Jacob.**
>
> Genesis 35:1-5 (Emphasis mine)

As Jacob decided to go back home, he told the people who worked with him and would be following him, to get rid of all their idols and cleanse themselves. It is our responsibility to cleanse ourselves; I could not say that enough. He knew that they had a decision to make: go with God all the way and dissociate from the old altars and build a new one.

As they made their way, after ridding themselves of their idols, amulets and things dedicated to other gods, "a terror from God" came upon anyone who would pursue them in order to harm them. What happened was that, as they got rid of the idols, the *Presence of God* enveloped them. For some of us, we may have to destroy idols or ornaments dedicated to any deity that is not Jehovah. There are Christians (especially in the west) who go on holiday and buy things like buddha statues as souvenirs. Such things will have to be done away with (1 Corinthians 10:19-22). There are believers who have had strange negative occurrences in their lives and even untimely deaths because of such. We must consciously break any known or even unknown covenants, so that we can have the fullness of all that Jesus died for us to receive.

One Decision Breaks the Curse

When you look at the life of King Ahaz and his son Hezekiah, we see a glaring contrast between both men. Ahaz was a king of Judah, but he was also an idolater. He even went as far as sacrificing his sons to demons (2 Chronicles 28:1-4 NIV).

Ahaz gathered together the utensils of the house of God and cut the utensils in pieces. He then shut the doors of the LORD's temple and set up altars at every street corner in Jerusalem. Instead he built shrines and altars to other gods in every town in Judah. This action provoked the LORD, the God of Israel, to anger. This man was quite evil. Idolatry in the Old Testament usually opened the door for a family to come under a generational curse (Deuteronomy 5:9).

Before Hezekiah became king at the relatively young age of 25 years old, temple worship had been abandoned in Judah. When Hezekiah became king, he restored the temple and the Davidic pattern of worship. Desire for God was restored. He also restored Israel's consecration to God.

During his reign, he destroyed all the idols that Israel worshipped. He even went as far as destroying the brazen serpent that Moses built because people had begun to worship it. He is the only king on account in the Bible to completely destroy idolatry in Israel and Judah. No other king before or after him pulled it off.

The result of Hezekiah restoring the temple worship and purity to the land was the presence of God. Because of God's presence with him, Hezekiah was made to prosper (1 Kings 18:7). Hezekiah is on record as one of Israel's (and Judah's) greatest kings; he is put in the same class as David and Solomon. Now that's some company to belong to!

Both Ahaz and Hezekiah had the opportunity to make the same or similar choices; Hezekiah chose the Lord and Ahaz did not. Hezekiah was passionate for God. We recall that God's curse comes upon idolaters "punishing the children for the sin of the parents to the third and fourth generation of those who hate Him," but He lavishes His unfailing Love on those who love Him and obey His commands for a thousand generations (Deuteronomy 5:9-10 NLT). The decision that breaks the curse is the decision to love the Lord.

God spoke through the prophet Ezekiel that, "the son shall not suffer for the iniquity of the father, nor the father suffer for the iniquity of the son" (Ezekiel 18:20). From the scriptures, we can conclude that the generations to come who suffer the punishment of the fathers' sins, are those who hate God. How this comes about is not exactly explained in the Bible, but we understand that when the father's sins are visited on the children, it is because the children remain sinful or continue the practice of the previous generation.

You don't have to suffer the consequences of your father's sins. I don't know what your father did or what your grandfather was involved with, but you can start a generational blessing in your own family. Your decision to develop a deep love, a lifestyle of obedience and passion for God will break every curse and establish you in the *Blessing*. You are not your father; you are not your grandfather or those before him. If you are in Christ, you have been "re-gened." You belong to a new family. You have the bloodline of God's family. You are part of a *Blessed* generation. The era of the generational curse is over in your life!

Chapter 5

BREAKING BARRENNESS

Everyone who carries the *Blessing* often goes through certain struggles. The enemy's primary instrument for bringing limitations into the life of the individual who carries the *Blessing* is the spirit of barrenness. The Holy Writ reveals to us that our spiritual patriarchs encountered and overcame barrenness in their lives. God called Abraham at the age of 75, and gave him the promise of a child. There was just one minor hurdle: Sarah, his wife, was barren.

Isaac, the promised child, did not manifest until 25 years later. The same pattern is seen in Isaacs's life. He got married at 40 and waited 20 years for Esau and Jacob to be born.

Jacob fell in love with and married Rachel. Though he was given Leah by trickery and she bore his children, Rachel, the one whom he truly loved, was barren for quite a number of years before she gave birth to Joseph. Before anyone is crowned a champion, they must go through a test. For example, before someone earns a degree from the university, they must go through a series of exams. Before anything is declared fit for use, especially as it pertains to manufacturing, it endures rigorous testing. For us to see the power of the *Blessing*, we must see its ability to overcome the *curse* and its fruit of barrenness.

The point here is that, even though your promise comes from God, the enemy will try you with a stumbling block. But I've got good news for you from Glory. The Blessing is more potent than barrenness. The Blessing is much stronger than any manifestation of the curse. Our covenant of blessing is stronger than any climate or circumstance. It will outlast any opposition. If you stay with the Blessing, it will put you over all the time and cause you to make progress from the doldrums of barrenness and unfruitfulness to the wealthy place of fruitfulness

Definition (Hebrew and Greek words)

When a person is barren, they are incapable of producing offspring; they are sterile, which means unproductive and unfruitful. When a woman is unable to conceive and birth a child, she is said to be barren. However, inability to bear children is just one form of barrenness. Barrenness manifests itself in various other facets of life. There is financial barrenness, ministerial barrenness, and personal barrenness. A territory can be said to be barren.

The spirit of barrenness can also manifest in a family. In the Bible, there are Hebrew words in the Old Testament and Greek words in the New Testament that provide a thorough understanding of what barrenness is. As we explore these words, we will have a clearer picture of how barrenness operates in the lives of people, as well as how to curtail its effects.

The first time the word *barren* is mentioned in the Old Testament, the word used is the Hebrew word *Aqar*[1]:

But Sarai was *barren*; she had no child

Genesis 11:30 (KJV)

The same word is used here:

He maketh the *barren* woman to keep house

Psalm 113:9 (KJV)

The second Hebrew word we will examine that is translated *barren* in the Old Testament is **Sakol**.[2]

None shall *miscarry* or be barren in your land; I will fulfil the number of your days.

Exodus 23:26 (KJV)

This word *Sakol* means to miscarry, to suffer abortion, to be bereaved of children. It also means to make childless, to lose children or to deprive. Another Hebrew word translated to mean *barren* is **Melaha**.[3] It means salted or desert, a barren land, or barrenness caused by salt. Enough salt will decrease the fertility of a land. Salinity in a garden will make it hard for plants to grow. Saltiness can represent an attack of the enemy to prevent a life or a business from being productive.

Oser,[4] is a Hebrew term that could mean closed, constraint, barren, oppression, prison or restraint. When a person is held in confinement, no matter how hard they can work, no matter the number of ideas they may have, they are not capable of making progress, simply because they are in prison. Many people are in various forms of mental and spiritual prisons that have blocked them from accomplishing or making any progress in their lives. In prison, there is activity without fruitfulness; effort without result.

A "mental prison" stops someone from going beyond their current position because of a "barricade" in their mind. They believe that what they have and where they are is the best they could ever achieve. Many people are not making progress because, in their minds, they've accepted their lot in life and are not motivated to fight to break the chains that bind them.

Siwwn[5] means parch, aridity, drought, or a dry or solitary place. Another name for an arid land is desert. The ability of plants to grow in a desert is very limited without irrigation. There is little hope of having plant life, or animal life for that matter, exist in a desert. When a person is in a prolonged dry season of fruitlessness, we can conclude that there is an activity of the spirit of barrenness in their lives.

The first Greek word we encounter in the New Testament that is translated as *barren* is the word ***Sterios***.[6] It means to be firm, hard, stiff or unnatural. It signifies being barren and not bearing children. It is basically used in connection with physical or biological barrenness.

In the days of Herod, King of Judea, there was a priest named Zechariah, of the division of Abijah. And he had a wife from the daughters of Aaron, and her name was Elizabeth, "And they were both righteous before God, walking blamelessly in all the commandments and statutes of the Lord. *But they had no child, because Elizabeth was **barren**, and both were advanced in years*" (Luke 1:5-6 ESV, Emphasis mine).

The second word used for barrenness in the New Testament is the word ***Argos***.[7] It is a word that denotes a state of being idle, barren, yielding no return because of inactivity. ***Katargeo***[8] is another compelling Greek term that connotes barrenness, meaning to abolish. It conveys the idea of being "reduced to inactivity." When a once productive person seems to lose their means of livelihood or a business steadily loses its relevance, we can conclude that the spirit of barrenness is in full force. More often than not, long-term sickness that renders a person inactive and unable to provide for themselves and/or their loved ones, typifies this form of barrenness.

From the definitions above, we can establish that barrenness represents unfruitfulness, restraints, constraints, limitations, imprisonment and unemployment. In this warfare against barrenness, our God has presented us with the weapons to combat and gain mastery over it. As you employ these weapons in your life, your life will become a testimony of victory over barrenness in every form. You will live a life of fruitfulness as the Lord has planned, purposed and designed for you. I will share with you two basic weapons by which we can overcome the activity of the spirit of barrenness is our lives.

Prayer

The first weapon we have been given to overcome the spirit of barrenness is prayer. As I mentioned earlier, Isaac had to combat this spirit in his life. Isaac met and married the love of his life; but for 20 years he was denied the pleasure of having children. This caused Isaac to seek the face of the Lord for a change.

> These are the generations of Isaac, Abraham's son: Abraham fathered Isaac, and Isaac was forty years old when he took Rebekah, the daughter of Bethuel the Aramean of Paddan-aram, the sister of Laban the Aramean, to be his wife. ***And Isaac prayed to the LORD for his wife, because she was barren. And the LORD granted his prayer, and Rebekah his wife conceived.***
>
> Genesis 25:19-21 (Emphasis mine)

As you engage the power of God through prayer, you will put pressure on the pressure points of your life. You will trouble that which has troubled you for years and made you feel incomplete.

> Now there was a certain man of Ramathaimzophim, of mount Ephraim, and his name was Elkanah, the son of Jeroham, the son of Elihu, the son of Tohu, the son of Zuph, an Ephrathite: And he had two wives; the name of the one was Hannah, and the name of the other Peninnah: and Peninnah had children, but *Hannah had no children.*
>
> 1 Samuel 1:1-2 (Emphasis mine)

Unless you lived or grew up in an environment where polygamy is a norm, you may not fully understand Hannah's predicament. Childbearing was one of the ways that she could stake her claim in the marriage and have some form of personal pride. Though we can say that she was loved by her husband, his love for her could not satisfy her desire to have children of her own. The other wife, Peninah (she was referred to as Hannah's rival) had a lot of children. To make it even worse, she scornfully laughed at Hannah. Hannah, aside from being unfulfilled, was in a state of depression.

> So Hannah rose up after they had eaten in Shiloh, and after they had drunk. Now Eli the priest sat upon a seat by a post of the temple of the LORD. And she was in bitterness of soul, and prayed unto the LORD, and wept sore.
>
> 1 Samuel 1:9

One of the first things you must do to break every hold of barrenness in your life is to "rise up." There has to be a "rising up" in our spirit and mind. There has to be change in our posture.

Hannah changed her posture and went into the house of the Lord. She poured out her heart in prayer. I'm sure she used God's Word in her time of prayer that "none shall be barren" (Exodus 23:26). She received the child, Samuel, as a response to her heart-filled prayer to God. The name Samuel means "asked of God" or "heard by God." As you ask of God in prayer, God will hear you and grant you an answer to your request.

> And this is the confidence that we have in him, that, if we ask any thing according to his will, he heareth us: And if we know that he hear us, whatsoever we ask, we know that we have the petitions that we desired of him.
>
> 1 John 5:14-15

A couple of years ago, in the city of Port Harcourt, Nigeria, one of my friends was experiencing an extraordinarily challenging moment in his life. He had lost his dad to a long-term sickness. During that course of time, he became born again.

After receiving his degree in Economics, he took part in the mandatory one-year post-university service programme in Nigeria. Many people are retained with companies that they work for during this period, thus earning their first post-university job. But this did not happen for him, even though he had graduated with relatively good grades. Things were very rough at that point and he had to live with his friends, who were still in university at the time. He also had to provide for himself. Without a job or business, this was nearly impossible. He began to seek the face of God in prayer for a change.

One day he received a letter of invitation for an interview, since this story seems pretty routine, please allow me to indulge you for a while. He also began applying for jobs, but there had been no positive response. A courier turned up at his uncle's house, which is the address he used for correspondence. When the courier arrived at the address, the house help told him that he must have had the wrong address, because the person with that name was a girl in primary school. Apparently, my friend was known by his middle name at home. As the courier was about to leave, miraculously, his uncle's wife who had heard the voices from inside the house, stepped out to know what was happening. She made further enquires and confirmed that the letter was for my friend. The house help was sent to deliver the letter.

Upon receiving the letter, he could not remember ever applying to that company for that position. He didn't even know they existed! He had the interview and the job was given to him. It was the kind of job he was looking for, the kind of boss he was looking for, and he was also the exact person who his boss was looking for.

Something else that is strange about this testimony is that the said boss did not remember ever sending out a letter of invitation for an interview to my friend; it became a standing joke between them. The barrenness of unemployment was broken in his life by the power of prevailing prayer.

Your testimony may not be as dramatic or sound as miraculous as my friend's, but I can assure you that our God is still a miracle-working God. What He does for one, He will do for another. He is not a respecter of persons.

Prophetic Intervention

Throughout scripture, we are presented with more than one way to deal with the same problem. For example, on the subject of healing, people have asked why in certain verses, we see that we can be healed by faith; other times we are asked to call for the elders of the church to pray and anoint with oil; while at other times we see the gift of healing in operation. The reason there seems to be many solutions to the same problem is because God is on the side of health; and, He is a dynamic and creative Healer.

In the same way, there is more than one solution to break the oppression of barrenness. For the purpose of this, book we will delve into one more. This is because the same practices that establish the *Blessing,* will also destroy the yoke of barrenness. We will talk about those seven pillars of the *Blessing* in subsequent chapters.

The second solution to barrenness is what I call the *Prophetic Intervention* or the influence of the anointing of the man of God. Every believer needs a man of God in their lives. This is someone who occupies a five-fold ministry office; who has been given spiritual authority that gives them the ability to provide supernatural covering. I agree that every believer is a priest in the New Testament, the same way that God made Israel a nation of priests; but God has chosen and graced certain individuals with special gifting and anointing for the purpose of the believer to walk in complete freedom.

We see many people in the Bible who needed the intervention of a Priest or Prophet, especially in the Old Testament, for their destinies to be released and their potentials to gain full expression.

The Prophet's Widow

In the book of 2 Kings, we see a woman who was married to a Prophet. The prophet died and left her in debt (2 Kings 4:1-7). Her husband's creditor came into her home and was about to take her sons into slavery in order to satisfy the debt. Not many things can be more devastating that losing a husband who we would call a good man and then losing both your sons into a system of slavery to pay off a debt.

The prophet left his family a legacy of debt. Whether you are in the clergy or laity, it behoves you to leave an inheritance to your children. We must begin to think about the legacy we are leaving behind. Every day we are building a legacy, whether we know it or not; therefore, we must invest our time and harness our God-given potential, talent, ability, education and experience to create not only a good life for ourselves and our family, but to also leave a legacy for subsequent generations.

The widow from our text went to see a prophet about the issue at hand. It is plain to see that there was a relationship with the man of God: the statement "my husband, your servant" is a clear indication that there was a relationship. Don't wait to get into trouble before you forge a relationship with your man of God. It brings to remembrance the account of the wedding at Cana, where the wine had been consumed during the reception. The couple invited Jesus and His disciples to the wedding even before they had the inkling that there was going to be an issue.

Elisha the Prophet asked the widow a simple question. "What do you have in your house?" Her response was "I have nothing but a little cruse of oil." More often than not, your breakthrough will always come from what you already have. What do you have that you have despised? What talent do you possess that you could employ for profit? Many of us are where we are because we've had an *"only"* mentality. There are many who have become great by using the same gifts and abilities that you possess but continue to ignore or despise. In fact, there are many people who are prosperous today, but had actually been dealt a worse hand than a whole lot of us have been dealt.

The man of God gave the widow an unusual instruction, "Go and borrow vessels, not a few." God has a sense of humour! Her family was in debt because her husband borrowed, and here is the Prophet asking her to borrow. She obeyed the instruction and poured out the oil into the vessels. As many vessels as she could borrow she did pour the oil into. She sold the oil and paid her debt, and she was delivered from the predicament of having her sons sold into slavery.

Like the woman with the cruse of oil, we must stretch our vision of what we have as a *Sent One* from the Father. The Lord Jesus was the most anointed Man who ever walked the earth. On one occasion He met Peter, who was a fisherman at the time, when he was about to close shop for the day. Christ borrowed Peter's boat to preach a sermon. I'm pretty sure that they all "had church" that day. After delivering His homily, He asked that Peter cast his net into the sea.

Now Peter who was quite an experienced fisherman, complained about his lack of success, though he had spent the night trying to catch fish. But he obeyed the Lord's command, and voila! A great catch. While we can argue that he let out one net (singular), when the Lord instructed him to cast nets (plural) into the sea, he still obeyed, albeit partially, but the result was as Jesus expected. The catch was so great that the net he employed was breaking and he also needed help from his colleagues.

A Divine Word

Never underestimate the power of one divine instruction. One Word from God can change your circumstance. A divine word can take you from the back to the front. A divine word has the ability to move you from zero to hero. A divine word can take you from penury into prosperity. Obeying a divine word can move you from obscurity into to an elevated status.

All Peter needed to spur his barren business was a Word from the Lord. From Peter's knowledge and experience, night time was the best time to catch fish, but one Word from God is actually all it takes. God's Word works even when it doesn't make sense. Then again, God's wisdom is sometimes antithetical to human logic (1 Corinthians 1:27), but a faith response will always produce the desired effect.

God answers prayer in two ways: by an instruction or through a manifestation. More often than not, when God responds to our cry for help, it is through an instruction. Many of us have not made the type of progress we ought to have made in life because we have either been deaf to divine instruction or just bluntly disobeyed. I pray that you will hear an instruction and by the obedience of it, your barren spell will come to an end, and you will come into a season of fruitfulness in Jesus' name.

Out of a Dry Ground

If you are going through a barren spell right now, you may just be in very good company. The Bible is filled with accounts of many people (women especially), who overcame barrenness and brought forth their joy. The greatest prophetic voice under the Old Covenant, John the Baptist, was a product of years of barrenness (Mathew 11:11). His parents, who were very old and past child-bearing age, were the most unlikely candidates for a child, but our God does work in amazing ways.

If you are barren right now, be encouraged because things can change:

> For he shall grow up before him as a tender plant, and as a root out of a dry ground:
>
> Isaiah 53:2a

The word *dry*, as used in Isaiah 53, is the Hebrew word *Tsiyah*, which means wilderness, aridity, or a solitary place. Barrenness can sometimes leave you in a place of aloneness. Elknanah did not understand Hannah's struggle; Eli thought she was drunk when she was praying. Barrenness can be a very lonely place, because you want to manifest that potential that God has placed inside of you, and until it is birthed, nothing else will do.

Life teaches us that most people do not want to associate with fruitlessness, but there is enough power in the Gospel of Jesus to help you overcome the assignment of the spirit of barrenness in your life or ministry. There are many other examples in the Bible of how greatness came out of barrenness. Isaac was born out of barrenness. Jacob and his twin brother, Esau, from whom emerged great nations, came out of barrenness. The nation of Israel (Israel was originally called Jacob) came about as a result of an answer to Isaac's prayer, dealing with the spirit of barrenness in Rebecca's life.

The boy who grew up to be one of Israel's greatest men, the Prophet Samuel, was a child who was born after years of barrenness. Joseph (whose name means addition) was the first child born to Jacob and Rachael, after her womb was opened by God, following many years of barrenness. Samson, the great judge of Israel, was also a child that came out of a barren womb. We see a pattern in the Bible that many prophetic voices were born after God opened the womb of barren women.

You may have been barren for a long time, but your story is about to change. Little wonder Isaiah said to the unfruitful, "Sing, O barren, thou that didst not bear; break forth into singing, and cry aloud, thou that didst not travail with child: for more are the children of the desolate than the children of the married wife, saith the LORD" (Isaiah 54:1).

Your song is an expression of your praise, and the Psalmist confirms that "God inhabits the praises of His people" (Psalm 22:3). The response to your praise is divine presence. Your praise will result in divine habitation, and you know that where the Spirit of the Lord is, there is liberty, freedom and deliverance (2 Corinthians 3:17).

"Sing O barren", because you are about to bring forth; sing because the potential that you carry on the inside of your spirit is about to find expression. You will bring forth in every area of your life.

Isaiah 53 is a Messianic prophecy that was fulfilled in the life of Jesus, more so on the Cross of Calvary. In the first part of verse 2, He is described as a root out of dry ground. He was born from the most unlikely situation.

We could say, as it were, that the Lord came out of a place of barrenness. Mary was a virgin, she had not known a man, so it was impossible for her to give birth to a child; but after the power of the Holy Ghost came on her, the seemingly impossible became possible.

Because of God's love for you, He will hear and answer your prayer; your praise will attract His presence and bring addition to your life, and bring you to a place of fruitfulness, causing your greatness to manifest by the power of His *Blessing*.

Chapter 6

MAINTAIN THE UNION

As I study the Bible, I come to the realisation that all that God has given us are accessible in Christ Jesus. The minute we accept Jesus as our Lord and Saviour, we are transported through time to that historic eternal event that happened around 29 AD. We are supernaturally identified with Christ in His death, burial, quickening, resurrection, ascension and His being seated on the Throne of Grace.

When we look at the four gospels, we see an illustration of the earthly life of Jesus. We are shown the incarnation, His human growth, His baptism and His teaching, healing and miracles. We also notice that a considerable amount of his time on earth is spent on His passion. Much of what we read in the gospels chronicle the scourging Jesus suffered; His crucifixion, death, burial and resurrection.

Though I run the risk of sounding redundant by repeating myself, Paul said he gave "a place of priority to this".

> Now I would remind you, brothers, of the gospel I preached to you, which you received, in which you stand, and by which you are being saved, if you hold fast to the word I preached to you—unless you believed in vain. ***For I delivered to you as of first importance what I also received: that Christ died for our sins in accordance with the Scriptures***, that he was buried, that he was raised on the third day in accordance with the Scriptures,
>
> 1 Corinthians 15:1-4 ESV (Emphasis mine)

In the Gospels, we see Christ suffering for our sins. The inspired writers provided us an account of what they saw. What they saw really happened, but what they saw was not all that happened. In the epistles, there is a radical dimension of thought. We observe beyond a picture of the events; we are actually given a peek into what God saw during these events, in that we were united with Him in His passion.

> But of him are ye in Christ Jesus, who of God is made unto us wisdom, and righteousness, and sanctification, and redemption
>
> 1 Corinthians 1:30

Jesus Christ became our substitute. He was the sin offering that died in our place. The sacrificial blood of animals that covered the sins of the Old Testaments saints foreshadowed what He did on the cross. He died on our behalf on the Cross of Calvary; but more than that, God included us in Him. When He was dying on the cross and pierced, blood and water gushed out of His side. By His blood, He cleansed us, redeemed us and reconciled us to the Father; by the water, we were regenerated and saved through His Life. God mysteriously included us.

Throughout the Gospels, all we see is a snapshot of these events. In the epistles, however, we come to an understanding that we were crucified with Him; we died with Him; we were buried with Him; we went to Hades with Him; we were made alive with Him; we were resurrected with Him; and, ultimately, we ascended into heaven with Him. Right now, we are seated with Him, in the place of power with the Father.

By the operation of God's wisdom and might, we are now in union with Christ. We are joined together with Him; laminated to Him. His Life has become our life and His condition is our condition; what an awesome privilege! This ubiquitous union we share together with Christ is so vital that the Apostle says that his aim was to be:

> Found in him, not having mine own righteousness, which is of the law, but that which is through the faith of Christ, the righteousness which is of God by faith:
>
> Philippians 3:9

In the Old Testament, in one of Moses' encounters with God, we witness a foreshadowing of our union with Christ. Moses had asked to see God's glory if he had received favour from God. God told him that he couldn't see Him and live (because He dwells in inapproachable light). But He will put Him on a *Rock* from where he could observe Him:

> And he said, Thou canst not see my face: for there shall no man see me, and live. And the LORD said, Behold, there is a place by me, and thou shalt stand upon a rock: And it shall come to pass, while my glory passeth by, that I will put thee in a clift of the rock, and will cover thee with my hand while I pass by:
>
> Exodus 33:20-22

1 Corinthians 10 describes Christ as that *Rock*, and from that very *Rock* there issued out water, which represents the Holy Spirit. The children of Israel partook in the articles of the *Blessing*: the heavenly *bread (Manna)* and the water from the *Rock*, even as the Church, in the wilderness.

Though it was physical rock Moses was placed on, he was, in a sense, metaphorically put into Christ. God said that there was a place on the rock by Him. There is a place in Christ for every believer; a place prepared from before the foundation of the world. Like Moses, we have received favour from God in Christ, and have been joined to Christ. In Paul's epistle, we see that we are joint heirs with Christ; we share in His inheritance.[1] We have been qualified to see His Glory in Christ Jesus.

Joined to Christ

One of the facts about our being in Christ is that we have been joined to Christ. The word *joined* primarily means to glue or cement together; then generally, to unite or to join firmly. To describe our union with Christ, Paul uses the analogy of grafting (Romans 11:23) to illuminate the concept.

The word *graft* is originally a horticultural term. It means to induce a plant or part of a plant to unite with another part of a plant. It is the process of joining a piece of plant tissue (the scion), normally a stem, with an established plant (the stock), which supports and nourishes it. Grafts are used to strengthen or repair plants, and increase fruit yields without requiring plants to mature from seeds.

We have been grafted into Christ, so that by His supernatural supply, He supports and nourishes us, and by His nourishment, we are endowed with the ability to become fruitful and productive. When plants are grafted, they become one; they share the same life, and the potential of the part that is grafted into the tree is determined by the parent tree. This point is highlighted in Paul, when he said that:

> But he that is joined unto the Lord is one spirit.
>
> 1 Corinthians 6:17

What an amazing privilege to be joined to the Lord and share His Spirit. This is a co-mingling or inter-mingling between our recreated human spirits and the Spirit of God. We've been fused together with Christ, merged and amalgamated, in fact. By our union with Him, He's got us "wrapped up, tied up, tangled up in Him." We are irrevocably connected with Him; what a privilege to be one with God!

> I am crucified with Christ: nevertheless I live; yet not I, but Christ liveth in me: and the life which I now live in the flesh I live by the faith of the Son of God, who loved me, and gave himself for me.
>
> Galatians 2:20

Our union with God is a result of our faith response to the love of God. It's akin to a marriage. Two people are united in wedlock, because of the faith in the words of love (covenant) said by both parties. Paul did not live in Jerusalem during the ministry of Jesus; he never had any personal encounters with Him during His sojourn on earth, but God opened Paul's eyes to this divine revelation that in His death, we were crucified with Him. Something supernatural took place during that *Passion* weekend. Our new life is now lived in Christ and Christ in us; this is our union with Christ. What a privilege to be One with Him, to be fused together, laminated to and merged with Him.

Blessed in Christ

Something else transpired in our being joined together with Christ, as described in in Ephesians 1:1-3

> Paul, an apostle of Jesus Christ by the will of God, to the saints which are at Ephesus, and to the faithful in Christ Jesus, Grace be to you, and peace, from God our Father, and from the Lord Jesus Christ. Blessed be the God and Father of our Lord Jesus Christ, **who hath blessed us with all spiritual blessings in heavenly places in Christ:**

We have been blessed with every spiritual blessing in Christ. God puts our blessing in the present perfect tense. Before we had the faintest idea of it, we had already been blessed. I could actually take this thought further that every person born into the world is already blessed in Christ. This is because God included every person in the *Passion* of His Christ. When we accept the sacrifice of our heavenly substitute, we enter into the work that He has already completed for us.

In my Physics class, I learnt about a phenomenon called diffusion. Diffusion is the movement of molecules or atoms from a region of high concentration to a region of low concentration. This is also referred to as the movement of a substance down a concentration gradient. The Bible describes The Lord as the One "who is blessed forever" (Romans 9:5). He possesses the *Blessing* in infinite proportions; He is the Source of the *Blessing*. By staying connected to Him, we can receive the *Blessing* from Him through the process of spiritual diffusion. The concentration of *Blessing* in Him is forever growing higher and stronger; and, as we stay "plugged" into Him our walk in the *Blessing* will increase in strength.

In identifying with Him, we are blessed with Him. If you are in Christ, you are not trying to get a blessing, you are already blessed! The same blessing that is in Christ is in every believer! The same identical life that is in Christ is in you. It is not just a good thought, but the reality of what we've been given as believers in Christ Jesus.

If we must stay in the *Blessing* and grow in its effectiveness, it's essential that we maintain our union with Christ. Let us see the various ways that we can maintain this union with God.

Fellowship

Possibly the greatest privilege any individual can have, is the privilege of having fellowship with God. God created man so that man could reflect and represent Him on earth. The only way to do that is by remaining in constant fellowship with Him.

Fellowship comes from the Greek word *Koinonia*. It means communion, or sharing something in common. It also means to share intimacy; close association with deep and detailed knowledge of each other. It is marked by very close association, contact or familiarity. It is developed through a warm friendship through long association.[2]

> God is faithful, by whom ye were called unto the fellowship of his Son
> Jesus Christ our Lord.
>
> 1 Corinthians 1:9

The Bible says that we have been called into the fellowship of Jesus Christ. The primary reason for our calling is so that we can share intimacy with Christ, intimacy with the God of the universe. As we share intimacy with the Lord, we maintain the union that we were graciously given to share in Christ.

The earthly ministry of Jesus was a result of his intimacy with Father God. He walked in great authority, because His authority flowed out of his prayer life and intimacy with God. He spent long hours, especially at night, in prayer, through a lifestyle of intimacy with God. Effective ministry can only flow out of a lifestyle of intimacy with God. For us to walk in the fullness of the *Blessing*, it will have to flow out of who you are in your relationship with God.

Intimacy with God

Having intimacy with God is the hallmark of a love relationship with Him. Intimacy with anyone is impossible if there is no love in the relationship. This could be the reason why we are commanded to love God. In His response to a question about what the greatest commandment is, the Lord's response was:

> …Thou shalt love the Lord thy God with all thy heart, and with all thy
> soul, and with all thy mind. This is the first and great commandment.
>
> Matthew 22:37-38

Loving God is the greatest commandment and privilege of all. We can only claim to love God, because He loved us first (1 John 4:19). His love for us is so deep that even when we were sinners, Christ died for us; The *Righteous* for the unrighteous and most unworthy (Romans 5:8). A revelation of His love for us necessitates us to love Him in return.

In loving God, we share relationship; we have fellowship and intimacy with Him. Our love for God is primarily expressed by our keeping His commandments. The Lord asserted that if we love Him, we would keep His commandments.

Whoever has my commands and keeps them is the one who loves me. The one who loves me will be loved by my Father, and I too will love them and show myself to them

John 14:21 (NIV)

The apostle in the early church, known as John the Beloved, also reiterates the same teaching in his epistles:

In fact, this is love for God: to keep his commands. And his commands are not burdensome

1 John 5:3 (NIV)

And this is love: that we walk in obedience to his commands. As you have heard from the beginning, his command is that you walk in love.

2 John 1:6 (NIV)

John equates our love for God to keeping His commandments and obeying His Word. When you look at both terms in detail, we recognise that **love** for God and the **fear** of the Lord are one and the same thing.

The Fear of the Lord

The fear of the Lord simply means deep reverence for God. It is a profound respect for God that produces obedience to Him and His Word, thereby making it our only option.

The word *Lord* means a person who has authority, control, or power over others; a master, chief, or ruler. The Supreme Being is God - the Being who, in the entire universe, is the One with the highest authority.

The fear of the Lord is not synonymous with being scared of God or afraid of Him; No, not at all. For instance, have you been so intimate with a person to the point that you enjoy such close fellowship with them that you don't want to let them go or see any harm done to the relationship? That is a more perfect picture of what it means to "fear the Lord." We have been given the privilege of intimacy and fellowship with Him, and we don't want anything to jeopardise that relationship; so we walk softly with Him. That, my friend, is what the fear of the Lord is.

The Bible says when we fear God, we tremble at His Word. Trembling at His Word means that are quick to obey it and do what it says. The Lord asserted that if we love Him, we will keep His commandments. Keeping His commandments is essentially the same as trembling at His Word.

> Thus saith the LORD, The heaven is my throne, and the earth is my footstool: where is the house that ye build unto me? and where is the place of my rest? For all those things hath mine hand made, and all those things have been, saith the LORD: but to this man will I look, even to him that is poor and of a contrite spirit, ***and trembleth at my word.***
>
> Isaiah 66:1-2 (Emphasis mine)

If we are consistently not keeping His commandments, then the depth of our love for Him should be called into question. The strength of our dominion as kings is determined by the depth of our devotion to God as priests. Dominion, which is the exercise of kingly authority, is an integral part of the *Blessing*, and our authority is only as effective as our priestly ministry.

> By mercy and truth iniquity is purged: and by the fear of the LORD men depart from evil.
>
> Proverbs 16:6

The headgear worn by the priests in the Old Testament had an inscription, "Holiness unto the Lord." As New Covenant priests, we have been called to live holy and think holy thoughts. Holiness is a function of the operation of the fear of the Lord in our lives.

> Having therefore these promises, dearly beloved, let us cleanse ourselves from all filthiness of the flesh and spirit, perfecting holiness in the fear of God.
>
> 2 Corinthians 7:1

In recent times, I have heard teachers claim that the fear of the Lord is an Old Testament concept, but that is not particularly true as we observe that it is discussed in the New Testament. Paul connects our holy lifestyle with the promises that God has given us. These promises were enumerated in the verses preceding 1 Corinthians 7. The Bible was not originally written in a chapter-and-verse format; the books were structured this way for us to easily compartmentalise them. The thought that Paul shares in verse 1, is a continuation of the final verses in Chapter 6.

The promises of God to which Paul refers, relate to separating ourselves from ungodliness. When we do this, we will have God's presence in our lives. When we became regenerated, one of the things that we gained is union with God. Because of our union with the Lord, He wants us to cultivate a certain lifestyle.

Our bodies have become members of Christ. As such, we are instructed by Paul to flee sexual sins. The act of sin obstructs our fellowship with God, in turn affecting our union with Him. God wants to deliver certain things to us and through us; but for this to happen, it is critical to maintain a certain type of lifestyle. Because of the benefits of the Presence of God that comes from our union with Him, we are instructed to perfect holiness by our reverence for God. Holiness may not be a popular message, but without a life of holiness, our union with God is suspect and our Christian walk futile.

Follow peace with all men, and holiness, ***without which no man shall see the Lord:***

Hebrews 12:14 (Emphasis mine)

In my mind, the thought of being in vital union with Christ is akin to having the presence of God in the Old Testament. Maintaining our union with Christ brings us to a place of having God's manifest presence in our lives. The presence of God is the difference maker.

Obed-Edom

As we study the life of the patriarchs, we see that they all had one thing in common: God was with them. Abraham feared the Lord and it was testified of him that God was with him. Isaac walked in the fear of the Lord and even his enemies affirmed that He had God's presence. The same was also said of Jacob and Joseph. Then, there is the unusual story of a man named Obed-Edom in the Old Testament.

After David had been established in his throne as King of Israel in Jerusalem, he wanted the Ark of God with him in Jerusalem. Long story short, while attempting to bring up the Ark of the Covenant from Kiriath-Jearim, the ox on which the Ark was being pulled stumbled. One of the men who kept the Ark, by name, Uzzah, tried to steady it and he died. The place was called Perezuzzah, because of the breach that happened.

This event took place close to the house of a man named Obed-Edom. David refused to carry the Ark to Jerusalem but rather had the Ark kept in the house of Obed-Edom.

> And the ark of the LORD continued in the house of Obededom the Gittite three months: and the LORD blessed Obededom, and all his household. And it was told king David, saying, The LORD hath blessed the house of Obededom, and all that pertaineth unto him, because of the ark of God. So David went and brought up the ark of God from the house of Obededom into the city of David with gladness
>
> 2 Samuel 6:11-12

The Bible does not tell us the state of Obed-Edom's life before the Ark was brought into his house, but there had to be a remarkable difference between the time before and after the arrival of the ark, because his neighbours noticed it, so much so that they brought news to David that the Lord had blessed Obed-Edom.

Before King David had the desire to bring the ark up to Jerusalem, the ark had been with a family for over 50 years. Israel went into battle with the Philistines at a time when they had turned their back on the Lord. They lost the battle to the Philistines, and the Philistines seized the Ark of the Covenant. The ark was kept in the house of their god, Dagon. After many dramatic happenings, they returned the ark to Israel in a cart with some offerings.

The ark was brought to the house of Abinadab, and his son Eleazar was consecrated to keep the ark (1 Samuel 7:1). They had the ark in their home before Saul became King of Israel up until his death. It was now David's seventh year as king at this time. If we make a modest calculation, we can conclude that for more than 50 years, this family had the ark, which bore the presence of God with no change in their life and circumstances. What a tragedy! The ark was with them in their house, but the ark was not in them. They did not let the ark influence their life and lifestyles.

How many of us have carried the presence of God for years without any positive change, radical or otherwise in our lives! It is recorded in the Book of Acts, that the disciples were first called Christians in the city of Antioch. The people must have seen something about those guys that made called them 'little Christs' (that's the literal meaning of the word Christian).

For 50 years, the family of Abinadab had the Ark of the Covenant in their house with no impact; while and Obed-Edom had it only for three months, and it produced radical change in his situation.

The reason for the difference can be found in the cause of Uzzah's death. 2 Samuel 6:6 says that Uzzah was killed *"because of his error."* That word *error* means negligence or a lack of reverence. We can now see the reason why for 50 years the ark did not profit one family, yet it did for three months in another.

When you study the life of Obed-Edom, you see a man who was addicted to the presence of God. You cannot be addicted to the presence of God without there being a change in your life. Obed-Edom might not have learned the protocols of the ark, but he reverenced God, he feared the Lord and his fear of the Lord attracted *Divine Presence* and the *Divine Presence* caused him to be *Blessed.*

One strange fact about this man's life is that his name means "servant of Edom." He is also referred to as the Gittite. The meaning of his name suggests that he may not have been a Jew. He was most probably a proselyte who loved what he saw about the Israelites (some commentators say David), and accepted the Jewish God, culture and became circumcised. Though his origins disqualified him, his attitude made him accepted. God is no respecter of persons; if you make time for God, He will make time for you.

During his sojourn on earth, God gave testimony about our covenant father, Abraham, that he feared the Lord.

And he said, Lay not thine hand upon the lad, neither do thou any thing unto him: *for now I know that thou fearest God,* seeing thou hast not withheld thy son, thine only son from me.

Genesis 22:12

In the following verse, we see the fruit of his reverence and profound fear for God:

That in blessing I will bless thee, and in multiplying I will multiply thy seed as the stars of the heaven, and as the sand which is upon the sea shore; and thy seed shall possess the gate of his enemies; And in thy seed shall all the nations of the earth be blessed; because thou hast obeyed my voice.

Genesis 22:17-18

Isaac also feared the Lord. His son, Jacob, referred to Jehovah as the God of Abraham, whom Isaac reverenced.

> Except **the God of my father, the God of Abraham,** and **the fear of Isaac,** had been with me, surely thou hadst sent me away now empty. God hath seen mine affliction and the labour of my hands, and rebuked thee yesternight.
>
> Gen 31:42 (Emphasis mine)

These Old Testament saints had the presence of God in their lives and it made all the difference. It was the key to their prosperity. Though it is true that we are New Testament believers, we must live our lives in a certain way to be a people of His *Presence.* This is not legalism; this is the truth of God's Word. As a result of our maintaining our union with Christ, we will become men and women who carry the tangible presence of God.

Abiding in the Vine

The Lord calls Himself the Vine and calls us, His people, His branches. The ability of a branch to bear fruit is tied to its staying connected to the vine. We have been grafted to Him, and the onus is on us to stay connected to Him. Without this connection, fruitfulness is impossible.

> Abide in me, and I in you. As the branch cannot bear fruit of itself, except it abide in the vine; no more can ye, except ye abide in me. I am the vine, ye are the branches: He that abideth in me, and I in him, the same bringeth forth much fruit: for without me ye can do nothing
>
> John 15:4-5

We can understand on a simple level, that when Jesus said for us to "abide in Him," it was possible for the people He was addressing to do the direct opposite; not abide in Him. As free moral agents, the decision and obligation to abide, remain and keep dwelling in Him lies with us.

I did say elsewhere that the *Blessing* is the empowerment to be fruitful. If we desire the *Blessing* and its fruitfulness thereof, then we must stay connected to the vine as branches stay connected to a tree.

The power to bear fruit is not resident in the branch; it is resident in the vine. Sap flows from the vine itself into the branch. That sap is the fruit-bearing enablement that the vine transmits into the branch. In the same way, we receive the Life of God from our Vine, so that we can manifest the Blessing in our lives.

We see that the key to fruitfulness is abiding in the vine. As the branches of the vine, without constant supply of sap from our principal, we cannot bear fruit. If we keep getting disconnected, we will not be in the vine long enough to bear any meaningful fruit.

> Wherefore, my brethren, ye also are become dead to the law by the body of Christ; that ye should be married to another, even to him who is raised from the dead, that we should bring forth fruit unto God.
>
> Romans 7:4

The analogy of marriage is here used. Without intimacy between a man and his wife, it is impossible to bear offspring. We have been espoused to Christ as his bride individually and collectively. If we must become fruit-bearers, then we must maintain spiritual intimacy with the One who redeemed us for the fellowship of union. Our empowerment for fruitfulness is tied to our union.

> Wives, submit yourselves unto your own husbands, as unto the Lord. For the husband is the head of the wife, even as Christ is the head of the church: and he is the saviour of the body. Therefore as the church is subject unto Christ, so let the wives be to their own husbands in every thing. Husbands, love your wives, even as Christ also loved the church, and gave himself for it; That he might sanctify and cleanse it with the washing of water by the word, That he might present it to himself a glorious church, not having spot, or wrinkle, or any such thing; but that it should be holy and without blemish. So ought men to love their wives as their own bodies. He that loveth his wife loveth himself. For no man ever yet hated his own flesh; but nourisheth and cherisheth it, even as the Lord the church: **For we are members of his body, of his flesh, and of his bones.** For this cause shall a man leave his father and mother, and shall be joined unto his wife, and they two shall be one flesh. *This is a great mystery: but I speak concerning Christ and the church.*
>
> Ephesians 5:22-31 (Emphasis mine)

In this relatively long text, Paul expounds on the relationship between husband and wife. At the end of the day, he called this talk about marriage a mysterious representation of our marital relationship in union with Christ. In this context, we are the bride (wife) of Christ, and we are commanded to submit ourselves to our Husband, Christ. Christ's love has been clearly displayed for us by His passion; therefore, we ought to allow the water of His Word come into our lives, sanctifying us and cleansing us from character flaws, so that we can be a church that is without blemish before Him.

Since we are joined to Him, as a man is joined to his wife, so that we can bear fruit, in order to make this marriage work, we must live in union with Him according to His terms.

Trembling before His Presence

The fear of the Lord also means Trembling before His Presence.

> Fear ye not me? saith the LORD: will ye not tremble at my presence, which have placed the sand for the bound of the sea by a perpetual decree, that it cannot pass it: and though the waves thereof toss themselves, yet can they not prevail; though they roar, yet can they not pass over it?
>
> Jeremiah 5:22

We see that if God's presence means so much to us, we would have to walk in a way that is pleasing to Him. When you treasure His presence, you don't want to live anywhere else.

We saw earlier in John 14:15, where Jesus equated our love for Him to keeping His commandments, the next verse starts with "and." The word "and" is a conjunction. In English lexis and structure, a conjunction connects two separate sentences together. So let's see what our keeping His commandments connects with:

> And I will pray the Father, and he shall give you another Comforter that he may abide with you for ever; Even the Spirit of truth; whom the world cannot receive, because it seeth him not, neither knoweth him: but ye know him; for He dwelleth with you, and shall be in you. I will not leave you comfortless: I will come to you.
>
> John 14:16-18

The indwelling presence of the Holy Spirit and His abiding with us is connected to our love for God, expressed by treasuring, keeping and obeying His commandments. The reward for our walking softly before Him, is the Father and the Son honouring us with their presence by the Spirit.

> Jesus answered and said unto him, if a man love me, he will keep my words: and my Father will love him, and we will come unto him, and make our abode with him. He that loveth me not keepeth not my sayings: and the word which ye hear is not mine, but the Father's which sent me.
>
> John 14:23

During his ministry on earth, our Lord walked in the fear of God. If Jesus Christ, while He was on earth, walked this way, and the Bible calls Him the author and finisher of our faith, then we don't have a choice but to also walk in the fear of the Lord like He did.

> Who in the days of his flesh, when he had offered up prayers and supplications with strong crying and tears unto him that was able to save him from death, *and was heard in that he feared*
>
> Hebrews 5:7(Emphasis mine)

And he was heard because of his reverent submission. (NIV)

And he was heard because of his reverence. (ESV)

And He was heard because of His piety. (NASB)

And God heard his prayers because of his deep reverence for God. (NLT)

And having been heard for his godly fear. (WEB)

And had his prayer answered because of the fear of God (BBE)

All the various versions point to the fact that His prayers were heard because of His deep reverence, submission, godly fear and piety; if He did, then we must. Truth be told, if we did what He did, then we can have what He had.

The Lord said that He and the Father are one (John 10:30). He was fully conscious of His union with God, but He also walked in godly fear. I would think that this should be the most valid reason for us to want to walk in the fear of the Lord.

> If a man abide not in me, he is cast forth as a branch, and is withered; and men gather them, and cast *them* into the fire, and they are burned.
>
> John 15:6

Maintaining our union with Christ should be our primary focus, because He says that anyone who doesn't go on abiding in Him is rejected as a branch. The result of being cast off as a branch is that the *cast-off* branch begins to wither. To wither is to dry up, become parched, shrivelled, and fall into decay and decline.

The withered branch becomes good for nothing. This is the harsh reality! I wish these were my words so that they could be easily disbelieved, but they are not. They are words straight from the mouth of Jesus. We need the sap that flows from Him. If our lives must become fruitful and productive for the kingdom, then we must stay connected, *hooked up*. The choice is ours.

> If ye abide in me, and my words abide in you, ye shall ask what ye will, and it shall be done unto you. Herein is my Father glorified, that ye bear much fruit; so shall ye be my disciples.
>
> John 15:7-8

We are given a blank cheque that is conditional on our maintaining our union with Christ. I have known these words for as long as I can remember, and it never fails to impact me any time I read it. If we will just *stay* connected, we can write our ticket with God. We can decide the amount that we want to cash; it's already signed for and the resources are available.

We have an Old Testament equivalent in the Psalms. The psalmist said, "delight yourself in the Lord and He will give you the desires of your heart" (Psalm 37:4 KJV). The word *delight* is likened to being pliable like putty before God; being easily moulded into whatever shape that He wants.

When that becomes us, our desires and His desires become one, and whatever ever we desire will be granted unto us. Our union with God is the key to everything. If we can just take care of our union with God, then we can be sure of every kingdom desire falling into place.

Standing before the Lord

In the Old Testament, the Priests were ordained to stand before the Lord and minister to Him in His Presence. Under the New Covenant, every believer is a minister; every believer has been called to stand before the Lord. Standing before the Lord is our greatest duty.

When the Prophet Elijah came on the scene, he declared himself as one who stood before the Lord (1 Kings 17:1). He had the authority to close the heavens and to release the rain in the nation of Israel. As a matter of fact, Elijah changed the nation of Israel because He stood before the Lord. We are called to be city-changers and world-shakers, and to do this, it behoves us to position ourselves to stand before the Lord.

In the book of Zechariah, we see a man who was supposed to stand before the Lord but was limited.

> And he shewed me Joshua the high priest standing before the angel of the LORD, and satan standing at his right hand to resist him. And the LORD said unto satan, The LORD rebuke thee, O satan; even the LORD that hath chosen Jerusalem rebuke thee: is not this a brand plucked out of the fire? Now Joshua was clothed with filthy garments, and stood before the angel. And he answered and spake unto those that stood before him, saying, Take away the filthy garments from him. And unto him he said, Behold, I have caused thine iniquity to pass from thee, and I will clothe thee with change of raiment. And I said, Let them set a fair mitre upon his head. So they set a fair mitre upon his head, and clothed him with garments. And the angel of the LORD stood by. And the angel of the LORD protested unto Joshua, saying, Thus saith the LORD of hosts; *If thou wilt walk in my ways, and if thou wilt keep my charge, then thou shalt also judge my house, and shalt also keep my courts, and I will give thee places to walk among these that stand by.*
>
> Zechariah 3:1-7

Joshua who was the high priest in Israel at the time the second temple was built was resisted by satan and had to be helped by the angel of the Lord. Joshua could not fulfil his responsibilities, because he was dressed in filthy garments. The priest was meant to be clothed in white garments that represented holiness. Filthy garments are symbolic of sin. Because of his filthy garments, he could not stand before the Lord. One of the jobs of the high priest was to bless the people. Without carrying a blessing from the *Presence* of God, he could not declare a blessing to the people and be a blessing.

His garments had to be replaced (forgiveness), and he was once again given headgear that speaks of a renewed mind:

> If we confess our sins, he is faithful and just to forgive us our sins, and to cleanse us from all unrighteousness.
>
> 1 John 1:9

We ought to be quick to repent and confess our sins, because God is waiting to forgive us and cleanse us from unrighteousness by the *Blood* of Jesus.

> But if we walk in the light, as he is in the light, we have fellowship one with another, and the blood of Jesus Christ his Son cleanseth us from all sin.
>
> 1 John 1:8

John shows us the process of the continual cleansing of the believer, as he stays in fellowship with God. The *Life* of God that has been given to us is the light of men (John 1:5). It is that divine illumination in our spirits that leads us in the way we ought to go. It is that quality of being that the believer has, that the optical eyes cannot yet see. Moreover, our walk with God is a walk in light. God is *Light* and dwells in unapproachable light; and, we have been united with Him, so by that union, we have been qualified to have fellowship with Him.

It is in this fellowship that we receive light into our condition, if, and when, we sin. As we recognise that we have missed the mark, we ask for forgiveness and the blood is ever ready to cleanse us from unrighteousness.

After his (Joshua the high priest) garments were replaced, and he was once again clothed in holy garments, the angel gave him a word from God, which applies to us today, "***If thou wilt walk in my ways, and if thou wilt keep my charge ... I will give thee places to walk among these that stand by.***" (Zechariah 3:7)

The Lord was saying, in essence, that if he lived in holiness, He would cause him (Joshua) to continually walk before Him in the eternal realm. The *Presence* of God, the *Eternal Realm,* is the place from where the *Blessing* originates. What a privilege to maintain our position that was acquired for us by the grace and mercy of God! God has given us access by our union with Christ. How we live will determine whether we maintain the access or not.

> Who shall ascend into the hill of the LORD? or who shall stand in his holy place? He that hath clean hands, and a pure heart; who hath not lifted up his soul unto vanity, nor sworn deceitfully. He shall receive the blessing from the LORD, and righteousness from the God of his salvation.
>
> Psalm 24:3-5

Sin sends us on a downward spiral from the eternal realm. Holiness sets us on an upward journey into God's presence. When we ascend the hill of the Lord, we encounter the *Blessing.* God says of His hill that "I will make them and the places round about My hill a blessing" (Ezekiel 34:26). In the hill of the Lord, we are filled with His *Blessing* and made into a *Blessing.* Whatever it takes, we should want to ascend into this realm.

The Lord said that "the pure in heart shall see God" (Matthew 5:8). The pure in heart will ascend into the hill of God. The pure in heart will enjoy the fullness of the *Blessing.* This is an invitation to be all that God created us to be, by the power of the *Blessing;* and this *Blessing* is only accessible when we cleanse our hearts and clean our hands, so that we can lay hold of that which the Lord has already qualified us for by His blood.

If we can stand before God, we can win against everything that stands against us. It is in the place of standing before the Lord that we are empowered to change the 'climate'. Elijah could hear the sound of the abundance of rain, as well as prophesy the rain and release the rain, because he stood before the Lord. We will be a people who release the rain of God's Spirit as we stand before the Lord; we will change the climate in our cities and localities. We will change the world!

Friendship with God

Friendship is a relationship of mutual affection between two or more people. The highest form of relationship between people is friendship. There are siblings and, sadly enough, spouses who are not friends with each other. People can be related by blood and not be friends. In the Old Testament, only two men were called friends of God: Abraham and Moses.

God's validation of Moses as His friend came in quite unique circumstances. Miriam and Aaron had started criticising and rebelling against Moses because he had married an Ethiopian woman (Numbers 12:1) and God responded on His behalf.

> And he said, Hear now my words: If there be a prophet among you, I the LORD will make myself known unto him in a vision, and will speak unto him in a dream. My servant Moses is not so, who is faithful in all mine house. With him will I speak mouth to mouth, even apparently, and not in dark speeches; and the similitude of the LORD shall he behold: wherefore then were ye not afraid to speak against my servant Moses?
>
> Numbers 12:6-8

It's kind of cool to know that God fights for His friends. During this encounter, God said that He spoke to prophets in dreams and visions, but He spoke to Moses mouth to mouth. This was because Moses was the friend of God. One powerful truth that should not be overlooked here is that you can be a prophet or minister and not be a friend of God. In the New Testament, the Lord said He only called those "who did what He commanded them to do" His friends (John 15:14).

> The friendship of the LORD is for those who fear him, and he makes known to them his covenant.
>
> Psalm 24:15 (ESV)

The Bible says that friendship with God is only for those who fear Him. He will reveal His covenant to them in a way that He wouldn't with others. The fear of the Lord is not a one-time event; IT IS A LIFESTYLE!

> Therefore the showers have been withholden, and there hath been no latter rain; and thou hadst a whore's forehead, thou refusedst to be ashamed.
>
> Jeremiah 3:3

The fear of the Lord is the key to the rain, and rain is what waters the earth and makes the crops grow. When we walk in the fear of the Lord, our lives are open to receive the rain from heaven. By the rain of *Heaven*, we walk in the fullness of the *Blessing*.

> *He will bless them that fear the LORD*, both small and great. The LORD shall increase you more and more, you and your children. *Ye are blessed of the LORD which made heaven and earth*
>
> Psalm 115:13-15

Walking in Love

Another way that we maintain our union with God is in our love walk.

> And we have known and believed the love that God hath to us. **God is love; and he that dwelleth in love dwelleth in God, and God in him**.
>
> 1 John 4:16

The scripture is quite plain in expressing to us that dwelling in love is synonymous to having a vital union with God. If we are not consciously walking in love with each other, I'm afraid to say, but the Bible says we have stepped out of God. Any step out of God, is a move away from union with God. Any move away from union with God, is effectively making a decision that we don't want live in the fullness of the *Blessing*.

We see in the *Word* that "we were chosen in love… accepted in love … so that we can have a share of God's inheritance (Ephesians 1:4; 6; 11). The *Blessing* is our inheritance and it is a gift of *Love*.

God is *Light* and He dwells in unapproachable *Light*. Who He is and what He is creates a force field of *Light*, and we have been brought into that *Light*. By the power of His grace, our spirits have been brought into this *Light*. As we dwell in *Love*, we dwell in God. The very essence of God is *Love*, and His *Love* is the source of *Life*, and in His *Life* is the *Light* produced.

When we cut off ourselves from His *Love*, we ultimately enter into darkness and our light without the *Light* of God is not strong enough to resist the influence of this darkness. The *Blessing*, being a manifestation of the *Life* of God, finds its source in His *Love*. As we maintain our union with God, we continuously dwell in His love, and we receive a constant supply of His *Blessing*.

Union with God: The Key to Dominion

When God blessed man in Genesis 1, included in that original *Blessing* was man's dominion in the earth realm. Man sinned against God and lost his place. Jesus came to restore man to his original position and give us the *Life* of God. Now, in Him and by Him, we can walk in dominion today.

> For if by one man's offence death reigned by one; much more they which receive abundance of grace and of the gift of righteousness shall reign in life by one, Jesus Christ.)
>
> Romans 5:17

Reigning is synonymous with dominion. Dominion is mastery over everything we face in life. It is the power to rule, and the supreme authority to reign in life. The opposite condition to dominion is impotence, which is a state of powerlessness. The Bible also reveals to us that we can reign in life through the wisdom of God.

> By me (wisdom) kings reign, and princes decree justice. By me princes rule, and nobles, even all the judges of the earth. I love them that love me; and those that seek me early shall find me. Riches and honour are with me; yea, durable riches and righteousness
>
> Proverbs 8:15-16

But the access to wisdom from God is the fear of the Lord:

> *The fear of the LORD is the beginning of wisdom,* and knowledge of the Holy One is understanding.
>
> Proverbs 9:10 (NIV, Emphasis mine)

We see a prophetic illustration about the Lord in Isaiah 11, where the prophet speaks of the Messiah and how that the effectiveness of His ministry is as a result of the Spirit that will rest on Him:

> And there shall come forth a rod out of the stem of Jesse, and a Branch shall grow out of his roots. And the spirit of the LORD shall rest upon him, the spirit of wisdom and understanding, the spirit of counsel and might, the spirit of knowledge and of the fear of the LORD; and shall make him of quick understanding in the fear of the LORD
>
> Isaiah 11:1-3a

The Lord was the prototype Man, and for us to get the same kind of results He had, we will have to be filled with the same Spirit. The spirits enumerated in the above scripture are the spirits known as the seven spirits of God in the Book of Revelation. They are as follows:

The Spirit of the Lord: After the Lord left the wilderness at the end of His prolonged fast, He announced that the *Spirit* of the Lord was upon Him. Quoting Isaiah 61, he asserts that this *Spirit* would enable Him to bring about changes in the lives of the people. It is the same empowerment that He said the disciples would receive on the day of Pentecost. It is also the same enabling that Peter said the Lord worked with in his message to the first Gentile converts (Acts 10:38). The *Spirit* of the Lord is a manifestation of the Holy Ghost as the *Spirit of Power*. It is the ability to bring about dynamic changes in people and situations.

The Spirit of Wisdom: The spirit of wisdom makes us unusually capable to think and act while utilising knowledge, experience, understanding, common sense, and insight beyond our natural experience. Solomon was given wisdom from God beyond his experience, and by the wisdom of God, he wrote books with sound wisdom that are still relevant, more than 3,000 years later. The wisdom of God made him the richest man in the world in his day. That is what the Spirit of wisdom can do for a man.

The Spirit of Understanding: It is the superior ability to understand, judge and discern.

The Spirit of Counsel: Before the Lord left the earth, He said He was going to send us the *Spirit* that would be our counsellor. The word counsel is from the Hebrew word *etsah*, which means advice or purpose. The *Spirit* of counsel allows us to access supernatural advice or guidance. Every person in the world today has a purpose, but without the *Spirit* of counsel one cannot access the knowledge of their purpose. With the *Spirit* of counsel, we can both discover and fulfil our God-given purpose.

The Spirit of Might: Might means strength or power, force, or vigour, especially of a great or supreme kind. This was what Samson operated in. The Philistines had to send Delilah to discover the secret of his strength.

Samson couldn't have been very muscular, because they would have at least guessed that his strength was based on a physically strong body. The *Spirit* of might permits us to carry out great feats beyond our natural strength without getting tired. God enables us by His *Spirit* to continue in carrying out great exploits for the kingdom.

The Spirit of Knowledge: The *Spirit* of knowledge provides the supernatural ability to know and perceive things that we could not naturally know.

The Spirit of the Fear of the Lord: The *Spirit* of the fear of the Lord is the activity of the *Spirit* of God in our lives that creates holy fear in the heart of the believer. It causes the believer to prize the Lord's presence above all else. The fear of the Lord is a *Spirit*; and, it is by this fear of God that we depart from iniquity (Proverbs 16:6). It is not something we conjure up ourselves, but a *Spirit* that comes upon us.

Of the fear of the Lord, the Bible says that:

> And wisdom and knowledge shall be the stability of thy times, and strength of salvation: the fear of the LORD is his treasure.
>
> Isaiah 33:6

Isaiah calls the fear of the Lord the treasure of the one who trusts in God. Another version illuminates this analogy:

> He will be a sure foundation for your times, a rich store of salvation and wisdom and knowledge; The fear of The Lord is the key to this treasure
>
> Isaiah 33:6 (NIV)

The fear of the Lord is the key to this treasure! Though the *Spirit* of the fear of the Lord is referenced (the last *Spirit* that is mentioned), if we juxtapose both passages of scripture, it is derived that the *Spirit* of the fear of the Lord is the key to walking in the other six dimensions of the *Spirit* of God. The fear of the Lord is the first step on the ladder. There is a level of demonstration of faith and power that is only accessible by the man who walks in the fear of the Lord. New dimensions in faith are the result of a breakthrough in revelation. Greater revelation comes from deep waters; and, these deep waters can only be accessed by those who are friends of God by reason of a walk of reverence with Him.

One of the reasons that the fear of the Lord is my passion is because during a time of seeking God, I heard Him say that "the coming revival and restoration of God's power to the church will be preceded by a release of the *Spirit of the Fear of the Lord.*" God is looking for people to use in this coming restoration. Let us make ourselves available by aligning ourselves with Him, His Word and His way.

Maintaining union with God is worth everything in life; it is the key to everything. To a very large extent, I think that everything about the *Blessing* is encapsulated in our maintaining *union* with God. If it is the fullness of the *Blessing* that we seek, then there must be some lifestyle adjustments. This is not a "feel good" message, but our feeling good depends on it. It will take the fullness of the *Blessing* to get work done, but we need to do some work to obtain and walk in the *fullnes*s of the *Blessing.*

Grace to Fear

Truth be told, a word on the fear of the Lord is not always the easiest message to digest. If the message seems impossible to obey and adhere to, it is because we've only heard half the message. John 1:17 says that, *"For the law was given by Moses, but grace and truth came by Jesus Christ."*

If you have only heard me say that you must keep his commandments, which by God, I hope you do, I must add that I only present to you the *grace* of God. The *grace* of God is the power for us to do His Word. *Grace* is God's empowering presence; it empowers us beyond our natural ability to do what God demands of us.

> And of his fullness have all we received, and grace for grace.
>
> John 1:16

What we've been given is grace upon grace, upon grace, upon grace; it is grace unlimited. As often as you need it, His *grace* is available. The depth of God's *grace* gives enables us to live out the requirement of the seemingly un-scalable height of His Truth.

> Wherefore we receiving a kingdom which cannot be moved, **let us have grace**, *whereby we may serve God acceptably with reverence and godly fear.*

Hebrews 12:28

Holiness, through the fear of the Lord, is a product of *grace,* and *grace* is only given to the humble (1 Peter 5:5).

> Let us therefore come boldly unto the throne of grace, that we may obtain mercy, *and find grace to help* in time of need.
>
> Hebrews 4:16

We have been given a free pass to approach the Father at the *Throne of Grace*, not timidly, but boldly, with the freedom to ask for *grace* to help us. We cannot do it ourselves, but when we decide to walk in reverence to God and ask for His *grace*, He will move all of heaven to fill our hearts with the *Spirit* of the fear of the Lord.

The saints in the Old Testament did not have the kind of access we have under the New Covenant. They only knew about a God to be feared, but we know about a God who is gracious beyond human capacity to understand graciousness. What we need today is an Old Testament understanding of the **Fear of the Lord** and a New Testament insight into the **Grace of God**. It will revolutionise the Church and cause us to maintain our union with Christ, walk in supernatural dominion over the kingdom of darkness and every work of the enemy, and experience the fullness of the *Blessing.*

Chapter 7

FAITH IN THE BLESSING

The truth that has been presented thus far in this book is this: God wants us to be a people who understand the *Blessing* and walk in its fullness.

When God made man, He blessed him and placed him in a garden. God issued a mandate to man to tend, keep and protect the garden (Genesis 2:8). In other words, God wanted man to expand the garden throughout the earth. We know how that panned out, but God's purpose for man hasn't changed.

> The heavens, even the heavens, are the LORD'S: but the earth hath he given to the children of men.
>
> Psalm 115:16

The Lord dwells in heaven and He put man on the earth. He actually bequeathed the earth to man as his inheritance. Basically, what God said to man: *In the same way I rule in the Heavens, you rule your world, have dominion on my earth*. The power by which God ruled in the Heavens is what He breathed into man (Genesis 2:7); this same power is the *Blessing*. The *Blessing* is the power that God gave to man, to enable us to bring forth His purposes on earth.

In an earlier chapter, we defined the *Blessing* as the empowerment to prosper. To prosper is to excel to the highest place in God. It also means to get to the zenith in something desired. God has designed paths for us in life and when we proposer it means that we are making progress and excelling in God's paths for us.

It is enlightening to know that, even though the devil was already on the earth, God did not mention anything about the devil to Adam. What God gave Adam to lord over the enemy was The *Blessing*. The *Blessing* gives us power over the enemy and all his works.

God's intention for man to live in The *Blessing*, like Adam did in the Garden of Eden has never changed. The *Blessing* that God spoke over Adam is very similar to the same *Blessing* that He spoke over Noah (Genesis 9:4). It is also the same *Blessing* that was spoken over Abraham when God called him. In the book of Galatians, the Apostle Paul shows us that we are blessed with the same *Blessing* with which Abraham was blessed:

> So *all who put their faith in Christ share the same blessing Abraham received* because of his faith
>
> Galatians 3:9 (NLT)

If we backtrack to verse 8, we read a powerful phrase, "God would justify the heathen through faith." The word *heathen* is from the same Greek word that means Gentile (or a non-Jew). When I hear the word *heathen*, the image that comes to mind is of someone who is involved in polytheistic worship or paganism. The wonderful thing about the *grace* of God is that it's not only for the goody-two-shoes; the *grace* of God is for everybody. It really doesn't matter who you are, where you are from, what your ancestors and forbears were involved in, faith in God has the power to justify you and declare you righteous.

Faith can bring you into the presence of God, where you can stand before him without any guilt or condemnation. Saving faith is our introduction into the *Blessing*; that is, faith in the blood of Jesus. To be established in the *Blessing*, we need to live a life of faith.

The Gospel Preached to Abraham

> Know ye therefore that they which are of faith, the same are the children of Abraham. And the scripture, foreseeing that God would justify the heathen through faith, *preached before the gospel unto Abraham, saying, In thee shall all nations be blessed. So then they which be of faith are blessed with faithful Abraham*
>
> Galatians 3: 7–8 (Emphasis mine)

The message that God gave Abraham – the message that Abraham accepted and had faith in - was the message about the *Blessing*. Isn't that exciting to know? When God "preached" to Abram and called him, the message that He delivered to him was the *Word* on the *Blessing*. The same message is what is being delivered to us today: God wants to bless us and cause us to bless others, families, communities and nations through us – the Church.

When God made man, He blessed Him. Adam disobeyed God, and his rebellion confined mankind to the curse. God began to search for a man through whom He could restore the *Blessing* on earth. God found Abraham and blessed him and promised that all the people of the earth will Blessed through him. God is committed to us living in the *Blessing*. It is His desire that we be blessed, and that we live in the fullness of the *Blessing*. All I'm doing in this treatise is to reiterate the same message that God preached to Abraham and to the Body of Christ; but for the message about the Blessing to be beneficial to us, the hearers, it has to be "mixed with faith" (Hebrews 4:2).

God wants us to walk in the fullness of the Blessing and become channels through whom the world can be blessed by Him. God wants us to take the Blessing to our sphere of influence. He wants us to take it to our workplaces, to the people and places where we conduct our business, to our families, schools and communities.

Seasons vs Systems

Throughout history we've experienced different eras when major shifts changed the world. Compared to the whole of history, they were nothing but a short burst of time. More often than not, they were also times of heightened spiritual activity.

In the New Testament there are two Greek words that are mostly interpreted as *time*. They are *Chronos* and *Kairos*. *Chronos* denotes a space of time, whether long or short; while *Kairos* primarily means due measure, fitness, proportion and is used in the New Testament to signify a season or a period of marked characteristics. The Lord Jesus is said to have come in *fullness of time* (*Kairos* time/season), but He came to introduce a system that operates in *Chronos*. By that I mean that Jesus came to show us how to live in God's fullness at any point in time.

A similar thought is presented in Paul's letter to the Roman church.

> But the righteousness which is of faith speaketh on this wise, say not in thine heart, who shall ascend into heaven (that is to bring Christ down from above:) or, who shall descend into the deep? (that is, to bring up Christ down from above:) but what saith it? ***The word is nigh thee, even in thy mouth, and in thy heart: that is, the word of faith,*** which we preach
>
> Romans 10:6-8 (Emphasis mine)

What we see in the above scripture is the description of a group of people who are asking for a special God-event. That He should be "brought down from heaven." The writer of Romans says our approach should be different, because the solution is already accessible and it is the *Word of Faith.*

While we cry out for 'seasons', God wants us to work by His system: Faith. At the expense of sounding irreverent, I liken it to an exact science, where you can predict the outcome of a certain experiment at every given point in time. An experiment that uses two molecules of hydrogen and one molecule of oxygen will always produce water. This experiment will produce the same result in Japan, Germany, Ghana, South Africa and Peru.

In most of our churches, we have a "word" for the year. It could be a year of favour, triumph, or double anointing. It could be whatever. While I don't have a problem with that, it is worthy to note that when the Lord announced His ministry after coming out of the wilderness in the *Power of the Spirit,* amongst other things, He declared that He came to announce "The Acceptable year of the Lord" (Luke 4:18). The era of God's abundant *grace* and *favour,* the time of His favour, victory, blessing, power, prosperity, wholeness, peace and fullness.

It is not "the year of favour," because any pastor says so; it is so, because 2,000 years ago, the Lord spoke it into being, then He went to the *Cross of Calvary* to make payment for the *Blessing* and its attendant favour. We receive every good thing, because of the sacrifice of *Calvary.* Jesus Christ, our Lord, is the One that brought us into the tide of the *Blessing.*

God's authorised system of living life is living by *faith.* God wants us to be in a stream of continuous fruitfulness, whether in special seasons or just regular seasons. It is the Father's desire that we are making steady progress and moving from glory to glory.

The only way we can make consistent and continuous progress in God is by a life of living faith. Paul, quoting the Prophet Habakkuk, concludes that "the just shall live by faith" (Romans 1:17). The just man, the man or woman who has been declared as the righteousness of God in Christ Jesus, his or her life becomes a life of faith.

The *faith* message has received a bad rap from many critics and naysayers calling it a "name it, claim it," "blab it, grab it" gospel. The preaching of the *faith* message has been termed the "Word of Faith" movement. The message of faith in God is not a movement; it is a lifestyle - the lifestyle of the believer. The real *faith* message places the *Word* of God in its rightful place as King, and overthrows human knowledge from the throne it used to occupy. We walk by faith, not by sight.

God has called us to live a life of faith. Faith is so important in the divine scheme of things that it is impossible to please God without it (Hebrews 11:6). If our ambition and primary goal in life is to please the Lord, then we must be a people who walk by *faith*. If the just must live by faith, then every moment of our lives must be lived by faith. Every day of every year, we have been called to live and walk by faith.

Hope

We are shown the key ingredient of faith in the Hebrews 11:1. We cannot talk about the subject of *faith* without making mention of the significant matter of hope.

I've never forgotten my answer in Bible School about the difference between *Faith* and *Hope*. I said, "Faith is from God and Hope is not." **Epic Fail!** Years later, I sat under a Bible teacher who thoroughly gave hope a real beating as a Christian virtue. For a lot of us, there is a poor understanding of what hope is and its power.

The Bible says "hope does not disappoint."(Romans 5:5a NASB) The word, *disappoint* means to fail to fulfil expectations or wishes. To be frustrated in one's dreams or have one's effect thwarted. What this says about hope is that the believer that possesses real hope will have their dreams come to pass. Hope, as used in the New Testament, is from the Greek word *elpis*. It means confident expectation of something good. It has to do with the unseen and the future.[1] The Lord is called the God of Hope (Romans 15:31).

Faith accepts as real and tangible today the dream (hope) that we expect to physically see in the future. Faith is present tense, while hope is future tense. Abraham's faith was fuelled by hope. When God showed him the picture of stars and grains of sand, He was giving him a depiction of the future. Visions and dreams are illustrations of our future. Hope is the confident expectation that the future will come to pass. The reason Abraham changed his name from Abram was because he believed in his God-given hope.

> Who against hope believed in hope, that he might become the father of many nations; according to that which was spoken, so shall thy seed be.
>
> Romans 4:18

Your vision or hope is the blueprint for your expectation. When a person desires to build a house, he consults with an architect who renders a drawing of what the house ought to look like when it is constructed. Our *Divine Architect* is the one that gives us vision for our future.

> For I know the plans I have for you," declares the Lord, "plans to prosper you and not to harm you, plans to give you hope and a future.
>
> Jeremiah 29:11 (NIV)

I could redefine hope to mean the confident expectation of your God-given dream or vision coming to pass. Hope is spoken of as the anchor of our soul (Hebrews 6:19). An anchor is a device dropped by a chain to the bottom of a body of water to hold a ship or vessel steady. When the anchor fails to hold, the vessel will move with the blowing current or wind. The vessel is held in place by the anchor.

When faith is tested by the winds of life, our anchor holds firm; it keeps us steady. This hope goes into the very presence of the Almighty. That is why the Christian hope is not just a wish for a better future, but a confident expectation of good fortune from the Throne of *Grace*. The hope that finds its source from that place will see its expectation become a tangible reality; thus, the refrain of the wonderful Methodist hymn, "*Will Your Anchor Hold?*"[2]

> We have an anchor that keeps the soul
> Steadfast and sure while the billows roll

Fastened to the Rock which cannot move
Grounded firm and deep in the Saviour's Love

Faith

If the effectiveness of a message is dependent on our faith in the message, what is Faith?

Faith is the substance of things hoped for; the evidence of things not seen.
Hebrews 11:1(Emphasis mine)

Faith, as translated from the Greek word *pistis,* is primarily defined as firm persuasion, a conviction based upon hearing. The main elements of faith, in relation to the invisible God as distinct from faith in man, are: 1) a firm conviction, producing full acknowledgement of God's revelation and truth; and, 2) a personal surrender to Him and conduct that demonstrates evidence of such surrender. Karl Barth believed that faith is trust that includes and stems from knowledge.[3]

Faith starts where the word of God is heard or read and the realisation dawns that this is the very truth of God. It is strong confidence and assurance in God, His Word, His Person and His character. Faith and belief are of the same Greek word, but *faith* and *belief* are not one and the same thing. *Believing* is where faith begins; the movement from belief to action is *faith.*

Faith is at the very heart of the gospel, for it is the vehicle by which we are enabled to hold on to the grace of God. The Hebrew word, as used in the Old Testament, for *faith* is *emunah*, which is translated faithfulness. The Hebrew language conveys the idea of faith with verb forms. Perhaps that is because the Hebrews regarded faith as something one does, rather than something one has; an activity rather than a possession. Fastening to the heart upon the *Divine* word of promise; a leaning upon the power and faithfulness of God. Faith echoes David's acknowledgement, "and now, O Lord God, thou art God, and thy words are true" (2 Samuel 7:28).

Philosophically, substance is that which supports accidents or attributes. *Substance* could be defined as substratum. It is something that is spread or laid under something else. It is any layer or stratum lying underneath another as a foundation.[4] Faith is the substratum of hope.

For a long time, I asked myself why God places such a high premium on our belief of Him and faith in Him. It's simply because it indicates that we take Him seriously. For any business transaction to take place successfully, both parties have to be sure of the veracity of their claims. If we don't accept God's claim, there is no way there can be any transaction between us and Him. If you don't take what God says seriously, you are making God out to be a liar, and God cannot lie. When we hear the Gospel message, we must employ the measure of faith He's given us to believe the Word and act on it.

Let's bring this to a human relational level. If you don't believe what I say, it affects our relationship. It means you don't trust my integrity and character. If you don't trust and have confidence in my integrity and character, we can only go so far.

In His integrity, it is impossible for God to lie. So it gives Him great pleasure when someone believes Him. If we don't respect God's integrity, He can hardly get anything to us and He can't do anything significant through and with us. God's purpose can only be birthed on earth by people who absolutely trust Him.

Faith arises and grows by revelation knowledge of God and His Word, and it is expressed through trust. You can only really trust a God that you know by relationship; therefore, *faith* is a function of relationship.

How Faith Works

Faith is the vehicle that moves the *Blessing* from its spiritual dimension to our natural experience:

> Paul, an apostle of Jesus Christ by the will of God, to the saints which are at Ephesus, and to the faithful in Christ Jesus, Grace be to you, and peace, from God our Father, and from the Lord Jesus Christ. Blessed be the God and Father of our Lord Jesus Christ, **who hath blessed us with all spiritual blessings in heavenly places in Christ:**
> Ephesians 1:1-3 (Emphasis mine)

The *Blessing* that has been given to us in Christ Jesus is in "heavenly places," but we need to experience it here on earth so that with it, we can fulfil the purpose of God for our lives. Faith is the power that makes real in our experience the treasures that Jesus, in His death, burial and resurrection, purchased for us. For us to receive our heavenly treasures from heavenly places, we must know how faith works. Incidentally, faith works the same way for everything in life.

Faith believes, but faith also speaks. In Jesus' popular Mark 11:23 classic teaching about faith to His disciples, he stressed more on the speaking type of faith than on the believing. He mentioned "believe" once and "say" thrice; therefore, for us to be established in the *Blessing* by faith, we say what we believe. As the Lord said, "he shall have whatever he saith." We are already blessed, but by our declaring what we believe about the blessing over ourselves, we shall "see what we say." For *faith* to work, it must be voice-activated; we must say something.

> We having the same spirit of faith, according as it is written, I believed, and therefore have I spoken; we also believe, and therefore speak
>
> 2 Corinthians 4:13

We release the spiritual force of the *Blessing* over our lives by *words* of *faith*. It is not enough to believe the *Blessing*, we speak the *Blessing;* that is how the spirit of faith works. That is how the force of faith is released for our victory and prosperity in life.

> That the communication of thy faith may become effectual by the acknowledging of every good thing which is in you in Christ Jesus.
>
> Philemon 1:6

Your faith cannot become effective if you are not saying something. There has to be a growth in consciousness about the good things that are in us in Christ Jesus. You may have been born with certain good things and natural talents, but I can assure you that you were born again with good things. Many good things were wrought into you the day that you got born again. As you discover those things, begin to say them.

You cannot become a great man or woman of faith if you don't say what you believe. Your confession of what you believe is the deal-breaker. It is what puts the *Blessing* that is in you, on you. Your satisfaction in life will be determined by what you are creating with the words of your mouth (Proverbs 18:20).

The Bible says that "death and life are in the tongue" (Proverbs 18:21). We see that the word *death* appears before life; this is a spiritual principle. When God called Jeremiah, He commissioned him over kingdoms to first "root out, and pull down and to destroy, and to throw down" before he would "build up and to plant" (Jeremiah 1:10). Before we speak life, we will have to kill some things. Before we build up, we will have to destroy some things. If you bought a piece of land that contained a raggedy old house, you don't build on the house; you first of all destroy the house and clear all the debris on site before you start the building process. You will have to speak the death of certain things that you see right now; this is blessing without the sorrow.

With the word of our mouths, let's begin to process the negative out of our families and our cities, and let us plant the positive in the places where they need to be. We must clear out the old ruin before we bring in new structures in the places where we want to see them manifest.

Your tongue determines the course of your life. Our vocabulary should be filled with the *Blessing*. What you say about yourself is as important as what God says about you:

> That he who blesseth himself in the earth shall bless himself in the God of truth; and he that sweareth in the earth shall swear by the God of truth; because the former troubles are forgotten, and because they are hid from mine eyes.
>
> Isaiah 65:16

The word for *blesseth* is the Hebrew word *barak*. What we see from God's word is that we can speak the *Blessing* over our lives. We bless ourselves in the name of the God of truth. We speak God's word about the blessing over ourselves.

> Though while he lived he blessed his soul: and men will praise thee, when thou doest well to thyself.
>
> Psalms 49:18

Talking about a blessed man that had gone on to glory, the psalmist said that this man blessed himself while he was alive. As long as you have breath in your lungs, bless yourself. The New English Translation of the Bible explains the concept further:

> *He pronounces this blessing on himself* while he is alive: "May men praise you, for you have done well!"
>
> Psalms 49:18 NET (Emphasis mine)

The Psalmist said men will praise you because of what you have done to yourself by blessing yourself. Not only will you see what you say, men will also see what you say. If you do not believe it, you won't speak. If you won't speak it, you won't experience its power. You have a responsibility to yourself to bless yourself. You are anointed. Speak words of power and favour over your life.

> And I have put my words in thy mouth, and I have covered thee in the shadow of mine hand, that I may plant the heavens, and lay the foundations of the earth, and say unto Zion, Thou art my people.
>
> Isaiah 51:16

When you are planting heaven, you are establishing the blessing by words from the mouth of God. The Word of God was first spoken before it was written; and, it was written so that it can be spoken. There are seasons when God gives us prophetic words - not just a general word from the scriptures, but a special, personal, **revelation** word for yourself. Meditate on that word, pray in the Holy Ghost if you are filled with the Spirit, and then begin to declare those words over your life. Plant the heavens in your life by blessing yourself.

The Word of God contains the very essence from which the *Blessing* is made. Everything we see was created by the Word of God; therefore, the Word of God, from His lips, will affect anything. God's word in the mouth of the believer is as powerful as if it were His speaking it.

When Ezekiel spoke forth God's word to him, the army that was dead came back to life (Ezekiel 37:1-14). Whatever God gives you to say over your life, say it and don't hold back. Declare over yourself in the name of Jesus, that you are blessed. "**The blessing is on me, it is in me. The water of the life of God is irrigating my life. I am like a green olive tree in the house of God.**"

This is not just positive confession; this is planting heaven on earth. His Will will be done on earth as it is in heaven as we speak words of power over our lives. This is God's method of transferring things from the eternal realm to the seen realm. "Believe in your heart and confess with your mouth." Nothing is impossible to the person who knows God's system of transference. God's system of moving things from the spiritual to the natural is by speaking the word of *Faith*.

113

The writer of the book of Hebrews reveals to us that the worlds were framed by the Word of God. The word *frame* is the Greek word, *katartizo*.[5] It means to mend what has been broken; to fit out, equip, put in order, arrange; to thoroughly adjust and restore. God's Word in our mouths has the ability to mend the parts of our lives that have been broken by the curse. By our speaking the Word of God, we can thoroughly repair and restore what was lost, as well as build up and put our lives in order.

The Word of God is alive, full of power, and contains enough power to bring itself to pass, when planted in the human heart through hearing. Faith comes as a result of hearing the Word of God (Romans 10:17).

When the believer declares his status as blessed, contrary to what he may have heard, he is not telling a lie. He is agreeing with his status in eternity as *Blessed*. He may not look like it, but that's who he is. He is affirming the truth of God's Word over his life. You may be barren right now, but declare you are fruitful! You may feel inadequate right now, but declare that God is your sufficiency, and that He has made you adequate and sufficient for your purpose.

My favourite healing in the ministry of Jesus is the healing of the woman with the issue of blood.

The Lord remarked that her faith made her whole . . .

She said it to herself. . .

She kept saying to herself. . .

The Lord said to the Israelites in the wilderness that He would do what He heard them say.

In life, we usually say what we see. That's why our spiritual eyes must be open, so that the eternal reality of the *Blessing* becomes more real to us than whatever temporal situation we are in. That was how I was set free from asthma. This is how we experience the power of the *Blessing*.

I was asthmatic for years, but by holding on to the Word of God that by His stripes I was healed, the stranglehold of asthma was broken in my life. The *Blessing* is all encompassing. It includes healing, deliverance, financial prosperity, raising great kids. It includes success and progress in everything. We don't make confessions to make what we are saying true, we say it because we believe it to be true.

Let's make this confession together:

> Jesus became sin for me that I might become the righteousness of God in Christ Jesus; I am the righteousness of God in Christ and because of His righteousness, I have inherited the *Blessing*. I have been redeemed from the curse. The Bible says cursed is everyone that hangs on a tree, that we might receive the blessing. Jesus was my curse bearer that I might become His *Blessing* carrier. I've been redeemed from sickness; Divine health is mine, in the name of Jesus.
>
> I am *Blessed*, I am not cursed. The *Blessing* is working in my life. I am making progress by the *Blessing*. I am fruitful and productive by the *Blessing*. I have dominion by the *Blessing*. I cannot fail in life. When men say there is a casting down, by the *Blessing* I am being lifted up because the forces of heaven have been released to work for me. I am blessed in the city; I am blessed in the field. The heavens are opened over my life. I have the rain of heaven and the dew of the earth; therefore, I am fruitful. I am righteous now; therefore, I am blessed.
>
> The favour of God is at work in my life. I am increasing in wisdom and in favour with God and with man. By the Power of the *Blessing*, I am fulfilling my God-given destiny. I am a problem solver. I am a gift to my generation. The *Blessing* of the Lord is making me rich. The *Blessing* of the Lord is causing me to walk in manifest abundance. By the *Blessing*, I enter into my wealthy place. I have been given all that I need for life and godliness. I have been given all I need to be prosperous and exceedingly successful in life. Thank you Lord, because the yoke of barrenness has been destroyed from my life.
>
> The *Blessing* is mine, in the name of Jesus, the favour of God is mine in the name of Jesus. I am in the *Blessed* place, the lines are fallen for me in pleasant places, I have a good inheritance, I have inherited the *Blessing*, I am walking on the

Blessed **path, I am a just man and my path is shining brighter and brighter, the Lord shows me the path of life, I have the presence of The Holy Spirit in my Life. I am prospering by the presence of God in the name of Jesus. God is on my side, Jesus is on my side, the Holy Spirit is in me and on me. I am** *Blessed***!**

Just begin to give God praise where you are right now. Hallelujah!

The Obedience of Faith

Abraham, who is known as our father of faith, "when he was called to go out into a place which he should after receive for an inheritance, he obeyed" (Hebrews 11:7). By faith, he followed God on a journey, even though he did not know the destination. Abraham also obeyed God in the most inconvenient of circumstances. He was instructed by God to sacrifice his son, the one whom he truly loved, Isaac, and he obeyed the voice of God. His obedience to sacrifice was called worship in Genesis 22:5.

The most acceptable form of worship to God is obedience to His Word; that's why Samuel told Saul that obedience is better than sacrifice (1 Samuel 15:22). Abraham's obedience would later be described as faith by the writer of the book of Hebrews. He believed God's promise about his Isaac to the point that he was sure that even if Isaac died, God was able to raise him from the dead (Hebrews 11:17-19). His belief in God's Word shaped his actions; the obedience of faith.

And there was a famine in the land, beside the first famine that was in the days of Abraham. And Isaac went unto Abimelech king of the Philistines unto Gerar. And the LORD appeared unto him, and said, Go not down into Egypt; dwell in the land which I shall tell thee of: Sojourn in this land, and I will be with thee, and will bless thee; for unto thee, and unto thy seed, I will give all these countries, and I will perform the oath which I sware unto Abraham thy father; And I will make thy seed to multiply as the stars of heaven, and will give unto thy seed all these countries; and in thy seed shall all the nations of the earth be blessed; Because that Abraham obeyed my voice, and kept my charge, my commandments, my statutes, and my laws. And Isaac dwelt in Gerar:

Then Isaac sowed in that land, and received in the same year an hundredfold: and the LORD blessed him. And the man waxed great, and went forward, and grew until he became very great

116

Genesis 26:1-6; 12-13

The above passages provide an illustration of faith and its connection with the *Blessing.* Isaac was in a land ravaged by famine and he decided to change locations. He was dwelling in a land that was experiencing an economic downturn. The sensible thing to do would be to move to a place that was flourishing. As he prepared to leave where he was, the Lord told him to stay.

Now this brings me to another point about faith. Faith is neither positive thinking, nor possibility thinking or positive confession. Positive thinking is a good thing. I would rather be around positive people. Sometimes, many of God's people are negative. A positive attitude trumps negativity every time.

Faith is not a blind trust either. Faith is not gumption or an assurance that events will work out. That is wishful thinking. It is based on pure conjecture. Bible faith is founded upon the Word of God. The word/voice of God is the stronghold or basis of *faith.*

> And it shall come to pass, if thou shalt hearken diligently unto the voice of the LORD thy God… And all these blessings shall come on thee, and overtake thee, if thou shalt hearken unto the voice of the LORD thy God.
> Deuteronomy 28:1-2

Israel's being blessed as a nation was determined by their response to the voice of God. When Isaac heard God's voice, he obeyed. It is really crazy to sow seeds in a famine when the land is in drought. But Isaac chose to obey God over the evidence. Now that's faith.

The result of Isaac's faith was a hundred-fold return and he was established in the *Blessing.* As you obey Gods voice, you will be established in the *Blessing.* God's instruction may not make professional or academic sense, but the result will always be miraculous.

Unbelief

Faith has many enemies that impair its effectiveness. Doubt, fear and unbelief are faith's most common adversaries. I would think that amongst these three, unbelief is probably the greatest enemy of living a life of *faith.* Unbelief is to *faith,* what Kryptonite is to Superman; unbelief is *faith's* Kryptonite.

In Matthew 17:14-20, we see the account of the disciples of Jesus' unsuccessful attempt to heal a boy that had epileptic seizures. Having just left the mount of transfiguration with Peter, James and John, Jesus was accosted by the boy's father to minister to his son, as the disciples couldn't heal him. Jesus granted his request and healed the boy.

When they were alone with Jesus, the disciples asked him why they couldn't heal the boy—they had healed the sick at other times—and the Lord's response was that it was because of their unbelief. It wasn't due to a lack of desire, but due to their unbelief, which had dismantled their faith. Unbelief robbed them of their ability to cast out the demon.

Now, not being able to cast out a devil is pretty bad—casting out demons in the name of Jesus is our heritage and right as believers—but not being able to enter into our promised land, flowing with milk and honey is far worse. That is the evil of unbelief.

The *Promised Land* is our wealthy place. It is The *Blessed Place*. It is the place in God where the *Blessing* is effectively at work in our lives.

> And to whom sware he that they should not enter into his rest, but to them that believed not? So we see that they could not enter in because of unbelief.
>
> Hebrews 3:18-19

The work was all done, the place of rest had already been prepared, but they were denied entry because of their unbelief. Unbelief has the potential to rob you of the experience of the *Blessing* of God in your life.

> Seeing therefore it remaineth that some must enter therein, and they to whom it was first preached entered not in because of unbelief
>
> Hebrews 4:6

The word translated *unbelief* is the Greek word *apisitia*. It is the direct opposite of the word for faith, *pistis*. It could be defined as a lack of faith, weakness in faith, or a lack of strength in belief. It also translates as unfaithfulness (or better still disobedience). Unbelief represents a lack of corresponding action to God's Word.

In the book of Hebrews, we see unbelief being related to the state of one's heart:

Take heed, brethren, lest there be in any of you *an evil heart of unbelief*, in departing from the living God.

Hebrews 3:12

The Bible was not talking about unsaved people; it was referring to the children of Israel as those whose hearts were evil because of the presence of unbelief. The result of a man's life is seen by from the condition of his heart. A heart of unbelief will never manifest the *Blessing* in its full measure. God wants us to live lives that are full of faith and cured of unbelief.

The Cure for Unbelief

In Mark 8:17, Jesus asked the disciples if their heart was still hardened, if they had no perception and if they still lacked understanding. The symptoms of unbelief are "an evil heart," "a lack of perception," and "a lack of understanding". These symptoms also point to the cure.

Repentance

Repentance is defined as a change of mind that produces a change in conduct. It is a renewal of the mind to build new mental models that align with the truth of God's Word. At the very fundamental part of it, repentance is a change of heart. We discover in the scriptures, that a person's life is a reflection of the condition of their heart (Proverbs 27:19).

I've met people who find it difficult to accept God's grace and unconditional love. This is the product of an evil heart of unbelief. It doesn't make them bad people, it just means that theirs hearts need work to accept the promise and the plan of God for them.

We cannot make ourselves deserving of what God has given us; He already made us deserving. We need to come to Him, in repentance saying "help thou my unbelief." From time to time we need help and cleansing from an evil heart of unbelief. If we are not careful, unbelief will rob us of God's *Blessing* for our lives. It won't be because we were not *Blessed*, but because our hearts were not cleansed of influences of the past that fostered in us an evil heart of unbelief.

Divine Illumination

You must have heard the expression, "seeing is believing". I've come to realise that even in spiritual things, this saying is true. You can't see it and not believe it. So the opening of our eyes beyond optical sight will cure unbelief. When we begin to see by revelation that which God desires for us, we can begin to have faith for those things.

> Cease not to give thanks for you, making mention of you in my prayers; That the God of our Lord Jesus Christ, the Father of glory, may give unto you the spirit of wisdom and revelation in the knowledge of him: *The eyes of your understanding being enlightened, that ye may know* what is the hope of his calling, and what the riches of the glory of his inheritance in the saints, And what is the exceeding greatness of his power to us-ward who believe, according to the working of his mighty power, Which he wrought in Christ, when he raised him from the dead, and set him at his own right hand in the heavenly places
>
> Ephesians 1:16-20 (Emphasis mine)

Paul prayed that the eyes of the Ephesian church and beyond be enlightened so they could know. The Greek word translated *know* in verse 18, is the word, *eido*. It means to perceive with the eyes, to get knowledge of, or to understand. It also means to experience any state or condition.[6] It can also be defined as to know by seeing. **Faith begins where the will of God is seen.**

To get an even clearer understanding of this word, *eido*, let's consider this example. As at the time of writing this book, the building called "The Shard" in the city of London is the tallest building in Europe. It has a very beautiful view of London. If someone tried to compare the view of London from "The Shard" with something else, they may have an idea of what it could look like, but they won't fully comprehend it. But when you make the same comparison to someone who has experienced the view from "The Shard," their response will be different. The reason is, one has experienced the view of the city of London from "The Shard" and the other one has not.

God told Abraham that the dimensions of the land that he was going to inherit was what his eyes could see (Genesis 13:15). The word for eye in Hebrew is the word *ayin*; it also means fountain. Your eyes are the fountain of your life. Jesus said that if your eye is good, your whole body will be filled with light. Your life follows the quality of your eye. What can you see? How far can you see? You become what you "see." You materialise what you visualise. We will always move in the direction of our vision. Our vision is what we can imagine through the inspiration of the Holy Ghost.

For the one who has had "the eyes of their understanding enlightened," they 'experience' what they 'see'; so unbelief is an almost impossibility for them. Therefore, the antidote to unbelief is the enlightening of the eyes of our hearts by the Spirit of wisdom and revelation.

The Believer's Labour

Let us labour therefore to enter into that rest, lest any man fall after the same example of unbelief.

Hebrews 4:11

The writer of Hebrews admonishes us to labour so as to enter into our rest. The labour that the author of the book of Hebrews is instructing us to partake in is the labour against unbelief. Unbelief robbed a generation of Israelites of their inheritance. We cannot allow unbelief to rob us of that which God has freely bequeathed to us in Christ Jesus. As you rise above unbelief, I see you walking into the fullness of your inheritance in Jesus' name.

When you research the word *belief* in the Greek text, it has the same root word as faith. Though *faith* and belief and two sides of one coin, it is safe to say that *believing* or belief is the central theme of faith. It is supported on either side by persuasion and trust. When persuasion and trust are lacking, unbelief soon replaces belief.

He staggered not at the promise of God through unbelief, but was strong in faith, giving glory to God; And being fully persuaded that, what he had promised, he was able also to perform.

Romans 4:20-21 (Emphasis mine)

The word *stagger* is the Greek word, *diakrino*; it means to withdraw, to put one's self at variance, or to separate one's self in a hostile spirit. Abraham had every reason to put himself at variance with God's promise. The possibility of the promise was more unlikely to happen than it was. The man was 100 years old, so his body was as good as dead, where receiving the promise of a child from his body was concerned.

The Bible says, "he did not consider his body now dead" (Romans 4:19). Your faith will either be strengthened or weakened by what you choose to focus on. In the final analysis, the responsibility of what to focus on depends on you. If you focus on the wrong thing, it will create unbelief; but, if you keep your eyes on the word of God, your faith will be strengthened. Unbelief will separate you from the manifestation of the promise of God to you. There will come times in our lives when we will have to choose the unseen reality of the *Blessing* over the seen evidence of the challenge that we face.

What our focus should be on is the promise, plan and purpose of God. God's promise to us can also be termed "the honey" of the Word. As with natural honey, there is sweetness in God's Word and promise, so it really should not be difficult for a faith man to believe them. The effect of the "honey" on the life of the believer should be restoration of strength for the journey and new vision.

> But Jonathan heard not when his father charged the people with the oath: wherefore he put forth the end of the rod that was in his hand, **and dipped it in an honeycomb, and put his hand to his mouth; and his eyes were enlightened.** Then said Jonathan, My father hath troubled the land: see, I pray you, **how mine eyes have been enlightened, because I tasted a little of this honey.** How much more, if haply the people had eaten freely to day of the spoil of their enemies which they found? for had there not been now a much greater slaughter among the Philistines?
>
> 1 Samuel 14:27, 29-30 (Emphasis mine)

Israel was in battle and Saul had placed a curse on anyone who ate food, but Jonathan did not hear the instruction. On his way to join the other soldiers, Jonathan found some honey and ate it. The honey changed his countenance and enlightened his eyes. The honey of God's Word will give us supernatural eyesight to see the *unseen*, so that we can believe the *invisible* and do the seemingly impossible.

> And **being fully persuaded** that, what he had promised, he was able also to perform
>
> Romans 4:21 (Emphasis mine)

Faith believes the ability of God to accomplish whatever He has promised to perform. As we walk with God and grow in Him, we will go through "the school of persuasion" where we will be eventually fully persuaded of divine ability to deliver as He had promised. So, the more I work on my persuasion by receiving revelation from God's Word, the more I walk above unbelief.

The term *fully persuaded* comes from the Greek word *plerophereo*. It means to make full; to carry through to the end; to accomplish; to fill one with any thought or inclination; or, to make someone certain. If there is full persuasion, then there has to be partial or no persuasion.

How do we become persuaded?

In Hebrews 11:13, we see a group of people who were said to have tasted the "honey of God's Word." They had a promise from God, though they "not having received the promises, but having seen them afar off, they were persuaded of them, and embraced them, and confessed that they were."

First of all, they saw the promise. They had a revelation of the promise of God to them, and the fact that they could *see* brought them to the place of persuasion. After being persuaded, they embraced the promise and spoke about the promise. The first key to persuasion is sight—we can never be persuaded of that which we do not see. We need supernatural eyesight to become persuaded of the promise of God.

Reaching the point of full persuasion is another matter altogether. We must embrace the promise; *embrace* is the Greek word, *aspazomai*, which means to joyfully receive, to welcome, to pay respect like it's a distinguished guest. The promise of God to us is special and we must treat it as such; holding on to it joyfully.

As we embrace it, we speak about it. We confess it. We say the same thing that God has said in His Word. To become fully persuaded, we have to keep saying what God has said about us. You have to see the promise to believe it; and, if you do not believe it, you won't speak. Finally, if you won't speak it, you won't experience the power of the *Blessing*. The place of *full persuasion* is what I also call the "stronghold of Faith."

In 2 Corinthians 10:3-6, we observe Paul talking about the on-going warfare in our minds. He talks about how we ought to be pulling down strongholds, casting down imaginations, and any high thing that is against the knowledge of Christ. He also talks about how we are to bring thoughts into the obedience of Christ.

The concept of *full persuasion* is seen in the reverse interpretation of this passage. Everything starts with a thought, and every thought has the potential to become something tangible. A thought that is dwelt on long enough becomes an imagination, and when the imagination is fostered and developed long enough, it becomes a stronghold. Our thoughts can determine the trajectory to which our lives follow. The word *imagination* is the Greek word, *logiosmos*. It refers to the analytical side of our mind. Most of our human training and education is in the realm of reasoning or *dialogismos*.[7] We must renew our minds with the Word of God until our imaginations are trained to think, see and visualise in alignment with God's thoughts.

God wants us to get to a place in our spirits where His word to us becomes a stronghold; where we build a stronghold of faith about His Word on the *Blessing*. In this place, we are more aware of what He has given us than we do not have; we are more convinced about the fact that we are *Blessed* than any curse, generational or otherwise.

God had Abraham walk with Him until he got to the place of the stronghold of faith (Genesis 17:1-2). It takes a continuous walk, persistent walk; learning while walking with God. There was a time in Abraham's life when God showed him the stars, figuratively asking if he could enumerate them, saying that that's how innumerable his descendants would be (Genesis 15:5). God had to take Abraham out of his house to give him new mental models; to open the eyes of his understanding, as it were.

Then again, God had another covenant with Abraham and this time Abraham did two things - firstly, he had to be circumcised, at the age of 99 years old. Imagine that! Secondly he got a new name. Picture him being called Father of many nations (that's the meaning of Abraham). He had to hear it every day and according to the chronology of the events, he had Isaac within one year.

God is trying to get us to produce the promise. As we travel along the journey of persuasion, there will come a time when we will be fully persuaded; then that which has been inside our spirits will began to manifest for the world to see. People will come to us because they will see that we are the ones with the answer.

Faith and Patience

I once attended a church meeting where the minister prayed for everyone who was named Patience, because their name was the source of the "delayed manifestation" of their breakthrough in life. I'm sorry to break this news to you: no anointing can deliver you from the need for patience. The Bible teaches us that "we have need of patience, that, after ye have done the will of God, ye might receive the promise" (Hebrews 10:36).

The writer of Hebrews says that we should be "followers and imitators of those who through faith and patience inherit the promises" (Hebrews 6:12). We saw in our key scripture that "the Blessing of the Lord makes rich." The word *makes* is a word that denotes a process. The space between when you receive the *Blessing* to when your profiting becomes obvious to everyone is time.

We would have to wait for certain things to come into fruition in life. When an orange seed is planted, it has the potential to grow and become a tree that could feed a community, but it must bide its time in the ground, before it becomes a shoot, then gradually grow into a tree that bears fruit in its season. The *Blessing* is a matter of growth.

> Desire without knowledge is not good, and whoever makes haste with his feet misses his way.
>
> Proverbs 19:2

We all desire to experience and express the fullness of the *Blessing,* but we must know and understand that, with the things of God, everything we receive is in seed form. The seed grows as we nurture it. If we make haste in these things, our intentions may be good but our failure to comprehend the principles will leave us lacking.

The connection between patience and the Blessing is also seen the first time early church received the fullness of the Spirit in the book of Acts.. We also realise that the *Spirit* of God is the benefit of the *Blessing* of Abraham when Paul asserts that "[Christ paid the price] so that the blessing promised to Abraham would come to all the people of the world through Jesus Christ and *we would receive the promised Spirit through faith*" (**Galatians 3:14** GWT, Emphasis mine).

The Lord had told them to wait in "the upper room" until the Spirit was poured out from on high. After His resurrection, Jesus was with them for 40 days, and it's plausible to think He fellowshipped and taught them certain things. Just before His ascension, He told them to wait. The Holy Spirit was poured out on the day of Pentecost. The day of Pentecost was 50 days after the Feast of Passover. This means the disciples had to wait for 10 days.

According to the scriptures, Jesus appeared to 500 people with this instruction, but only 120 people were there on that day of Pentecost. This suggests to me that 380 people were not patient enough for the initial outpouring of the Holy Ghost. Blessed are all those who wait for Him (Isaiah 30:18).

Just Do It!

Our faith cannot be said to be complete without action. As much as Christianity starts with a Big Done,[8] and we've so far spoken about the 'spiritual' key to walking in the fullness of the *Blessing*, for our lives to bear the fruit, we must do something with the *Blessing*. We must work!!

Jesus said, "I must work" (John 9:4), God the Father finished His work and rested from His work (Genesis 2:2) and The Holy Spirit works in, with and through us (Philippians 2:13). Every hero that we've grown to love in the Bible achieved greatness or fame because of their work. In his epistle, James asserted that faith without works is dead (James 2:26). For our faith in the *Blessing* to yield results, it must be translated into work.

From study, observation and experience, I have come to the realisation that the *Blessing* only works when we are engaged in doing some form of work. The *Blessing* becomes operational when we are about our Father's business. You don't exclusively have be the in classic ecclesiastical fivefold ministry to be about the Father's business; you just have to be in the place of destiny assignment, whether in your ministry or career calling.

One way the Lord has designed for us to see the *Blessing* in operation is in the work of our hands. God places a strong emphasis on work in both the Old and New Testaments. He wants us to bring glory to Him, through the work of our hands. One of the ways we bring *glory* to Him is by the avenue of doing the work we were designed to do.

Every believer is a minister, but not every believer is called into ecclesiastical ministry. We will have more believers on the frontline as market place ministers, who let their light shine at work, bringing glory to God, reaching the lost and influencing the world for the Kingdom of God.

If the *Blessing* is an empowerment to be productive, then we must produce something. One of the Greek words translated *barren* also means inactive, unemployed, lazy useless barren idle slow. One major reason for barrenness and unfruitfulness in the lives of certain believers is inactivity or outright laziness.

He becometh poor that dealeth with a slack hand: but the hand of the diligent maketh rich

Proverbs 10:4

The thoughts of the diligent tend only to plenteousness; but of every one that is hasty only to want.

Proverbs 21:5

You cannot be fruitful or great without applying yourself. More destinies have been truncated and wasted by laziness than by satanic orchestration and demonic manipulation. Mental laziness is the inability to apply the mind to create something. Physical laziness is oftentimes the refusal to apply oneself.

Laziness also includes not improving oneself or one's work:

I went by the field of the slothful, and by the vineyard of the man void of understanding; And, lo, it was all grown over with thorns, and nettles had covered the face thereof, and the stone wall thereof was broken down.

Proverbs 24:30

The above verse is quite intriguing, because it says that the lazy man had a vineyard in his field. Over time, some form of degradation had taken place. Your field is your career; it is the place that God has designed that you grow in. For us to experience the *Blessing* in our ministries (ecclesiastical or otherwise), we must employ continual effort. We can't stop cultivating that which God has given us; there has to be constant development. You should never leave your land fallow without purpose or be inconsistent at work.

The end result of laziness is unfruitfulness, poverty and a loss of relevance. God has given us our minds to think of more innovative ways to do what He has called us to. This is the work of faith; consistent growth and distinction in our God given roles.

Good understanding giveth favour: but the way of transgressors is hard.

Proverbs 13:15

In this life, to accomplish the great things that the Lord desires for you to accomplish, you are going to need favour. As much as favour is a spiritual energy that is given to us by God, there are certain principles that cause us to walk in favour, and one of them is "good understanding." In other words, the work that we create and produce has to be brilliant. Daniel was favoured but he also had an excellent spirit; he was brilliant. His work wasn't shoddy. Sometimes, as faith people, we do the least work while expecting great recompense; that is just foolhardy.

The Bible talks about a man named Bezaleel (Exodus 31:1). He received an extraordinary gift from God in the crafts. This man did not rest on his oars; he built the articles of the tabernacle. I discovered something about his work: the same brazen altar that he built was still functional 500 years later in the days when Solomon was king of Israel (2 Chronicles 1:5).

When you are brilliant at your work, you cannot be ignored. As the Lord shows us the career paths to take in life, let's become like Daniel, who was seen to be ten times better than his contemporaries (Daniel 1:20). Not only was Daniel a spiritual man, but he was astute in his career path. The *Blessing* is not just an entitlement, but an empowerment to work and create brilliant masterpieces that will endure if Jesus tarries. You have been given the power; the onus is now on you to be brilliant, and excellent, whether in ecclesiastical work or otherwise. *You are Blessed!*

Great Works

Verily, verily, I say unto you, He that believeth on me, the works that I do shall he do also:

John 14:12a

The phrase "what would Jesus do?" (often abbreviated as WWJD) gained popularity in the church in the 1990s, especially in the Unites States, as a personal motto for adherents of Evangelical Christianity. The phrase was used as a reminder of their belief in a moral imperative to act in a manner that would demonstrate the love of Jesus. The acronym WWJD was used for a type of bracelet or wristband, which became a popular accessory for members of Christian youth groups.

While the aim is not making this a popular phrase, when we read that the Lord said we would do the same works that He did, we should ask ourselves, "what did Jesus do?" What were the things He did during His sojourn on earth as the God Man? He healed the sick, cast out demons, cleansed the lepers, reformed people, created kingdom concepts, raised the dead and simply answered the cry of the people with whom He came in contact. He has commissioned us to do the same things.

> And as you go, preach, saying, 'The kingdom of heaven is at hand.' Heal the sick, raise the dead, cleanse the lepers, cast out demons. Freely you received, freely give.
>
> Luke 10:7-8

In what has come to be known as the Great commission in Christian circles, Jesus said similar words to His disciples and they are still true today:

> And these signs shall follow them that believe; In my name shall they cast out devils; they shall speak with new tongues; They shall take up serpents; and if they drink any deadly thing, it shall not hurt them; they shall lay hands on the sick, and they shall recover.
>
> Mark 16:17-18

God wants us to believe in the power of the *Blessing* the same way Peter and John replicated it at the gate called Beautiful (Acts 3). Before they healed the lame man, they made a statement that we ought to be able to make: *such as I have*. This phrase exemplifies that they had made this ability their own to deploy. Yes, it was God's, but they had personalised it and claimed ownership of it. We are to come to the place where we believe in the *Blessing* working in us to the point we can boldly proclaim "such as I have."

Jesus said to the disciples "you shall receive." The Greek word *receive* is the word *lambano*. It means "to take with the hand, lay hold of, any person or thing in order to use it; to take what is one's own, to take to one's self, to make one's own."[9] We have been given, but we now ought to *receive*. Make it your own, claim ownership of it. You are a co-heir with Christ; you are the continuation of the ministry of Jesus. Such as you have, give unto the people you come in contact with. Heal sick the sick, cleanse the lepers, raise the dead, by the power of the *Blessing*.

In the Old Testament, we meet a man called Gideon. When we are first introduced to him, he was in hiding from the enemies of Israel but God had called him to be the nation's deliverer. There are many of us in hiding today, because we have poor perceptions about who we are and what God has given to us. As we believe in God, we must also believe in ourselves. This is what Jesus meant when He said "have the faith of God."[10] God believes that what He says will come to pass, so we must believe not just what God says, but also that which He has wrought into our spirits.

During Gideon's encounter, he asked a question that we have all asked in different ways. He said "Where are all the miracles we heard about growing up?" (Judges 6:13) Gideon, like the other Israelites, had forgotten one thing: the miracles that they had heard about were performed by God, through men that had availed themselves to God. For us to see great works in our generation, we must be ready to make ourselves available to the Lord. The only ability that God is looking for is availability. If you are available to Him, He will use you for the great works that He purposed you to do before you were born. Gideon eventually became the great man as God saw him.

Faith Works by Love

We receive the *Blessing* the same way Abraham received the *Blessing*: by *faith*. However, for faith to be operative, it must "work by love." Our ability to walk in faith is dependent on the depth of our knowledge of God's Love for us. God's promise to us is an act of His love for us. He commends His love towards us and because of our assurance of His love for us; we can easily accept anything His Word says to us and about us. Faith in the love of God gives us the confidence to tap into the ability and provision of His *Blessing* for us.

> For in Jesus Christ neither circumcision availeth any thing, nor uncircumcision; **but faith which worketh by love**.
>
> Galatians 5:6 (Emphasis mine)

The word *worketh* is the Greek word *energeo*. It is from the same root word that we get the word *energised*. It means to make operative, to be effective, and to be actively efficient.[11] Without walking in love, our faith will not be energised to produce results. God is the source of our faith and the Bible says that in His very essence is *Love*. The atmosphere of the love of God is the only environment where faith can effectively be energised.

Faith is our entry ticket into the *Blessing*. We continue in the blessing by faith, experience it by faith and enter into the *fullness* of it by faith. Faith has no power in itself; its efficacy is based on what it holds on to. Our faith is founded on the *Word* of God, the source of the *Blessing*. As we grow in faith, we will grow and increase in our experience and expression of the *Blessing*.

Chapter 8

THE COMMANDMENT

When the Lord delivered Israel out of Egypt, He wanted them to be a people set apart unto Himself. He called them to be a kingdom of priests, dedicated to serving Him alone (Exodus 19:6). As a result, He gave them a law to distinguish them from all other nations. If they walked in obedience to the law that He had given them, then they were guaranteed to remain blessed.

> And it shall come to pass, if thou shalt hearken diligently unto the voice of the LORD thy God, to observe and to do all his commandments which I command thee this day, that the LORD thy God will set thee on high above all nations of the earth. *And all these blessings shall come on thee, and overtake thee, if thou shalt hearken unto the voice of the LORD thy God.*
>
> Deuteronomy 28:1-2 (Emphasis mine)

As born again believers and members of the Body of Christ, we are now the people of God on the earth. The command to Israel in Deuteronomy 28:1-2 has strong correlation to us as New Testament Christians. When we come into a relationship with God, we become united with Christ; and, by virtue of this union, we are made to sit in heavenly places with Christ Jesus, at the right hand of the Father, far above every other *nation* on the earth. As we continue in our walk with the Lord, the *Blessing* flows in our lives.

Essentially, God gave the Old Testament saints a law to live by; Israel had to walk in the law to stay within the confines of the Covenant and the *Blessing* that comes with it (Leviticus 26:2-5).

Conversely, if they disobeyed the commandments that they received from the Lord, they were to lose the benefits that came with their status as the people of His *love* and come under the curse:

> But it shall come to pass, **if thou wilt not hearken unto the voice of the LORD thy God**, to observe to do all his commandments and his statutes which I command thee this day*; that all these curses shall come upon thee, and overtake thee:*
>
> Deuteronomy 28:15 (Emphasis mine)

During the dedication of the temple, Solomon echoed the words of the Law of Moses that spoke about the consequences of forsaking the commandments that God gave Israel to follow after other gods to serve them:

> **But if you turn away and forsake My statutes and My commandments** which I have set before you, and go and serve other gods and worship them, then I will uproot you from My land which I have given you, and this house which I have consecrated for My name **I will cast out of My sight** and I will make it a proverb and a byword among all peoples
>
> 2 Chronicles 7:19-20 (Emphasis mine)

We are not under the Old Covenant; we have been made partakers of the New Covenant that is founded on better promises. Jesus, who is the author and finisher of our faith, has fulfilled the Law, and also abolished it (Ephesians 2:15). Whilst we agree on that, we must also realise that, in the same way that Israel was established under the Old Covenant to live by the Law, under the New Covenant we have also be given a Law; it is called the *Perfect Law of Liberty*. It is the law that not only liberates us, but ensures that we enjoy the benefits of our redemption. It is the *Law of Love*.

> A new commandment I give unto you, that ye love one another; as I have loved you, that ye also love one another.
>
> John 13:34

134

It behoves us, as New Testament Christians, to walk in love as commanded by the Lord. Paul asserts that we have been called unto liberty, but we should not use this liberty that we enjoy as an excuse to live for the flesh. We are to live by love and serve one another. The reason for this is because all the commandments of the law under the Old Covenant is fulfilled in one statement, which is, ***"Thou shalt love thy neighbour as thyself"*** (Galatians 5:13-14).

In his letter to the church in Rome, Paul taught that we owe a duty to each other, which is love. The debt of love is a debt from which we can never be free. The basis of the Old Covenant that God had with Israel was *love*. His nature is *love*; the very essence of His Being is *love*. So, all the commandments, "thou shalt not commit adultery, thou shalt not kill, thou shalt not steal, thou shalt not bear false witness, thou shalt not covet" can be surmised and understood by this one command:

> …Thou shalt love thy neighbour as thyself. Love worketh no ill to his neighbour: therefore love is the fulfilling of the law.
>
> Romans 13:8-10

Loving your neighbour is not just a nice thing to do; it is the commandment of the New Testament. The Lord takes the Old Testament concept of walking in love to another dimension. We are commanded by the Lord to love one another the way He loved us. Now the questions we should ask ourselves are: *How did He love us? How does He continue to love us?* He loved us by giving His life for us. He sacrificed Himself at Calvary for us. The most popular verse in the Bible is still "For God so loved the world that He gave His only Son…" (John 3:16). The love of God is a love of sacrificial giving; therefore, if we are to love one another, it must be sacrificial.

Possibly the most important present-day ministry of Jesus is His intercession for the believer. The Bible reveals that He is seated at the right hand of the Father, constantly making intercession for us (Hebrews 7:25). We can live rest assured that the love of Jesus is continually expressed through His ministry of prayer for us.

We can also express our love to each other by interceding one for another. In his letter to the various churches, Paul would always say that he was praying for them, or he would simply send them a prayer. The ministry of Epaphras to the church in Colossae included his intercession for them: that they may stand firm, and be fully established in the will of God (Colossians 4:12). When we intercede for one another, we are agreeing with the Lord in prayer as He is currently doing for each and every believer.

Love Defined

I define *Love* as the response of the recreated human spirit to God, people and things. This is because the love we are talking about is not an emotion; it encompasses emotions, but it goes beyond emotions. It is a decision to treat people the same way God in Christ treats us.

In the King James Version of the Bible, the word *charity* is used in place of *love*. In the New Testament, there are two Greek words that are interpreted as *love*; they are *Phileo* and *Agape*. P*hileo* more nearly denotes tender affection.[1] This is the more natural or human type of love between friends and family members. This is love on a more emotional level, where you treat people based on their response to you - for instance, what they do for you or what they can give you.

Agape is used in the New Testament to characterise the attitude of God toward His Son, mankind, and those who believe in the Lord Jesus Christ, in particular. It also conveys His will to His children concerning their attitude, one toward another, as well as to express the essential nature of God."[2] In 1 Corinthians 13, we see a clear definition and elucidation of this *agape* type of love.

This chapter continues from the discourse about the things of the Spirit or spiritual gifts:

> Love endures long *and* is patient and kind; love never is envious *nor* boils over with jealousy, is not boastful *or* vainglorious, does not display itself haughtily. It is not conceited (arrogant and inflated with pride); it is not rude (unmannerly) *and* does not act unbecomingly. Love (God's love in us) does not insist on its own rights *or* its own way, *for* it is not self-seeking; it is not touchy *or* fretful *or* resentful; it takes no account of the evil done to it [it pays no attention to a suffered wrong]. It does not rejoice at injustice *and* unrighteousness, but rejoices when right *and* truth prevail. Love bears up under anything *and* everything that comes, is ever ready to believe the best of every person, its hopes are fadeless under all circumstances, and it endures everything [without weakening]. Love never fails [never fades out or becomes obsolete or comes to an end]. As for prophecy (the gift of interpreting the divine will and purpose), it will be fulfilled *and* pass away; as for tongues, they will be destroyed *and* cease;

as for knowledge, it will pass away [it will lose its value and be superseded by truth].

1 Corinthians 13:4-8 (AMP)

Paul teaches us that there are three Christian virtues that are eternal: faith, hope and love (1 Corinthians 13:13). Furthermore, he asserted that the greatest of these three was love, that is, the *Agape* type of *Love*. If we can meditate on these qualities of divine love as expounded in the Amplified version's rendering of 1 Corinthians 13, there will be an amazing transformation in how we treat others.

Love Authenticates the New Birth

We know that we have passed from death unto life, because we love the brethren. He that loveth not his brother abideth in death.

1 John 3:14

As new creation people, the Bible says that the love of the Father is in us. Our father is essentially love by nature, and when He gave birth to us in the new birth, He gave us the same nature that He has. The *Love of God* is the essential ingredient in our spiritual DNA.

You cannot truly be a Christian without possessing love. You may close your heart to its flow, but it's in there.

It is comparable to a water reservoir designated to a house. Usually, the reservoir is connected to pipes that are linked to the taps throughout the house. If the taps are closed, there will not be a flow of water. When you open the tap, the water flows. The fact that the water did not flow, was never related to unavailability of water, it was the result of the tap being closed.

In one of his epistles, John asked this question: "But whoso hath this world's good, and seeth his brother have need, and shutteth up his bowels of compassion from him, how dwelleth the love of God in him?" (John 3:17)

When we became born again, the love of God was poured into our hearts by the Holy Ghost (Romans 5:5). So, love is not something that we are trying to obtain; love is something we already have. Love is the essence that defines us in the New Birth. John concludes that the way we know that we have moved from the realm of death into the realm of light is because we now love other Christians. The primary characteristic of the Christian is that he or she has become a *love* man or woman.

Love your enemies

Having been consciously born again for 27 years at the time of writing this book, I have seen many things become popular in the body of Christ. There is a stream of the church that goes about praying death to other human beings who they call their enemies (this is a very popular practice in certain cultures). It would be foolhardy for me to believe that we do not have human enemies or even human beings that avail themselves to the devil to try to cause pain, misfortune or even death on believers. As Christians, we do engage in spiritual warfare, but we must recognise that our battle is not against human beings.

> For we wrestle not against flesh and blood but against principalities and powers...
>
> Ephesians 6:11

That said, it is evident from scripture that divine judgment could, at times, result in the death of certain individuals and people groups according to divine wisdom. Such action is left to divine prerogative. The same God who killed King Herod (Acts 12:23), the firstborn of Pharaoh and all of Egypt (Exodus 12:29), punished Nebuchadnezzar's offence by making him graze as an animal for seven years (Daniel 4:32-33). It is my opinion that, while we seek God's righteous judgment on our behalf in spiritual combat, it is entirely His decision and prerogative on what transpires.

When Jesus was teaching his popular sermon of the mount, He made this popular statement that we often ignore:

> Ye have heard that it hath been said, Thou shalt love thy neighbour and hate thine enemy, But I say unto you, Love your enemies, bless them that curse you, do good to them that hate you, and pray for them which despitefully use you, and persecute you;
>
> Matthew 5:44-45

Who had said "hate thine enemy"? It was Moses in the Old Testament. The Lord Jesus is described as the "express image of God" or the very "representation of His essence" (Hebrews 1:3). So, if you want to know what God is really like, look at Jesus. During His transfiguration, there was a voice that came from heaven that said, "This is my beloved Son, listen to Him." To live like God wants us to, we must listen to Jesus. We must accept His perspective on any matter. On the issue of who to love, the Lord admonishes us to "love our enemies." If I love someone, I will not pray for his or her violent death.

> That ye may be the children of your Father which is in heaven: for He maketh his sun to rise on the evil and on the good, and sendeth rain on the just and on the unjust.
>
> Matthew 5:46

We are most like God when we walk in love with those who hate us. In verse 45, the Lord said that we should "pray for them that despitefully use us." When He said pray for them, he didn't mean pray against them. He meant pray for their well-being. The Bible in Basic English renders that phrase as "make prayer for those that are cruel to you." In the book of Acts of the Apostles, when Stephen was being stoned to death, he asked God to forgive his killers and "lay not this sin to their charge" (Acts 7:58).

> For if ye love them which love you, what reward have ye? do not even the publicans the same?
>
> Matthew 5:47

At the time of Jesus' earthly ministry, the publicans were seen as the most despicable of men. Jesus said that even the publicans loved the people who loved them. What He is saying here is that it is nothing special if the only people you love and treat kindly are the people who treat you well. If that's you, you have not impressed God; that is a life lived on a minimal level. God has called us to live life on the highest plane.

To live like God, we will have to be good to people who are very unkind to us. God actually commands us to bless those who curse us. The word used for curse there is an interpretation of the Greek word, *kataraomai*. It means to imprecate or invoke evil on another to bring about doom. Usually anyone that invokes evil is someone who is trying to truncate another's destiny. So, Jesus is simply saying "bless those who try to truncate your destiny". This is antithetical to normal human reasoning.

139

I mentioned earlier the stream of Christianity that believes in cursing people. When you contrast this with Jesus on the *Cross of Calvary*, He prayed for the forgiveness of the people - Jews and Gentiles - who put him on the cross.

If the nature of Jesus, which is the nature of God, is loving one's enemy and forgiving the people who harm you, what is the root of the prayers that cause harm; the prayers that wish death upon enemies? This does not sound like the character of God or like anything that can emanate from the Divine nature. The same people that are being 'killed' in prayer are human beings for whom Jesus died on the cross. I would rather listen to Christ than man. Let every man be a liar, and let God and His Word be true.

> Be ye therefore perfect, even as your Father which is in heaven is perfect.
> Matthew 5:48

It is only in our love walk that we can attain the perfect will of our heavenly Father. God is essentially *Love* and when we walk in love, we are radiating our Father's nature of perfection. Anything outside of a love walk is a walk outside of God; it is a life in imperfection.

The Love Test

The *Blessing* we have received is the *Blessing* of Jesus, but the Bible also calls it the *Blessing of Abraham*. If we must receive what Abraham had, then we must look at his example. In his first epistle to the Corinthians, Paul admonishes us that the *Law* and the *Prophets* were "written for our admonition"; because whatever occurred in those accounts are for us to use as a standard.

> But when the Pharisees had heard that he had put the Sadducees to silence, they were gathered together. Then one of them, which was a lawyer, asked him a question, tempting him, and saying, Master, which is the great commandment in the law? Jesus said unto him, Thou shalt love the Lord thy God with all thy heart, and with all thy soul, and with all thy mind. This is the first and great commandment. And the second is like unto it, Thou shalt love thy neighbour as thyself. On these two commandments hang all the law and the prophets.
> Matthew 22:24-40

When God called Abraham, Abraham brought his nephew, Lot, on the journey. Lot, who was like a son to Abraham, became great because of his association with Abraham. The people we are connected with in life are very important. By God's grace, I have developed many strategic relationships with various men and women of God whose faith and influences have been a great blessing to me.

There came a point in their lives when Abraham and Lot prospered so much that the land could no longer contain them. They had more livestock and staff than they had resources. As a result, their herdsmen began to contend with one another. When Abraham heard about the situation he went up to Lot:

> And Abram said unto Lot, Let there be no strife, I pray thee, between me and thee, and between my herdmen and thy herdmen; for we be brethren. Is not the whole land before thee? separate thyself, I pray thee, from me: if thou wilt take the left hand, then I will go to the right; or if thou depart to the right hand, then I will go to the left.
>
> Genesis 13:8-9

It is suggested to us that they lived in a community where seniority was given the highest priority. It was Lot's responsibility to go to Abraham to explain and broker peace. This entire debacle didn't have to get to Abraham; Lot should have tried to douse the flames before it became a significant issue that led to their eventual separation, but it didn't happen.

Abraham's humility, despite his greatness, is quite an example for us follow. More often than not, because we are right, we kick up a fuss. Abraham took the moral "high ground" and worked to diffuse the tension. Being from a culture where seniority always has topmost priority, I would expect Lot to apologise and try to broker peace between the rival herdsmen and his uncle, but we do not have any record of that taking place.

Instead, Lot took Abraham's offer without giving him first place. He did not honour the relationship and the place Abraham had in his life. He had a very low relational intelligence. Let's see the next verse:

> And Lot lifted up his eyes, and beheld all the plain of Jordan, that it was well watered every where, before the LORD destroyed Sodom and Gomorrah, even as the garden of the LORD, like the land of Egypt, as thou comest unto Zoar. Then Lot chose him all

the plain of Jordan; and Lot journeyed east: and they separated themselves the one from the other. Abram dwelled in the land of Canaan, and Lot dwelled in the cities of the plain, and pitched his tent toward Sodom.

Genesis 13:10-12

Against every cultural and natural sense of what is right, Lot chose first and chose what he thought was the better option and separated himself from Abraham. After Lot left, God spoke to Abraham. Incidentally, the name *Lot* means a veil, a covering. By implication, after the covering was separated from Abraham, he received Divine instruction. He was shown what he couldn't have seen with Lot in his life. I pray that the Lord will separate you from very covering cast in your life.

Sometimes to get to our next level in life, we need to be separated from certain relationships. Not every connection we have at the moment will be necessary for where God wants us to go. As unpalatable as this may sound, sometimes many friendships that we have are harmful to our progress in our God-given paths. I pray that God opens your eyes to see and know who you should cleave to and who you ought to go away from. Separation may not be easy, but it can sometimes be very necessary. The gain of our Divine destinies and purposes are far greater and worth every pain of separation that we may ever encounter in life.

And the LORD said unto Abram, after that Lot was separated from him, Lift up now thine eyes, and look from the place where thou art northward, and southward, and eastward, and westward: For all the land which thou seest, to thee will I give it, and to thy seed for ever. And I will make thy seed as the dust of the earth: so that if a man can number the dust of the earth, then shall thy seed also be numbered. Arise, walk through the land in the length of it and in the breadth of it; for I will give it unto thee. Then Abram removed his tent, and came and dwelt in the plain of Mamre, which is in Hebron, and built there an altar unto the LORD.

Genesis 13:14-18

Abraham was already blessed before this encounter, but by his walking in love with Lot, he was further established in the *Blessing* of God. Interestingly, both the land where Abraham was and the land Lot chose and beyond, were ultimately bequeathed to Abraham. Don't worry about who stole from you or cheated you out of a deal or promotion, God has something even greater planned for your life. As I am writing this, I have a smile on my face thinking about the many times we have fought needless battles not knowing that God already had a miracle in store for us; something that would literally blow our minds.

In the next chapter, Genesis 14, news reached Abraham that Lot had been kidnapped with many other inhabitants of Sodom and Gomorrah. This was Abraham's time to gloat. I mean, look at what had happened to Lot! In certain church streams, of which I had been part, this called for a great testimony of how God "punished" the person who had chosen the better part or taken what belonged to us. However, instead of Abraham revelling in Lot's predicament, he gathered his 375 trained warriors and went to war on behalf of Lot. He went to deliver Lot from captivity. What a man!

This man, Abraham, passed the love test! In the most uncommon circumstance, Abraham did what many "spiritual" people would point out as senseless. He put his life on the line for someone who had treated him poorly. No wonder when Melchizedek met him after the battle, he declared, "Blessed be Abram of the Most High God."

Forgive One Another

In the Lord's popular teaching on the subject of faith, as recorded in Mark 11, He said that when we stand praying, we should forgive (Mark 11:25). It is our responsibility to make peace with the people who have offended us, regardless of whether we think they are wrong.

Without sounding overly critical, someone once tried to explain a great doctrine to me about the seven stages of forgiveness. It seemed impressive, but there are no seven stages or five steps to forgiveness, just one: and that is, *forgive*! There are two very common acts of love: giving and forgiving. I can honestly say that sometimes, it is easier to give than it is to forgive, because forgiveness robs us of "our right" to feel offended.

> Let all bitterness, and wrath, and anger, and clamour, and evil speaking, be put away from you, with all malice: And be ye kind one to another, tenderhearted, forgiving one another, even as God for Christ's sake hath forgiven you.
>
> Ephesans 4:31-32

The Lord taught his disciples that we cannot live through life without ever having reasons to be offended (Luke 17:1). Bitterness, wrath and anger, are emotions that are stirred up in our hearts when we feel hurt or get offended. Offence is annoyance or resentment brought about by a real or perceived insult or disregard to oneself. There will always be reasons to become offended and bitter, but we will have to decide to take the high road and walk in love.

Walking in love is not for wimps. The love walk is the result of a force that emanates from a place of strength that we have been given because of the new nature that we have. Forgiveness is not always easy, but we owe it to ourselves to walk in forgiveness. I heard this statement years ago that unforgiveness is like drinking poison and expecting the person who offended us to become unwell. Unforgiveness poisons our souls.

The writer of the book of Hebrews admonishes us to not allow any "root of bitterness" to spring up and cause trouble, and by it many become defiled (Hebrews 12:15b). Bitterness is stirred up in the emotion and when we allow it to fester long enough, it affects our spirits and blocks our divine supply. We are called to be tender-hearted with one another. The word translated tender-hearted is the Greek word, *eusplanchos*. It means to be kind, compassionate and good hearted. We forgive and display compassion with one another because we are beneficiaries of God's forgiveness.

There are many sicknesses that are traceable to the emotional poisons of anger, unforgiveness, bitterness and offence. A CNN article quoted experts in the field of psychological sciences as saying that feeling bitter interferes with the body's hormonal and immune systems. Studies have shown that bitter, angry people have higher blood pressure and are more likely to die of heart disease and other illnesses. The reports illustrate overwhelmingly that negative mental states cause heart problems, to the same degree as smoking.

Physiologically, when we feel negatively towards someone, our bodies instinctively prepare to fight that person, which leads to changes such as an increase in blood pressure. We run hot as our inflammatory system responds to dangers and threats. Feeling this way in the short term might not be dangerous — it might even be helpful to fight off an enemy — but the problem with bitterness is that it lingers. When our bodies are constantly primed to fight someone, the increase in blood pressure and in chemicals such as C-reactive protein eventually takes a toll on the heart and other parts of the body.[3]

This is one reason why Paul says that we should not let the sun go down on our anger (Ephesians 4:26). There are many believers who are sick today, who may be able to trace the root cause of their aliments to these negative emotions. Walking in love secures your health; it frees you from the manifestation of the curse in sickness.

I had to spend an extra year to finish my first degree at a university in Nigeria because that was one of the lowest periods of my life. During that time, people who I considered as friends and members of same Christian Fellowship, peddled a rumour about me that I was a homosexual. Now, this is a very big deal for an African Christian, more so a minister. Homosexuality is frowned upon, both within and without the church in Nigeria. It took a lot for me, but I had to forgive people who questioned my sexuality.

For the record, I'm not gay, never have been and never will be. For many years, this rumour stigmatised me in certain places. I remember feeling sorry for myself when the rumour was still fresh and God spoke peace into my heart. This may be strange for certain people, but I still have a friendly relationship with the person who was the primary creator of the rumour. In the heat of the brouhaha, I spoke to him, and told him that I had forgiven him.

In the same vein, I've had to live through false allegations about financial misappropriation and downright stealing, which actually threatened my reputation and destiny. I can honestly say that it was not easy to deal with, but God's presence is worth more than any negative feeling.

Joseph's Example

More often than not, we get the worst treatment from our friends and families. There are siblings, cousins and all kinds of people who are related by blood that may never speak with each other again because of an offence. I will not belittle how you feel because I know it really hurts. The reasons for your offence and anger may be valid, but we are called to live by a higher reason: the *Love of God*.

The Bible can be a real soap opera sometimes, when you see the betrayals, the hate, and the connivance to do evil. There is almost nothing that you have gone through in life that we cannot find as an example in the Bible. If you think you have a dysfunctional family, then you may not have met Joseph and his family in the Bible.

Joseph was violently separated from his family and sold into slavery by his brothers. He went into Egypt as a slave; he was sold to a man named Potiphar. From Potiphar's house, he was sent to jail for a crime he did not commit. With all the humiliation that Joseph suffered, he could have developed anger and unforgiveness. But instead of animosity and resentment, he remained steadfast in his love for God and his care for people in the midst of his troubles. When he came into the place of power, he expressed his love by forgiving his brothers who had sold him into slavery. Joseph could have retaliated, but he forgave his brothers and provided a livelihood for them in Egypt.

When Joseph's father, Jacob, died, his brothers were afraid that he was now going to repay them for what they had done to him. However, instead of repaying them, he made what has now become a rather popular statement in Christian circles - that though they thought evil against him, God meant it for good.

I was once in a conversation with someone who unpacked this statement for me. The expression, "you meant evil against me," which Joseph used for his brothers, contains a Hebrew verb that traces its meaning to "weave" or "plait." He was literally saying, "you wove evil against me, but God unwove and then rewove it for good."

As we walk through life, people may weave our lives into complicated yarns of thread that put us in a bind, but as we stay in love and maintain our love walk, God, the *Master Weaver*, will unweave and re-weave again to create a masterpiece out of our lives.

Imitators of God

It is not redundant to emphasise again that walking in love is not something that is presented to us as an option. Walking in love is not a nice idea; walking in love is a **command**. Our love walk is compared to the sacrifice of Jesus on the cross and goes up to heaven like sweet smell of a sacrifice.

> Be ye therefore followers of God, as dear children; and walk in love, as Christ also hath loved us, and hath given himself for us an offering and a sacrifice to God for a sweet smelling savour.
>
> Ephesians 5:1-2

We are called to be imitators of God. We can only imitate someone when we believe we have the same or similar capabilities. As new creation beings, we have also received an impartation of the *love of God* in our spirits. We imitate our Father when we walk in love. His self-sacrificing *love* was displayed in the dying of Jesus for His enemies. He died for the unrighteous and the self-righteous. In God we see a Being who will rather die for His enemies than put them to death.

The Bible calls our right living a *living sacrifice*. Walking in love is not always easy; that is why it is considered a sacrifice. Acceptable sacrifices that are offered to the Lord attract *Divine Presence*. Sometimes we refuse to forgive, because our egos have been bruised and our emotions hurt. I think we would all agree that the *Presence* and pleasure of the *Blesser* is more than worth any offence or ill-feeling we may harbour.

The Love Advantage

Christ told us to love each other, in line with the original command. As we keep His commands, we live deeply and surely in Him, and He lives in us. And this is how we experience His deep and abiding presence in us: by the Spirit He gave us (1 John 3:23-24, The Message).

Let's consider some benefits of walking in love:

Love keeps us in the Light

Anyone who loves their brother and sister lives in the light, and there is nothing in them to make them stumble.

1 John 2:10 (NIV)

We said in a previous chapter that the *Love of God* is the source of the *Life of God* and the *Life of God* became the *Light of men*. At the very heart of the matter, living in the love of God keeps us in the light. When we have the light of God in our spirits, there is no occasion for stumbling in our lives.

An "occasion of stumbling" means to be caught in a trap or snare. It means any impediment placed in the way to cause one to fall. The plan of God in the *Blessing* is that we walk above everything that will cause us to be entrapped. The purpose of the curse is to have us trapped in snares. Living in love delivers us from the snares that the enemy has planned for us.

Some time ago, the Lord showed me how offence can keep us trapped in self-imposed spiritual jail cells. If you are offended and walking in unforgiveness, you could unwittingly be your own jailor, while praying for your freedom. God wants us to stay in the light, walk in freedom and live in the fullness of the *Blessing*. Release yourself from every prison and live in the freedom that Jesus purchased for you with His blood.

Filled with the Fruits of Righteousness

There are many prayers throughout the Bible, but there are also prayers in the New Testament, especially the Pauline epistles, that directly relate to us in lieu of what Jesus Christ did on the cross. Let's look at one of these prayers that speak about our growth in love:

> And this I pray, that your love may abound yet more and more in knowledge and in all judgment; That ye may approve things that are excellent; that ye may be sincere and without offence till the day of Christ; Being filled with the fruits of righteousness, which are by Jesus Christ, unto the glory and praise of God.
>
> Philippians 1:9-11

When our eyes are open to the *Love of God* in the full disclosure of knowledge, we will understand that our love walk is the most important part of our lives as believers. Love is the more excellent way. Walking in love keeps us sincere and unsullied. A solid love walk will enable us to live our lives without offence until the *Great Day* of the Lord's return.

We have received the gift of *Righteousness* from the *Righteous One* and have been made trees of righteousness. As trees of righteousness, we must bear fruit of righteousness. Our ability to bear these fruits in *Life* is tied to our love walk. Love is the life that flows through our root system. Being planted and rooted in love (Ephesians 3:17); rooted in Him (Colossians 2:7), who is *Love* in essence. It is safe to conclude that the major reason for poor fruit-bearing among us in the Body of Christ is our failure to walk in love.

There are church leaders who don't speak with each other. There are Christians who have vowed to never share relationship with certain believers because of offence. It ought not to be so. Do we want vengeance or to bear fruit for the *Kingdom* of our God?

There are things and paths in life that are good, but there are other things and paths that God has designed for us that are excellent: the highest value. When we abound in our love walk, our discernment will be clear. Love is the source of light and when we stifle our love flow, we dim the light that we receive in our spirits. This *New Creation Life* is a life that is lived by light. Love clarifies the plan of God for your life.

The Lord taught that the man who walks in the darkness stumbles because there is no light in him (John 11:10). John, in His epistle, elucidates this thought, saying that the man who hates his brother walks in darkness and lives without direction:

> But he that hateth his brother is in darkness, and walketh in darkness, and knoweth not whither he goeth, because that darkness hath blinded his eyes.
>
> 1 John 2:10

The believer without light can stumble through life. Oftentimes, in our stumbling, we attribute the lack of light for direction in our lives to God; as if God wants us to struggle through life. Because our step out of love puts us in the darkness, we light our own fires and live outside of the will of God for our lives. This is far from God's ideal for us. He wants us to have light; but light is a function of love. By the purity that comes from this love, our eyes are open to choose the highest and the best.

Love connects us with *The Blessing*

> Let brotherly love continue
> Hebrews 13:1

The Bible says that we should be good to all men, but especially to fellow believers as members of one family. The word translated to mean *brotherly love* is the Greek word *Philadelphia*. It means the love of brothers and sisters, the love which, as Christians, is demonstrated through cherishing each other; it is fraternal affection.[4] Every person who is born again is your brother or your sister. We are called to continue loving each other, which means forgiving every wrong and looking after the best interest of your brother in Christ.

The operative word in Hebrews 13:1 is "Let." That word proves that we are the ones who determine whether or not we walk in love. We are the ones who control our responses when we feel insulted or mistreated. Let means to allow; to permit, to enable, to authorise. These are all words of power, but they are also words of responsibility. God has given us the ability and responsibility of walking in love with each other; so whether we do or not is our choice. If we permit it, as with every godly virtue, it comes with a reward:

> Finally, *be ye* all of one mind, having compassion one of another, *love as brethren, be* pitiful, *be* courteous: Not rendering evil for evil, or railing for railing: but contrariwise blessing; knowing that ye are thereunto called, *that ye should inherit a blessing*
>
> 1 Peter 3:8-9 (Emphasis mine)

Our relationship with one another in the family of God facilitates our receiving our inheritance: *The Blessing*. Let's see the same verse in the Amplified Version of the Bible:

> Finally, all [of you] should be of one and the same mind (united in spirit), sympathizing [with one another], loving [each other] as brethren [of one household], compassionate and courteous (tender-hearted and humble). Never return evil for evil or insult for insult (scolding, tongue-lashing, berating), but on the contrary blessing [praying for their welfare, happiness, and protection, and truly pitying and loving them]. **For know that to this you have been called, that you may yourselves inherit a blessing [from God—that you may obtain a blessing as heirs**, bringing welfare and happiness and protection].
>
> 1 Peter 3:8-9 (Emphasis mine)

I love the Amplified Version of the Bible. It expounds certain verses of scripture, opening our eyes to sometimes hidden truth in God's Word. It explains to us that there are certain things that we cannot afford to do in our love walk with each other. We are called to be "compassionate and courteous (tender-hearted and humble)" to people who act towards us in a manner that directly opposes us; and to "never return evil for evil or insult for insult (scolding, tongue-lashing, berating)," where we can be easily tempted to insult those who insult us, just to prove that we can or that we are not weak.

It is easier to fight back than to ignore someone who has rubbed us the wrong way, but the essence of the spirit in us is love; therefore, we have the ability to respond in the love of God to the most obnoxious and uncouth of people. We should, as the Lord admonished us to do, leave a **blessing**; that is "praying for their welfare, happiness, and protection, and truly pitying and loving them." By doing so, we are sowing the seed of the *Blessing* and will "obtain a blessing as heirs."

We must understand that *love* is not weak. If you did not already know this, let me break it down to you. It takes more strength to ignore an insult or someone's misdeed against you—especially when you have the capacity to fully respond—than it does to get even with them. The amount of self-control that is required to not engage in the exchange of insults cannot be measured on a Richter scale. But that is what we have been called to do: not to pay evil with evil, but instead go out of our ways to do good to those who hurt us.

If we would maintain our love walk in the most difficult circumstances, we have a promise of inheriting the *Blessing*. I would think that with what we've seen about the *Blessing* so far, inheriting the *Blessing* is worth everything, including sacrificing that "good feeling" that we derive from retaliation.

The *Blessing* and *love* work hand-in-hand, because the *Blessing* is a result of the *love of God*. Because we've been blessed, we respond with love to Him and others. We can't love God without loving people. Keeping ourselves in the love of God holds us in position to stay in the light of His love, which releases a continuous flow of His *Blessing*.

In 2 Corinthians 7:1, Paul talks about how we ought to live, because of the promise of God's presence in the preceding verses: "I will dwell among them, and walk in them." These promises from God are indicative of us having God's tangible *Presence* in our lives, both individually and collectively.

John, in his epistle, asserts that we experience God's deep and abiding presence by our love walk. Our God is the *Blesser*, the originator of the *Blessing*. I would think that it is right for us to do whatever it takes to keep His presence in our lives. What a privilege to have both the *Blessing* and the *Blesser*.

Chapter 9

THE HONOUR PRINCIPLE

Let me emphasise it again, as I've repeatedly done in this book, that God wants us to step into the *Blessing*, remain established in the *Blessing*, and enjoy the fullness of the *Blessing*.

According to Ruth Paxson, "every Christian has inherited untold riches. As a child of the King and a joint heir with Christ, he is a spiritual multimillionaire. But comparatively few Christians bear the mark of spiritual affluence."[1] One of the many reasons we do not walk in spiritual affluence as we should, is failure to appreciate the *Honour Principle*.

> Wherefore the LORD God of Israel saith, I said indeed that thy house, and the house of thy father, should walk before me for ever: but now the LORD saith, Be it far from me; *for them that honour me I will honour,* and they that despise me shall be lightly esteemed.
>
> 1 Samuel 2:30 (Emphasis mine)

These words were uttered by the Lord Himself, and should, therefore, command special attention and regard from us. God said to Eli that if he would honour Him, in return Eli would be honoured by Him. It is *quid pro quo.*

Honour is the currency of the spiritual life. We trade or do business with currency. What we do when we honour the Lord is carry out a spiritual transaction that, as we honour Him, in return we receive honour from Him.

I think one of the ways God honours a man is to give him the *Blessing* in a greater measure.

In the first chapter of this book, we considered the three dimensions of God's moral character and one of them is justice. God is a just God; He administers His kingdom in conformity with his law. The justice of God means that He administers His law fairly; not showing favouritism or partiality. Only a person's acts, not his or her station in life, are considered in the assessment of consequences or rewards.[2] As the Supreme Being, who created and is greater than every other being, person or thing, the primary object of our honour is the Lord.

The words translated *glory* and *honour,* respectively, are interrelated and often used interchangeably in the Bible. But there is a subtle difference between them. The word *honour*, as used in the Old Testament, is from the Hebrew word, *Kabed.* It means to be heavy; in a bad sense (burdensome, severe dull) and in a good sense (numerous, rich, honourable). The other word translated *honour* is the word, *Kabod.* It means glorious, splendour, copiousness.[3] It is the word that is mostly translated as *glory.*

In Greek, the word translated to mean *honour* is *time* (pronounced tee-may), meaning "a valuing by which the price is fixed," "the price paid or received for a person or thing bought or sold." It also means the honour which one has by reason of rank and state of office. By analogy, it is esteem given, especially of the highest degree.[4]

Conversely, the Greek word for *glory* is *doxa,* which is the opinion, estimation or view of a person. In the New Testament, it is always a good opinion. It also means splendour, brightness, dignity, grace, pre-eminence, or majesty.[5] The word for *glory* also means *radiance.*

In a sense, we could also see honour as a defining theme in the Bible. God created man and included man in His glory, but man dishonoured God by disobeying His command; consequently, man lost his place and the glory associated with it.

We see throughout the Bible how this theme plays out. The Bible is an account of how people's lives were transformed based on whether or not they honoured God or gave Him priority in their lives. The outcome of a person's life was measured by whether they honoured God. Eventually, the universe, encompassing our world, will be turned over to God. When this occurs, He will again be given all the honour and glory by His creation and all creatures. Our lives on earth and in the hereafter are designed for us to give God the glory He deserves.

Give God Glory!

The Bible exhorts us to give God glory and honour. The primary way that we are admonished to give Him honour is by worship:

> Ascribe to the LORD the glory due to His name; Worship the LORD in holy array.
>
> Psalms 29:2

The word *worship* means the feeling or expression of reverence and adoration for God. We worship God because His attributes deserve it and His glory demands that reverence and adoration be given to Him In the study of biblical theology, there is something called the *Law of First Mention*. The *Law of First Mention* is the principle, in the interpretation of Scripture, which states that the first mention or occurrence of a subject in Scripture establishes an unchangeable pattern, with that subject remaining unchanged throughout Scripture.

In the Genesis account of the first mention of worship, God had instructed Abraham to sacrifice his only son, Isaac, to Him. No questions asked, he took Isaac and some servants, and went on a journey to the place where he was going to lay him on the altar. What he told his servants is quite instructive:

> …Abide ye here with the ass; **and I and the lad will go yonder and worship**, and come again to you.
>
> Genesis 22:5 (Emphasis mine)

The first time we see worship mentioned in the Bible, we see a man about to sacrifice his future on the altar. In his heart, as far as he was concerned, the boy was already dead; but God came on the scene and intervened, to prevent the sacrifice, because God does not accept human sacrifice.

What followed was a remarkable release of blessings:

> And said, By myself have I sworn, saith the LORD, for because thou hast done this thing, and hast not withheld thy son, thine only son: That in blessing I will bless thee, and in multiplying I will multiply thy seed as the stars of the heaven, and as the sand which is upon the sea shore; and thy

seed shall possess the gate of his enemies; And in thy seed shall all the nations of the earth be blessed; because thou hast obeyed my voice.

Genesis 22:16-18

The Hebrew phrase translated *to worship*, as it was first mentioned, is the word *shachah*. It means to bow down or prostrate oneself before a superior in homage, or before God in worship.[6] By his obedience to God, Abraham received the fullness of the *Blessing*.

Worship is a way of giving honour to God, and Abraham expressed his worship to God through obeying in a most significantly dire of circumstances: his choice to kill his son as a sacrifice. Because of Abraham's act, God once again declared an eternal blessing over him. From this definition and example of worship, we can easily conclude that *worship* goes way beyond singing songs. Yes, it includes songs of praise, but it comprises much more than that.

As earlier mentioned, the Hebrew language uses concrete ideas to give imagery to words. The Hebrew words translated *worship* include the following actions: serving, lighting up hands, bowing down, dancing, prostrating, and a few more. When we honour God, we are demonstrating the great esteem we have for Him. We are reflecting His glory back as praise and worship.

By him therefore let us *offer the sacrifice of praise to God continually*, that is, the fruit of our lips giving thanks to his name.

Hebrews 13:15

In the Old Testament, the priests were commanded to make sacrifices to God. Under the New Covenant, we have all been made priests (Revelation 5:10) and the sacrifice that we offer to God is our praise and worship to Him. We are called to offer sacrifices of thanksgiving to His name as a part of our priestly obligation. We are told that thanksgiving is the first portal into God's presence (Psalms 100:4).

Paul explains that the ungrateful and unthankful are cut off from God's goodness (or for our purpose, the *Blessing*) (Romans 1:21). Our continuous offering with the fruit of our lips, which is our thanksgiving, keeps us fastened to the presence of the *Source* of the *Blessing*.

Worship in Spirit and in Truth

But the hour cometh, and now is, when the true worshippers shall worship the Father in spirit and in truth: for the Father seeketh such to worship him. God is a Spirit: and they that worship him must worship him in spirit and in truth.

John 4:23-24

Worshipping God in truth means that we worship Him in the reality of who He is. We must **see** Him as He is, for our worship experience to be true worship. In Paul's second missionary journey, he found an altar in Athens with the inscription "TO THE UNKNOWN GOD" (Acts 17:23). One of the pivotal messages of Christianity is that not only can God be known as our creator, but that we can know Him personally and have a relationship with Him. Our worship is meant to stem from the knowledge of *Who* He is as a result of our relationship with Him.

The angels of heaven have been around God's throne for eons, yet they continually cry, "*Holy! Holy! Holy!*" In this sense, the word *holy* doesn't only mean pure; it also means *distinctive*, otherworldly; in a different class from them. He is amazingly awesome beyond what they could ever articulate. They see a new side of Him each day. When the Prophet Isaiah saw Him, he said that He is high and continually exalted. Our God enters a new dimension of exaltedness with such "speed" that is faster than the angels can grasp.

Honour is given to the degree of knowledge about the person to whom we are giving. If you met an older lady, you will show her courtesy, but the minute you realise that she is the Queen of England, there would be an immediate adjustment in your estimation of her. As it is in the natural, so it is in the spiritual. When we catch a glimpse of God's awesomeness, we will then realise that He is worthy of more honour and glory than we could ever muster. Oh, that our eyes may see the King in the beauty of His holiness!

This is the class of people for whom God seeks. The only time we see a similar concept in scriptures is in 2 Chronicles:

For the eyes of the LORD run to and fro throughout the whole earth, to shew himself strong in the behalf of them whose heart is perfect toward him.

2 Chronicles 16:9

When our hearts are right with God, we are giving Him real worship and He will show His magnificent power on our behalf. In the early church, we see a group of prophets and teachers who gathered together to minister to the Lord and fasted (Acts 13:2), and God spoke. Worshipping God is the way we minister to Him. It is our releasing of a reservoir of worship to an audience of One. The voice of God can never be scarce in the place where He is constantly being worshipped, honoured and held in high esteem.

The Sacrifice of our Bodies

God's Word is quite straightforward on the issue of honouring God in our bodies. In the Old Testament, the place where God dwelt was the Holies of Holies in the Ark of the Covenant, which was always situated either in the temple or the tabernacle. The word tabernacle means a fixed or moveable dwelling place. In the New Testament, we are told that our bodies are the temple of the Holy Spirit. If you are born again, God's new address in the world is your body. Whether moving or static, as a believer you have become the dwelling place for God. You are the house of God; so you have a great responsibility to take care of God's house.

If you knew that God was in a room and you could see Him physically, how would you act? God lives inside of you by His Spirit; so how you act with His Presence inside of you determines the type of host that you are. We can grieve the Spirit of God by how we act.

You were bought at a price. Therefore honour God with your bodies.

1 Corinthians 6:20

Paul tells us that we have been bought with a price. The primary reason for our consecration is the fact that we do not own our bodies. We live in a borrowed suit. If you loaned someone your car for the day and they brought it back smashed up, I am quite convinced that you would not be well pleased. Not just because they destroyed your car, but also because you would not feel honoured. God has loaned us our bodies; therefore, it behoves us to honour Him with them.

> I beseech you therefore, brethren, by the mercies of God, that ye present your bodies a living sacrifice, holy, acceptable unto God, which is your reasonable service.
>
> Romans 12:1

In his letter to the church in Rome, Paul tells them that because of the narrative he had given them about God's mercy in choosing them, Gentiles, to be fellow heirs in the *Divine Life*, they should present their bodies as living sacrifices. In the Amplified Version, presenting our bodies holy to God is equated to "our spiritual act of worship."

> Whether, then, you eat or drink or whatever you do, do all to the glory of God.
>
> 1 Corinthians 10:31

Our physical body is what qualifies us to be legal entities on earth. Without our bodies being healthy and strong, we would not be able to carry out our God-given purpose to its maximum. What we eat and drink, and how we manage our bodies is a sign of honour to God. Your body is a gift from God and what you do with it is your gift back to Him; that is why we are instructed in Paul's epistle to "honour God in our bodies." Physical exercise, right eating and good health practices are also ways in which we can honour God in our body.

Tithes and Offerings

Having been in church much of all my life, I can say that I know a few things about church and church traditions. Whenever someone steps up on the podium and mentions the book of Malachi, the first thing that comes to our minds is money: "Here he comes, about to take money out of my hands!" The tithe was even rechristened "Malachi" by my friends.

As I studied the Bible, I came to the realisation that the book of Malachi is about much more than money; it is about honour for God. In the first chapter of Malachi, God asks a question:

> *A son honoureth his father, and a servant his master.* **if then I be a father, where is mine honour?** *and if I be a master, where is my fear? saith the LORD of hosts unto you, O priests, that despise my name. And ye say, Wherein have we despised thy name?*
>
> Malachi 1:6 (Emphasis mine)

As our Father, we agree, without an iota of dissent, that God deserves our honour. One of the ways we honour Him, as revealed throughout the Bible and highlighted in the book of Malachi, is through our finances. I would like to reiterate here that the message about the *Blessing* is not fundamentally about financial empowerment, but about standing in a place of power on earth and in the heavens.

> **Honour the LORD with thy substance**, and with the firstfruits of all thine increase: So shall thy barns be filled with plenty, and thy presses shall burst out with new wine
>
> Proverbs 3:9-10 (Emphasis mine)

The verse above mentions the *first fruit offering* as a means to honour God. This verse brings us to a common practice in many churches -the *first fruit offering*. I don't think it is a New Testament concept. What the *first fruit offering* typifies is Jesus, as the first amongst many brethren (Romans 8:29). As the first man in the New Creation, He was declared as *blessed*, and anyone who follows in accordance with His order is also *blessed* (Romans 11:26). Adam was a first fruit of the old creation, while Jesus is the first fruit of the new.

Does that mean I disagree with the practice of it? No. The reason is that God is not a respecter of persons. The Lord said it is more *blessed* to give than to receive. So as you sow your seed (first fruit) offering, the *One* to *Whom* it is offered, will no doubt bless you for it. But if the question is the giving of *first fruit offering* as a New Testament ordinance, then the answer is a resounding No.

The key thought we can derive from the Proverbs 3 passage is that we can honour the Lord with our substance. When the issue of honouring God in our finances is raised, we cannot talk about it without delving into the subject of tithing. There are possibly as many opinions on tithing as there are books today. The tithe is defined as one-tenth of earned or received income, usually the first ten per cent.

There was a time in Israel's history when God accused them of robbing Him. They asked how they robbed Him, and He said it was by their non-remittance of tithes and offerings:

> Will a man rob God? Yet ye have robbed me. But ye say, Wherein have
> we robbed thee? In tithes and offerings.
>
> Malachi 3:8

When God says you have robbed me, He is not particularly saying "you have stolen money from Me," even though it alludes to that. What He is really saying is that He has been robbed of His honour and the one who doesn't honour Him, especially in that area, is denying Him the opportunity for Him to cause His *Blessing* to flow through to them.

Personally, I know many people who do not agree that we should tithe in the New Covenant, especially because it is not explicitly stated in the New Testament epistles. There are others who say that the idea of bringing the tithe wasn't restored to the Church until many years after the early disciples had passed on to glory and Constantine became the Emperor of Rome.

In all fairness, these are valid points. In response to these points, I will say that, for many years, and even in some Christian circles today, there are many truths in God's Word that have been restored that are not accepted in every stream of the Church. For instance, until the Azusa Street Revival in 1906, being filled with the Holy Spirit with the initial evidence of speaking in tongues was literally unheard of. Even now, healing, as a part of the atonement, is still not a generally accepted truth by many Christians and theologians. Baptism by immersion was recovered only after the Reformation. Several other biblical truths were practiced in the early church were not recovered until many centuries after the disciples had gone to be with the Lord.

The earliest record we see in the Bible about the tithe is in Genesis 14, where Abraham met Melchizedek after his defeat of the armies of four nations:

> And Melchizedek king of Salem brought forth bread and wine: and he was the priest of the most high God. And he blessed him, and said, Blessed be Abram of the most high God, possessor of heaven and earth: And blessed be the most high God, which hath delivered thine enemies into thy hand. *And he gave him tithes of all.*
>
> Genesis 14:19-20

When Abraham met Melchizedek, Melchizedek brought the elements of what we call the Holy Communion, and they shared this meal together; then, he blessed Abraham. We see that in the New Testament, the Lord refers to the bread and the wine as symbols of His *Life* (John 6:57). We bring the tithe, because the Lord has shared His *Life* with us in the New Covenant.

When Abraham met Melchizedek, he (Abraham) gave him tithes of all his spoils from war. This was his first interaction with a priest, as recorded in the Bible, and when he met this priest, he gave him tithes. We also see that Melchizedek blessed Abraham before Abraham gave the tithes. God had already blessed him, and he was financially prosperous as proof of God's hand on his life.

In the same vein, as believers, we don't tithe to get the *Blessing*, because our *Blessing* was given to us "in Christ Jesus" (Ephesians 1:3). We enter the *Blessing* solely by entering into the finished work of Jesus by the New Birth. What then does the tithe achieve? Why then should we tithe? We tithe not to become *blessed*, but as a sign of love, gratitude and honour to our King.

After these events, which included giving his tithes to Melchizedek, Abraham had another encounter with God:

> After these things the word of the LORD came unto Abram in a vision, saying, Fear not, Abram: I am thy shield, and thy exceeding great reward.
> Genesis 15:1

Abraham had just given tithes to Melchizedek, spurned the wealth of Sodom and Gomorrah, and declared God as his source. Then the Lord appeared on the scene, saying to Abraham in a vision that He was Abraham's protection and "exceedingly great reward." The same thought is presented in Malachi 3, where the Lord promised to rebuke the devourer for the sakes of His people. Honouring God with our finances keeps us in the flow of the *Blessing*.

One of the rewards of the tithe is God's *Blessing* in form of open heavens:

> Bring ye all the tithes into the storehouse, that there may be meat in mine house, and prove me now herewith, saith the LORD of hosts, if I will not open you the windows of heaven, and pour you out a blessing, that there shall not be room enough to receive it.

Malachi 3:10

In the original Hebrew, it doesn't read "a blessing," it reads "The Blessing," with a definite article, "The." It is our love and honour to our King, the One who owns the universe, which causes the opening of the heavens and the release of the *Dew of Heaven* to come down on our lives.

Under the New Covenant, we don't tithe out of fear of the curse, as non-payment of the tithe doesn't bring a curse; Jesus became a curse and bore it for us (Galatians 3:13). We tithe out of love. Our motivation for doing anything for God is an outcome of the energisation of *Love* that works in our hearts. In the New Covenant, what matters is faith working by love (Galatians 5:6). Anything we do in faith must be motivated by love, not fear.

There are many arguments in blogs, messages, teachings, books and articles against the tithe being for the New Testament Christian today. I will not go to lengths to rebuff every claim or counterclaim against the tithe, but I will give two reasons why I pay my tithe and why I believe the tithe is not only a way to honour God, but also a way to keep ourselves in the flow of *The Blessing.*

Jesus endorsed it

During His earthly ministry, Jesus talked about the tithe. Though He did not make a substantial statement about it, He did not discount the significance or the necessity of paying tithe, either.

> Woe unto you, scribes and Pharisees, hypocrites! for ye pay tithe of mint and anise and cummin, and have omitted the weightier matters of the law, judgment, mercy, and faith: these ought ye to have done, and not to leave the other undone.
>
> Matthew 23:23

While the Lord taught that *Justice, Mercy* and *Faith* carried more gravitas in the Kingdom of God, He added that they shouldn't neglect paying the tithe. So we can conclude that the only time He spoke about it, He wasn't against paying it. Since He endorsed it, we might as well not neglect it.

The Everlasting Priesthood of Jesus

When talking about the fact that the New Covenant is greater than the Old, the writer of the book of Hebrews says that the Levites, those who received the tithes under the Old Covenant, paid tithes in their forefather, Abraham (Hebrews 7:5). Then he asserts that, on earth, men who died received the tithe, but in the order of Melchizedek, Someone who lived forever received the tithe.

Jesus is said to be our High Priest, whose Priesthood is in the Order of Melchizedek (Hebrews 6:20). Not only is this Priesthood not based on a law of physical requirement, but it is both everlasting and powered by an indestructible *Life* (Hebrews 7:16). It is evident that the Person who receives the tithe, and lives forever is the Lord Jesus Christ.

Under the New Covenant, men are given the tithe, but the One who receives it is the Lord. Whenever I give my tithe, I say to the Lord **"I am doing this in honour of You, I bring it to you, the One who lives forever; thank you because I am blessed, and I stay in the flow of the Blessing, my heavens are open, in Jesus name, Amen."** With those words or similar, I bring my tithe to Him. When we bring our tithes, we are not bringing it to man, but to Jesus. A man may collect it, but it is Jesus who receives it.

Now, I have heard many people connect the tithe under the New Covenant to financial abundance. While I agree with that, it is my opinion that the *Blessing* is an intangible and powerful substance, which produces financial and all-encompassing prosperity; it is *Spiritual Power*.

On a final note, if you are adamant that the tithe is not part of the New Testament church tradition, I have no qualms with that; I will not be legalistic about it. What is important is that you are honestly sanctifying the Lord in your heart where the area of financial giving is concerned. Though our giving must emanate from a place of willingness, we must let it be established in our hearts that we are honouring God in our finances.

Offerings

I do believe that, after the tithe is brought, our offerings are empowered to produce a harvest. As we give our offerings or sow our seeds, something supernatural happens:

> And God is able to make all grace abound toward you; that ye, always having all sufficiency in all things, may abound to every good work: Now

he that ministereth seed to the sower both minister bread for your food, and multiply your seed sown, and increase the fruits of your righteousness;)

2 Corinthians 9:8; 10

In the verse above, our financial gift is considered "seed." What you do when you are giving your offering is that you are sowing a seed. One of the very first spiritual laws that we recognise in the Bible, is the *law of sowing and reaping*. You cannot be guaranteed a harvest, except you sow seeds. Money is one of the most important seeds that we can sow in the Kingdom of God. The Bible says that "He gives seed to the sower;" the reason that God gives us the gift of seed is so that we can experience the pleasure of harvest.

Life is measured by time, and we spend most of our time trying to earn a livelihood. In essence, we invest our lives for money. When we give our monies to the Lord, we are trading our lives for His *Life*.

And Jesus answered and said, Verily I say unto you, There is no man that hath left house, or brethren, or sisters, or father, or mother, or wife, or children, or lands, **for my sake, and the gospel's**, But he shall receive an hundredfold now in this time, houses, and brethren, and sisters, and mothers, and children, and lands, with persecutions; and in the world to come eternal life.

Matthew 10:29-30 (Emphasis mine)

There is a promise that comes with giving to the Gospel. There are ministries that are dedicated to reaching unreached people groups, and sometimes they organise gospel campaigns across the world. As much as we support our local churches financially, it will be noble for us to also give to these works. Not everyone can go into the field to reach the lost and train people, but some of us have to. Giving to this particular work of God on earth is crucial; it is one of the ways we honour God.

There is also the spiritual principle that, if anyone ministers spiritual things to you, you should minister material things back to them. In teaching this principle, Paul highlights the spiritual law that states, "whatsoever a man sows, that shall he also reap" (Galatians 6:7).

Our giving to ministers of the Gospel is an essential way to sow our financial and material seeds. God instructed that after the Israelites had brought their treasure before the Lord, the priest should bless them. When you are placing a demand on the blessing, you must release something. After their giving, the priest would declare a blessing on them. Though it was man declaring these words, it was God placing His name on the people; it was God engraving the *Blessing* on their lives (Numbers 6:27).

Giving: The Key to True Riches

> If therefore ye have not been faithful in the unrighteous mammon, who will commit to your trust the true riches?
>
> Luke 16:11

The true wealth of which the Lord speaks, is not necessarily multi-millionaire status; He is talking about the *Blessing*. The *Blessing* is the true wealth. What we do to activate the *Blessing* after every encounter with the Lord is giving of our treasure. When you honour God by being faithful in finances, the reward is the *Blessing*.

As I said earlier about the Hebrew concept of faith, it is more an act than a fact. We respond to God in faith by doing something: giving of our treasure. **Let me emphasise that the tithe, which is ten per cent of earned and received income, should be the starting point, the bare minimum.**

According to eminent theologian, N.T. Wright, "The regular habit of giving money is a further practice which forms the hearts and lives of God's people. Once more, this can become a hollow ritual or can, even worse, transform itself into the settled habit of people's minds which thinks, 'The church is always asking us for money' or 'God owes me a favour because I've written him a check.' Don't let the parodies put you off. The habit of giving, of giving generously, is not an extra option for keen Christians. It is absolutely obligatory on all – because our whole calling is to reflect God the creator, and the main thing we know about this true God is that his very nature is self-giving, generous love. The reason why 'God loves a cheerful giver' (2 Corinthians 9.7) is that that's what God himself is like. Someone like that is a person after God's own heart. Making a regular formal and public practice of giving of money is designed to generate the habit of heart which forms a key part of what meant by agape love."[7]

In closing, I'd like to state, without being legalistic, that whatever you choose to give financially, let these two principles be followed:

1. Giving should be Spirit-led. We are children of God who ought to be led by His *Spirit*. So, as with our living, our giving ought also to be *Spirit-led*. In giving, especially our tithes (because who you partner with in giving and receiving is very important), we should speak to the Lord about where He wants us to distribute it. Truth be told, the totality of our monies belong to the Lord - He owns it all; therefore, our giving should be according to His instruction.

2. "Sanctify the Lord in your hearts" (1 Peter 3:15). The word, sanctify means to treat with deference, venerate and exalt. The word, Lord is from the Greek word, *kyrios*. It means a person who has absolute ownership rights. It also means master or owner. To sanctify the Lord in our hearts would mean to put Him on the throne of our lives and if He is on the throne as the One with full authority over us and what we own, it will definitely be reflected in our giving. The Lord sent His disciples to get a donkey from a man with the instruction that "the Lord has need of it". The donkey was released no questions asked (Mark 11:1-6). If our giving would stem from a place of loyalty to God and recognition of His Lordship, our giving will always reflect our honour of God.

With these two principles in place, we can never go wrong.

I have heard some Bible teachers say that Adam's fall was a result of his eating the tithe. I beg to differ. What Adam ate was not the tithe, as there were more than ten trees in the garden. But the principle is still the same, as Adam's high treason was a result of dishonour. Adam lost the *Blessing* simply because he did not sanctify God in heart. Conversely, we can walk in the fullness of the *Blessing*, as we sanctify God in our hearts and honour Him in the area of our finances. **If we are giving God esteem of the highest degree in our finances, I would wonder how much that would be.**

Honouring People

As much as we must honour the Lord, we also have a duty to honour other people. Our faith walk cannot be all about loving and honouring God, while despising people. I'm afraid to say, but if your faith doesn't include honouring people, especially the ones who God said to honour, then "your faith is futile" (1 Corinthians 15:17 ESV).

We honour other people to the degree that we consider the significance of their position and contributions. We are commanded to honour people because of their position, not their performance. The next part of this chapter catalogues the people that the Lord admonishes us to honour.

The Aged

Thou shalt rise up before the hoary head, and honour the face of the old man, and fear thy God: I am the LORD

Leviticus 19:32

Among the people who God wants us to honour are the elderly, whether in the church or outside the church. "Reverence for the old is inculcated as being a part, not merely of natural respect, but of the fear of God. In the East this virtue, implying deference on the part of the strong to the weak, and of the inexperienced to the wise, exists in larger influence for good than in the West, where, however, its place has been, but only partially, supplied by the greater deference paid by man to woman."[8]

In his letter to Timothy, even though he was the Pastor of the church, Paul admonished him to respect and honour the older ones who were parishioners in his Presbytery.

Do not rebuke an older man harshly, but exhort him as if he were your father ... older women as mothers

1 Timothy 5:1-2 (NIV)

You may be the Pastor and the anointed man of God, but divine responsibility and character still holds you accountable to treat these relationships with the utmost respect.

Peter, who walked with Jesus on earth and was one of the lead apostles in the early church, also admonishes the church in similar matters.

> Likewise, ye younger, submit yourselves unto the elder. Yea, all of you be subject one to another, and be clothed with humility: *for God resisteth the proud, and giveth grace to the humble.*
>
> 1 Peter 5:5 (Emphasis mine)

We are exhorted to pay deference to the elders, as younger people. Your being more gifted than the elder is irrelevant here. This is a divine injunction by which we all must abide. If we do not adhere to God's Word in this matter, what it reveals is pride in our hearts; and, "God resists the proud."

I don't think any one of us in our righteous mind would like to have God as the resistance before us. Let us do what is right, because it is good; and, moreover, for the reward that comes with it.

The Parental Connection

God told the Israelites as part of the Ten Commandments to honour their parents (Exodus 20:12). Paul goes on to reiterate this commandment in the New Testament as the only commandment that carries with it a direct reward from God.

> Children, obey your parents in the Lord: for this is right. Honour thy father and mother; (which is the first commandment with promise;) That it may be well with thee, and thou mayest live long on the earth.
>
> Ephesians 6:1-3

It "being well" with you basically means you will prosper in your endeavour. One of our definitions of the *Blessing* is an empowerment to prosper; therefore, if parental honour can be responsible for prosperity, then it carries with it part of the blessing force that enables us to walk in the fullness of the *Blessing.*

Because of the ways our families and various family relationships have become, I believe that this parental honour includes step-parents, foster-parents, de facto parents, spiritual parents, grandparents and of course, natural and biological parents. As a Father, parental honour is something that God gives a special place in His heart. You cannot disregard your parents and respect God; it is just impossible.

In Esau's losing out on the *Blessing*, we see a salient issue that we could easily gloss over: Esau rejected his parents' opinion on whom to marry, and the Bible says that it grieved them. Please do not give your parents grief.

> And Esau was forty years old when he took to wife Judith the daughter of Beeri the Hittite, and Bashemath the daughter of Elon the Hittite: Which were a grief of mind unto Isaac and to Rebekah.
> Genesis 26:34-35

When the One who sees the end from the beginning said, "Jacob have I loved but Esau have I hated." He wasn't talking about them personally; He was referring to hating their characters. We can conclude that one of the character flaws that God did not like in Esau was his disobedience to his parents. Esau disqualified himself from the *Blessing* by his lack of parental honour.

Contrary to what the law in any country says, we are mandated by the God of Heaven to honour our parents. Parental honour or the lack of it can make or mar your destiny. If you are guilty in this matter, please repent and seek their forgiveness.

> The eye that mocketh at his father, and despiseth to obey his mother, the ravens of the valley shall pick it out, and the young eagles shall eat it
> Proverbs 30:17

One of the potential impairments that can come to anyone as a result of parental dishonour is the loss of vision. Your vision is the picture of your future. Your life will most likely follow your vision, but if you live in perpetual dishonour of your parents, then you could be in danger of losing your ability to "see."

Reuben was Jacob's first son, but because of his dishonour for Jacob, he lost both the *Blessing* and the birth right. The *Blessing* of birthing the Messiah went to Judah and the double portion reserved for the firstborn went to Joseph. His other brothers, Simeon and Levi, who were next in line, lost out because of disobedience. Paul warns about people who will be disobedient to parents in the last days, and we are in those days.

Reuben, thou art my firstborn, my might, and the beginning of my strength, the excellency of dignity, and the excellency of power: Unstable as water, ***thou shalt not excel***, because thou wentest up to thy father's bed; then defiledst thou it: he went up to my couch.

Genesis 49:3-4 (Emphasis mine)

Reuben's crime was that he had sexual relations with one of his father's concubines. The words his father spoke over his life were very strong words. One of the ways that blessing and curses are released is through the spoken word. Jacob told Reuben, "you shall not excel." The word *excel* means to reach the *zenith* of your potential; to prosper in life. Reuben had it going on; he had the potential to be great, but dishonouring his father truncated his destiny.

I am certain that most of my readers will not dishonour their parents in that fashion, but we can be cut from that supply *(the Blessing)* that should cause us to excel, if we tread the dangerous road of parental dishonour.

David honoured Jesse, his father. Imagine this anointed future King of Israel feeding dirty, stinky sheep in the wilderness. When he was sent on an errand by his father to go and see his brothers, who had gone to battle and deliver cheese to the captains and take their order back, David got someone else to look after the sheep, not his father. These little things sometimes have great ripples of effect on our destiny. May God have mercy on us wherever we have missed it!

For many of us, especially those of us in the West, we ought to re-examine how we treat and speak to our parents. Sometimes I see people who show more respect to their boss at work than their parents.

Bless Your Parents

As much as it is within your means, you ought to give to your parents, especially if they are in circumstances where they require help. This is one of the ways by which we unlock the *Blessing* that the Lord placed in them for us.

One of the most difficult dynamics of giving unto parents, is when giving to wealthy parents. Because, think about it, what can you really give to wealthy people, who are your parents? If I would be honest, the answer is nothing. The thinking is, "it should be the other way round, because they are wealthy". But permit me to say that even if your parents are wealthy, give things to them. Buy gifts for them; give them monetary gifts. It is not because they need anything per se, it is because you need the *Blessing* to keep flowing in your life.

Isaac asked for the food he loved before he released the *Blessing*. This was from his biological son. As he grew old and thought that it might soon be time to go, he decided to release the *Blessing* that he received from his father. There is a strong chance that he received the *Blessing* under similar circumstances. He said:

> Now therefore take, I pray thee, thy weapons, thy quiver and thy bow, and go out to the field, and take me some venison. ***And make me savoury meat, such as I love, and bring it to me, that I may eat, that my soul may bless thee before I die....*** And he said, Bring it near to me, and I will eat of my son's venison, that my soul may bless thee. And he brought it near to him, and he did eat: and he brought him wine, and he drank
> Genesis 27:2-4; 25 (Emphasis mine)

The man had to be in a state of excitement to release the *Blessing* over his son and that was why he asked for something that his soul loved. This was what happened when his soul was satiated:

> And he came near, and kissed him: and he smelled the smell of his raiment, and blessed him, and said, See, the smell of my son is as the smell of a field which the LORD hath blessed: ***Therefore God give thee of the dew of heaven, and the fatness of the earth, and plenty of corn and wine:***
> Genesis 27:27-28 (Emphasis mine)

With these and many words, he blessed him and released him into an upward spiral of fruitfulness and abundance. It is clear from God's Word that to unlock the parental aspect for the fullness of the *Blessing*, there has to be honour in our transactions with our parents.

The *Blessing* has the power to define the lives of people. Parents can shape the lives of their children by speaking the *Blessing* over them. Before Jacob died, he spoke words that defined the lives of his children. He spoke words over Reuben, that carried the *Blessing* in reverse, and Moses had to reverse the effect of those words on the lives of the tribe of Reuben (Deuteronomy 33:6). Jacob literally defined the destiny of his sons with his words of *Blessing*. He spoke Judah's becoming king. He spoke the prominence of Ephraim over Manasseh, which made it possible later in Israel's history that the nation was called Ephraim. Reuben's descendants had become small and inconsequential and could have been on the brink of extinction. Moses spoke words of *Blessing* to buck the trend (Deuteronomy 33:6).

If you are reading this book and you are a parent, please speak words of *Blessing* over your children. Your words can define their future. Bless your children every day. Say what you want their lives to become. Seek God's face about their destinies and begin to call those things that exist in the spirit realm until they are established in the earth realm on their lives.

Husbands and Wives

Most messages about marriage and submission is about the woman submitting to the man. Taking a look at scriptures, it is a mutual honour for each other. I get that the man is the head of the family, but as my dad would say "the woman is the neck on which the head sits." If the neck is stiff, then the head can't turn. There has to be a symbiotic honour in marriage.

Beyond that, God expects married folks to walk in honour with each other, especially in the area of sexual fidelity.

> Let marriage be held in honor among all, and let the marriage bed be undefiled, for God will judge the sexually immoral and adulterous.
>
> Hebrews 13:4 (ESV)

Marriage is God's idea and He wants the husband and wife to honour the commitment that they've made to each other. If they don't honour the marriage union, the Bible says God will judge them.

The word judge is from the Greek word *krino*. It means to "separate, select, choose, hence to determine, and so to pronounce judgment."[9] It invokes the picture of being taken to court as a plaintiff and more often than not receives punishment.[10]

Women are also meant to love. I've often heard people say that God did not instruct the woman to love, because she was built to love naturally. I beg to differ. Paul told Titus to tell the older women to teach the younger women to love. If they had to learn how to love their husbands, then they ought to love their husbands.

More popular is the injunction from God for men to love their wives even as Christ loved the church. Women are instructed to honour their husbands, because the angels of God are watching. If the angels are watching, then it could mean that dishonouring the man over your life could close your heavens.

> That is why a wife ought to have a symbol of authority on her head, because of the angels.
>
> 1 Corinthians 11:10

Peter admonished the men to treat their wives with understanding or their prayers will not be heard. Heaven closed; no access to the rain of God.

> Likewise, ye husbands, dwell with them according to knowledge, giving honour unto the wife, as unto the weaker vessel, and as being heirs together of the grace of life; that your prayers be not hindered
>
> 1 Peter 3:7

This makes clear that the subject of honour in marriage is strongly connected to our walking in the fullness of the *Blessing*. When Peter said, "giving honour unto the wife," he meant "treat her with kindness," "take her shopping, buy her gifts," "pamper her." So guys, if you were not sure how to do it, that is definitely one way to honour your wife.

> Therefore as the church is subject unto Christ, so let the wives be to their own husbands in everything.
>
> Ephesians 5:24

That the wife should submit to her husband in marriage is not an ancient cultural practice that is designed to stifle women, but the divine wisdom of God at work to release the woman to be the best that she can be. The relationship between the husband and wife is symbolic of Christ and the Church. There is a supernatural supply that comes to us as we humble ourselves before our Lord and Master. In the same vein, as women respect and submit to their husbands, the God of the heaven releases the *Blessing* that He alone is able to give.

Spiritual Leadership

We must honour God's leadership on earth. That is one way to receive the fullness of the *Blessing*. This could stand as its own individual pillar, but I think it falls under the same principle of honour.

There are people whom God has specially graced with His mercy, who carry *Great Grace*. These people have been ordained as a part of the church for our benefit and profit. There is the argument that this is not a New Testament principle, because, unlike the Old Testament, we are all priests before God in the New Testament.

However, we must know, first of all, that God called Israel to be a kingdom of priests to him. Though the priesthood that was instituted, there were still people who came out of their tents on a daily basis to go near the tabernacle to seek God and worship. Moses and Aaron were Israelites, but God chose him and set him apart to be used as a conduit of His *Power* and *Blessing*.

Though God had blessed the nation of Israel and the people therein, there was an additional dimension from which they were able to obtain the same *Source* of the *Blessing*, by reason of their appointment, call and consecrated living. This is what the fivefold ministry (Ephesians 4:11) in the New Testament represents. To receive what God has deposited in our spiritual leadership on earth, we must honour them.

> Let the elders that rule well be counted worthy of double honour, especially they who labour in the word and doctrine.
>
> 1 Timothy 5:17

It is God's idea that the church leadership be given, not just honour, but double honour. Sometimes, we try to "over-spiritualise" certain concepts, but God sets men and raises them to bless us. This principle is very well documented in the Bible with respect to the relationship between Moses and Joshua. The Bible calls Joshua Moses' minister. Minister is simply a fancy name for servant. Joshua served Moses with all his heart, not so much his head. When it was time for Moses to depart, God did not choose the most skilful warrior in Israel, he chose the humble servant. Moses blessed Joshua and transferred what he carried to him.

Joshua qualified for it, not just because of divine choosing but by his service.

> And Joshua the son of Nun was full of the spirit of wisdom; for Moses had laid his hands upon him: and the children of Israel hearkened unto him, and did as the Lord commanded Moses.
>
> Deuteronomy 34:9

We also observe this modelled in the relationship between Elijah and Elisha. As much as we believe in impartation by the laying on of hands, and we will also talk about that later, there are certain habits, attitudes and lifestyles that qualify us to receive another man's God-given blessing.

> But Jehoshaphat said, Is there not here a prophet of the LORD, that we may inquire of the LORD by him? And one of the king of Israel's servants answered and said, Here is Elisha the son of Shaphat, which poured water on the hands of Elijah. And Jehoshaphat said, The word of the LORD is with him. So the king of Israel and Jehoshaphat and the king of Edom went down to him.
>
> 2 Kings 3:11-12

When Israel would go into battle, the King of Judah asked if there was no prophet in the land. There were prophets, but I'm sure the person who responded to the King knew that there are prophets and there are *Prophets*. Elisha's qualification was that he washed the hands of Elijah. That was his Bible School Certificate; a Master's degree in washing the hand of the man of God.

When Jehoshaphat heard the "subject" on which Elisha had his degree, he said "Bring him, the man carries the answer for that which we seek. The word of the LORD is with him." Astonishing! To paraphrase this statement, Jehoshaphat said, "The power of the *Blessing* is with him." As Yoda from the Star Wars movies would say, "the force is strong with him."

Jehoshaphat didn't hear about any miracles performed by the hands of Elisha, or any prophetic word given that was fulfilled. All he had was his service credential and that qualified him.

We've heard many times that service is the key to greatness. Actually, service is not the key to greatness - service is the greatness. God places a high priority on servants in His Kingdom. His rewards on the day of His return will be for good and faithful servants.

For Elisha to receive Elijah's blessing, he had to go through a process. He served Elijah for ten years, and when it was time for Elijah to be taken up to heaven by God, Elisha had to follow him until he saw him "taken up." They both went through Gilgal, Bethel, Jericho and Jordan before Elisha received a "double portion of Elijah's spirit." It wasn't a double portion of God's Spirit, but Elijah's. What Elisha received is what Elijah had developed in his spirit during his adventure with God on earth. Elisha served faithfully and his service qualified him for the *Blessing* that Elijah had received.

There is a place and a reward for being faithful to God, but there is also the place and reward for being faithful to man. Jesus highlighted this principle in one of his teachings:

> And if ye have not been faithful in that which is another man's, who shall give you that which is your own?
>
> Luke 16:12

As much as this concept has been abused by some in the church, it does not change the fact that it is a genuine spiritual principle for leaders, especially ecclesiastical office holders, to be held in high esteem. There are certain things that the Lord can never release to us until we prove ourselves faithful in that which belongs to another. There is that which belongs to you and no other, the Lord calls it "your own."

Faithful service is the path that leads to the Divine bestowal of that which is exclusively yours. True promotion in life and ministry can only come from God; He lifts one up and brings down another (Psalm 75:6). As the judge of our faithfulness and the One who sees everything, He determines who qualifies for the next level. How we faithfully serve in our current places of assignment to people in leadership, will, to a large extent, be the determining factor on when and how God elevates us.

Another way to receive a man's God-given blessing is by partnering with him financially. In the New Testament, Paul called the church in Philippi partakers of his grace:

Even as it is meet for me to think this of you all, because I have you in my heart; inasmuch as both in my bonds, and in the defence and confirmation of the gospel, ye all are partakers of my grace

Philippians 1:7

The Bible always has a way of disrupting my theology. I would have thought that grace always comes from God, but Paul calls the Philippian church a people who shared and received of his grace. If they were sharers of his grace, then it is possible for God to bless someone or a group of people through their partnership with the right spiritual authority.

I am aware that this message can be misused; but we cannot abandon the truth of God's Word because of people whose god is their belly, or deny the church the supply that comes with partnering with the man of God financially or otherwise.

The Philippians gave to Paul and he made this noteworthy statement in the same letter to them:

But my God shall supply all your need according to his riches in glory by Christ Jesus.

Philippians 4:19

Many times we quote this scripture as part of our confession. I don't have any issue with that whatsoever, but to put it in context, what Paul was saying that, "his own God" not theirs, would supply their needs. What did he mean by that? Every God-ordained ministry carries with it *grace* from the *Caller* – God. Paul was saying here that by reason of what he had received from God, their giving to him was now graced to produce fruit in their lives. Their giving had released a supply from the God that Paul encountered. This is not just an Old Testament idea; this is a spiritual principle that we see here modelled in the New Testament in none other than a Pauline epistle.

Why did the Philippians receive Paul's grace and become partakers of what he had received from God? Why was he confident that *his God* would supply all their needs, according to His riches in glory? It was because of what they did, as we see in the next verse:

Now ye Philippians know also, that in the beginning of the gospel, when I departed from Macedonia, no church communicated with me as concerning giving and receiving, but ye only.

Philippians 4:15

You cannot claim the *Blessing* of Philippians 4:19 without carrying out the responsibility of Philippians 4:15. Personally, I have been a recipient of certain graces because of these practices. God has spoken to me directly and through words of prophecy about receiving certain graces. It is not necessarily because I did anything special, but because I positioned myself to receive by service.

As you honour God, your parents, and spiritual authority, you will no doubt experience the fullness of the *Blessing*.

Favour: The Reward for Honour

As brilliant as it is, merely giving God outward honour is not sufficient. Our God desires that the honour we bestow on Him come from our hearts. We see this point being emphasised in the book of Isaiah, where the Lord says, "These people come near to me with their mouth and honour me with their lips, but their hearts are far from me..." (Isaiah 29:13).

Our honour for God should flow from the depths of our hearts of love and faithfulness to Him. Honour finds its origins in our hearts and denotes the importance that we personally place on something or someone. Honour that doesn't flow from the heart is not honour at all.

Speaking in purely human terms, when you honour someone, they will become favourably disposed to you. The difference between the relationship between children who honour their parents and the ones who do not is quite clear. In the same vein, when we honour the Lord from our hearts, we provoke His favour.

In the book of Malachi, we see the Lord Himself establishing the connection between honour and favour:

When you offer blind animals in sacrifice, is that not evil? And when you offer those that are lame or sick, is that not evil? Present that to your governor; *will he accept you or show you favor?* says the LORD of hosts.

Malachi 1:8 (ESV, Emphasis mine)

Honour is the key to favour. Jesus honoured the Father. No wonder the Word says that "He grew in favour before God and man" (Luke 2:52). The dictionary meaning of *favour* is "friendly or well-disposed regard, goodwill; the state of being approved or held in regard; excessive kindness, unfair partiality or preferential treatment".[11]

What will God's preferential treatment and "unfair partiality" look like? Truth be told, favour is very fair; it is *Divine* response to human action. Favour also means *access*. When we honour God, He grants us the type of access to Himself and His wonders that is not granted to everyone.

> In the light of the king's countenance is life; and his favour is as a cloud of the latter rain.
>
> Proverbs 16:15

In every kingdom there is a king, and we are citizens of the *Kingdom of God*. In our kingdom, the One who is the Monarch of the universe and the King of all kings is our King. The outcome of the favour of God in our lives is the release of His rain from heaven. When a geographical region lacks rain, the people suffer drought, and without irrigation, there will be no harvest when the season of harvest comes. God wants to give us the full harvest; He wants to pour out His rain, and it is in His being pleased with us that we experience His rainfall in life.

The rain of God is symbolic of the presence of His *Spirit*. Honour is the key:

> **Shower, O heavens, from above, and let the clouds rain down righteousness; let the earth open, that salvation and righteousness may bear fruit; let the earth cause them both to sprout; I the LORD have created it.**
>
> Isaiah 45:8 (Emphasis mine)

Chapter 10

SPIRIT FOOD

The Bible presents man as a tripartite being; that is, he is made up of three parts: spirit, soul and body. Man is a spirit, has a soul and lives in a body.

> And the very God of peace sanctify you wholly; and I pray God your whole **spirit and soul and body** be preserved blameless unto the coming of our Lord Jesus Christ.
>
> 1 Thessalonians 5:23 (Emphasis mine)

Everything that God does in or through man is carried out through the agency of his spirit. When man gets born again, the part of man that God touches is not his body but his spirit. Man's body, through his ears, may hear the message; his mind and will, respectively, decode and decide to accept the Gospel. It is in his spirit, however, that God does the work of regeneration. This spirit is the part of man known as *"the hidden man of the heart."*

Every virtue God releases to us is always deposited in our spirits:

> The Lord Jesus Christ be with thy spirit. Grace be with you. Amen.
>
> 2 Timothy 4:22

The *grace of God* cannot be seen, but its effect can be felt; and, this *grace* is deposited in our spirits by God through his Spirit. The spirit of man is the part of man through which God transmits His life into us. As with *grace*, the *Blessing*, which is an intangible, ethereal force that causes us to prosper, is also deposited in our spirits by God.

The hidden man is the part of man that doesn't die. It is part of man, but also an independent entity. As an entity on its own, the spirit also needs care and nourishment. The food that man's spirit needs to live by is the Word of God. The Word of God is regarded as food in the Bible:

> Your words were found and I ate them, and Your words became a joy to me and the delight of my heart; For I have been called by Your name, O Lord God of hosts.
>
> Jeremiah 15:16 (AMP)

Any living organism that goes without its food or nutrition will be very weak and could eventually die. No matter how strong a warrior is, if he goes two weeks without food, he will be dominated by his weaker enemies. A warrior must eat well to gain ascendancy in battle. The spirit and the flesh are in a constant battle; for the spirit of man to gain ascendancy over the flesh, it has to be constantly fed and nourished.

In the battles of life, we are either exercising dominion or we are being dominated. In a battle, the stronger, fitter, more experienced or wiser warrior wins. A strong spirit will sustain you (Proverbs 18:14). A strong spirit will enable you to overcome in life. God has designed the spirit to feed on spiritual things, primarily the Word of God. Strength, fitness, wisdom and experience in life's battles come as a result of your spiritual diet on the Word of God:

> And he humbled thee, and suffered thee to hunger, and fed thee with manna, which thou knewest not, neither did thy fathers know; *that he might make thee know that man doth not live by bread only, but by every word that proceedeth out of the mouth of the LORD doth man live.*
>
> Deuteronomy 8:3 (Emphasis mine)

The physical part of man needs bread (physical food) to exist, while the spirit in man is dependent on the Word of God for its life.

The passage in Revelation 22:1-3 reveals some fundamental truths: it describes a prophetic account of when God and His Presence take over the world, recreating it and ruling in it. We see that in this invasion of earth by heaven, the curse it is utterly banished (verse 3). I have become a bit of a health food enthusiast; I make "green smoothies" almost on a daily basis, especially when I'm not travelling to a different part of the world. In case you don't know, a green smoothie is a type of smoothie that consists of fruits and vegetables blended together. It tastes great as far as I'm concerned - at least the way I make it does.

Within a few weeks, I realised that I had lost some weight and my general health had improved. I became less fatigued and I felt better. This is because most of the fruits and vegetables that I use contain anti-oxidants. Fruits and leaves are edible parts of a tree or plant, "The leaves were for the healing of the nations." It is clear that the fruits and the leaves from the *tree of life* were ingested for them to get rid of the curse and its effects:

> And ye shall serve the LORD your God, and he shall bless thy bread, and thy water; and I will take sickness away from the midst of thee. There shall nothing cast their young, nor be barren, in thy land: the number of thy days I will fulfil.
>
> Exodus 23:25-26

When the Israelites came out of Egypt, one of God's promises was to keep them in good health, by blessing their bread and water. In this dispensation, the Lord also wants us to partake of His *Blessed* bread and water. As you feast on the Word of the Lord, sickness and barrenness are destroyed in your life.

Bread typifies the *Word of God,* while water is symbolic for the *Spirit of the Word.* Both the Word of God and its attendant Spirit are *Blessed*; so, by feasting on the Word, we are partaking in the very essence of the *Life of God.* In His promise to Israel, the Lord said that ingesting the *Blessed* water and word destroys the both the *aqar* and the *sakol* types of barrenness we discussed in Chapter 5.

Throughout the Word, we commonly observe God creating avenues to get the *Blessing* to us in order to deliver us from the shackles of the curse. We must eat the Word, we must drink the Word, and by so doing we overcome every trace of the curse and live the *Blessed Life.* The mechanism by which we *eat* God's Word is by meditation on it.

What is Meditation?

Meditation is the devotional practice of pondering on words of a verse, or verses of scripture, with a receptive heart, allowing the Holy Spirit to take the written Word and apply it as the living Word to the inner being. Meditation is inwardly receiving the Word of God, illustrated by eating or feeding.[1] Other words used that are synonymous with *meditation* to describe the meditation process are *think, contemplate, ruminate* and *confess.*

> **Blessed is the man** that walketh not in the counsel of the ungodly, nor standeth in the way of sinners, nor sitteth in the seat of the scornful. But his delight is in the law of the LORD; **and in his law doth he meditate day and night. And he shall be like a tree planted by the rivers of water, that bringeth forth his fruit in his season**, his leaf also shall not wither; **and whatsoever he doeth shall prosper.**
>
> Psalm 1:1-3 (Emphasis mine)

The word *Blessed*, in Psalm Chapter 1, is from the Hebrew word *Asher,* which means happy or to be given good fortune. It is the state of *blessedness.* It is the state of the man who has been imparted and impacted by the *Blessing.* The word translated as *happy* here is not the same as the usual *happy* in the English Language. The English word *happy* is derived from the Latin word *hap. Hap* is related to luck and favourable circumstance. It is where we get the word *happenstance* from. The Blessed man's countenance is not dictated by what is happening in his life or the outcome of his circumstances. His life is dictated by something stronger than mere happiness; he has what the Bible defines as **joy**. Joy is an attitude of contentment and pleasantness that comes as a result of the Spirit of God dwelling in us, "the joy of the Lord is our strength" (Nehemiah 8:10).

This *blessed man* doesn't form his opinions based on the counsel of the ungodly. We are always surrounded by the counsel of the ungodly in the form of reports from the media and comments from friends, family members, doctors and, sometimes, even spouses. Any word that is opposed to God's revealed truth is the counsel of the ungodly.

Like this archetypal blessed man, our delight should be in God's Word. We should be excited about God's Word. The word *delight* from the Hebrew is the word *chephets*, which means, "pleasure; concretely a valuable thing; something that one takes delight in."[2] The blessed man is someone who delights in God's Word and sees it as his source of spiritual indulgence.

Delight also means to be pliable or malleable. Whenever we come before the Word of God, our hearts must be in a state of pliability. We must be willing to receive what the Word says. Not enforcing our preconceived notions on the Word, but be willing to accept what the Word tells us, and change our lifestyle and worldview if required by it. The act that releases the *Blessing* from the Word is not just the *delight*, but the action that the *delight* produces: **meditation**.

The result of this *Blessed man's* meditation is that whatsoever he does, prospers. We can prosper in all our endeavours. The key to complete prosperity is meditation. We already defined the *Blessing* as the empowerment to prosper. What happens, therefore, as we meditate on the Word of God, is that we stay in the flow of the *Blessing* and receive that power that facilitates our prosperity. The *Blessing* is released to work in our lives. Our ministries prosper, our businesses prosper, our jobs prosper, everything we do prospers, because we engage and stay in the flow of the *Blessing*.

I've often said that I began to walk in healing by simply meditating on Mark 16:17. I've seen many healings as a result of that one verse. Before I perceived that I'd received any special gift to minster healing to the sick and see them healed, meditation on the Word of God made it happen. As you make meditating on God's Word your habit, I see you riding on the wings of the supernatural.

I like the fact that Psalm 1 doesn't just talk about one river but "rivers" of living water. A lifestyle of consistent meditation on God's Word connects us to an unending supply of supernatural resource for all year round fruitfulness in every area of our lives.

If you ever travel along a creek, you will find a perfect view of a mangrove swamp. You see trees that are planted by or within rivers. Those trees are evergreen and keep producing fruit throughout the year. Their fruitfulness is not determined by the geographical seasons of their location, because come rain or shine, they are plugged into to a life source. So are the people who meditate daily on the Word of God; they are in a constant, irreversible cycle of fruitfulness, because they are hooked up to the *Source* of manifest abundance.

> My root was spread out by the waters, and the dew lay all night upon my
> branch.
>
> Job 29:19

The fruit-bearing part of a tree is the branch. The bible describes the believer as a *tree of righteousness*. When our root system is connected to the water source, the dew of heaven will rest on our "branches" and in due season, our fruitfulness will manifest.

> This book of the law shall not depart out of thy mouth; but thou shalt meditate therein day and night, that thou mayest observe to do according to all that is written therein: for then thou shalt make thy way prosperous, and then thou shalt have good success.
>
> Joshua 1:8

After the death of Moses, the mantle of leadership fell of Joshua. Joshua was not particularly confident in his ability to lead the people, much less lead at the level of Moses. God, however, met him and told him to be courageous and audacious. To fulfil our God-given destiny, we require a level of audacity and boldness, because God will always call us into uncharted territories. You may have seen other people do it, but sometimes you will need to overcome fear to do what you've seen someone else do.

To come to this place of boldness, God instructed Joshua that the key to his progressing in his new God-ordained path was meditation on the Book of the Law; this was the key to his prosperity and success. A lot of times we ask God to bless us or prosper us. Truth be told, He has already prospered us in the *Blessing*, and the way to experience it is by meditating on his Word.

The Amplified Bible translates the last part of Joshua 1:8 as *"For then you shall make your way prosperous, and then you shall deal wisely and have good success."* To succeed in life, we need to be a people of astuteness in wisdom. If the *Blessing* is an empowerment for success, and wisdom guarantees success, then we must be engaged in the activity that secures our receiving the *Wisdom of God*.

> If the axe is dull and he does not sharpen its edge, then he must exert more strength. Wisdom has the advantage of giving success.
>
> Ecclesiastes 10:10

We need the Wisdom of God to succeed in life. A man without wisdom will expend more energy. Life lived without wisdom is burdensome and is bereft of true success, but by meditating on God's Word our wisdom is guaranteed.

Because of Joshua's mediation, he walked in a great degree of revelation, which increased the authority in which he walked, giving him remarkable victories and success as a leader. How did he know to speak to the sun to stand still (Joshua 10:12)? He could do that because of his constant meditation on God's Word. Meditation opens us to new vistas of spiritual reality. Meditation gives us a supernatural mind-set and mentality. A blessed mind thinks differently. One of the first things that happens to the person that will be used greatly by God is that their mind is transformed. Meditation on God's Word is the key to a renewed mind; it releases us to begin to think on the frequency of supernatural thought.

The same way God instructed Joshua, He is telling us today to mediate on His Word. If we want to see the fullness of the *Blessing* in our lives, then we have no choice but to follow God's prescribed order and meditate on His Word.

> Meditate upon these things; give thyself wholly to them; that thy profiting may appear to all.
>
> 1 Timothy 4:15

Paul instructed Timothy to continue meditating on the Word and that by doing so, his progress would become evident to everyone. It is possible to be blessed and for it not be noticeable. As we constantly meditate on the Word, something will happen on the inside of us. We will make progress in our various endeavours. Don't be discouraged that your progress is not yet evident. As you continue in meditation, there will come a day that the *Life* in the *Word* will have prevailed so much that your progress will no longer be debatable.

> All scripture is given ***by inspiration*** of God, and is profitable for doctrine, for reproof, for correction, for instruction in righteousness:
>
> 2 Timothy 3:16 (Emphasis mine)

Every word of God in the Holy Scripture is inspired. The word *inspired* means to be breathed out. When God spoke the *Word*, it was breathed out of His mouth. With it came the life that only He possesses. The breath of

God is what animated Adam, who was just a lump of clay. The breath of God carries the *Life of God*; therefore, every word in the Holy Book is a divine agency of *Life* and *Power*. As you feast on the word, you are breathing in that which God breathed out. You are inhaling His *Life*; you are inhaling His *Power*; you are inhaling His *Anointing*; you are inhaling the *Blessing*. The Lord and His Word are Life-giving Spirits. The more *Word* we receive, the more *Life* we receive; the more *Life* we receive, the more of the *Blessing* we receive and express.

How to Meditate

We will have to accept as true that the enemy attempts to counterfeit everything that God has given to believers, and meditation is not exempt. The Christian mediation is not transcendental meditation or any other New Age meditation practice. We don't focus our minds on nothing; the object of our focus during our times of mediation is the Word of God (it can also be words from an inspired Christian literature or message).

I would propose that we do it first thing in the morning and just before going to bed. You could also meditate during your short break at work or whenever you can find time during the day. No matter how we go about it, we have to find the time. If you are too busy to meditate of God's Word, then you are indeed too busy, and not in a good way.

Questions commonly asked are: How do I meditate? On what do I meditate? Yes, I agree that every word in our canon is inspired, but as you read the Bible, at certain times particular words, phrases or verses stand out for us. I would recommend that we fix our gaze on what the Lord emphasises to us at any given moment and feed upon it.

Thy words were found, and I did eat them; and thy word was unto me the joy and rejoicing of mine heart: for I am called by thy name, O LORD God of hosts.

Jeremiah 15:16

The Prophet Jeremiah said that the words that he ate were the words that he found. The word you find is that word or group of words that "jump at you." After reading the chapter, go back to those words and begin to feast on them. Our definitions of meditation, such as think, confess and ruminate, give us an idea of what to do in this feast.

As you "find" the word, you engage your mind on it and begin thinking on it. Another way to meditate is to gently mutter these words to yourself. That is why God told Joshua that the *Book of the Law* should not depart from his mouth. The *Blessing* is a product of what you do with your mouth; and, it just so happens that we eat with our mouths. As you mutter God's Word, you are ingesting the *Life* that is the *Word*.

The process of contemplation is one of the actions that describe meditation. It is the action of looking thoughtfully at something for an extended period of time. We contemplate on the Word by thoughtfully looking into it, and musing and reflecting on it. The word *contemplation* found its way into the English Language through the Latin word, *contemplātiō*, which comes from two Latin words: *con* and *templum*. The word *con* is a prefix that denotes joint action. The word *templum* was used to denote the defined area piece of land that is designated for a temple, within which a seeker would ponder and worship.

The dynamics of contemplation comes from an ancient Christian practice that saw the priest or seeker figuratively "cut out" a small piece of the "temple," where, by a joint action of mind and spirit, he comes to an awareness and consciousness of the presence of God. In our meditation, what we do is "cut out" a part of the Word of God, and fix our gaze on it, communing with the Eternal Spirit and enjoying the *Life* that flows out of union with God.

Another word that meditate is synonymous with is *ruminate*. Rumination is an agricultural term used to describe the digestive process of certain farm animals. The process of rumination is called *chewing the cud*. On a farm, when certain herbivores like cows graze, they eat as much grass as they can. When they've had their fill, they sit down and regurgitate what they had swallowed, and then they start chewing it again. By *chewing the cud* they are siphoning every nutrient that is in the grass for their nourishment. As we mediate on God's Word, we are extracting the nutrient and life that is in the Word.

> My son, attend to my words; incline thine ear unto my sayings, Let them not depart from thine eyes; keep them in the midst of thine heart. ***For they are life unto those that find them***, and health to all their flesh.
> Proverbs 4:20-22 (Emphasis mine)

We defined the *Blessing* as the experience of the *Life of God* in Christ for our enjoyment. Solomon, the writer of Proverbs, instructs us that we can only enjoy the *Life* that is in the *Word* when we find it. *Life* is in the *Word*, but the *Life* in the *Word* is only accessed by those who mediate on the *Word*. The *Word* also gives us health in our flesh. Your flesh is your natural life. The *Blessing* not only affects the spiritual aspect of your life, but also has visible and tangible effects in parts of your life that are observed by yourself and others. Form the Word, we realise healing from the various diseases of the soul and obtain the panacea from every curse. Let us feast on the *Word* and feed on the *Word* and appropriate the *Life* that is embedded within it.

You are What You Eat

Experts in human nutrition have a saying that "you are what you eat," meaning that you take the life of whatever you eat. I remember being on a week of fasting, where all I ate was cereal and milk. After a few days, I began to smell like milk! It occurred to me that I had, for lack of a better expression, in a sense received the life of the cow. In the same token, when you meditate on God's Word, you are receiving the *Life of God*. That is one fact that I cannot emphasise enough.

One of the things used to figuratively describe the Word of God is milk:

As newborn babes, desire the sincere milk of the word, that ye may grow thereby:

1 Peter 2:2

As new believers, we are instructed to desire the milk of God's Word. The first key to spiritual growth is that we, first of all, have the right desire: God and His Word. As we desire the milk of God's Word, we drink and grow because of it. In the natural, milk is an important component of a young child's diet. It is a good source of energy and protein. It also contains a wide range of vitamins and minerals, including calcium, which growing children and young people need, to build healthy bones and teeth. Because it is a good source of protein and calcium, milk forms part of a healthy diet. Our bodies need protein to work properly and to grow or repair themselves. Calcium helps to keep our bones and teeth strong.

As it is in the natural, so it is in the spiritual. The Word of God contains spiritual nutrients that help us grow and restore our lives as we move along in life. It gives us strength to face all of life's challenges.

The word of God shows us another activity of milk; it is called the "churning of milk" (Proverbs 30:33). The churning of milk basically means the shaking of milk. This action is what produces butter. Butter is a type of the richness of God's Word. As we churn the milk of God's Word by meditating on it, we experience and enjoy the richness that can only be produced by it.

We see the story of Job in the Bible, who was possibly the greatest man of his generation. He gives us some insight into what empowered him to live a life that was vested with the *Blessing*:

> When I washed my steps with butter, and the rock poured me out rivers of oil;
>
> Job 29:6

Job said that he bathed his feet with butter. As already established, butter is the product of churning milk. As we stay in God's Word, mediating on it, day and night, we will begin to experience the butter, the abundance of revelation, and the outcome of our lives will be determined by the revelation of His Word. Our steps will be ordered by God; we will start to operate in the realm of manifest abundance.

As it was for Job, the result of our mediation will be "rivers of oil." Oil is a symbol of the anointing. There is an anointing that comes on our lives as we mediate of God's Word; that is the *Blessing*.

> He made him ride on the high places of the earth, that he might eat the increase of the fields; and he made him to suck honey out of the rock, and oil out of the flinty rock;
>
> Deuteronomy 32:13

When are you feeding on God's Word, you are literally receiving the life, power and anointing that is embedded in the Word. To take this thought a bit further, when eating the Word, you are actually eating the Lord:

> In the beginning was the Word, and the Word was with God, and the Word was God.
>
> John 1:1

God has given us His Word as our food. The Greek word translated as the *Word of God* is *Logos*. In John 1:1, we see that the *Word of God* is God Himself; this then implies that when we eat the Word of God, we are feeding on the Lord Himself.

The Bible presents God as being larger than our imagination. He fills the universe with Himself. But as big as God is, He has transformed Himself into spiritual food for us. He makes Himself available in bite-sizes without the diminishing of Himself. It is astonishing to realise that God is the *Word*, and He has given us the *Word* to eat. What a mighty God we serve!

This spirit food is a steady flow of the energy of God from His Logos into our spirits; it is the supernatural enablement and empowerment that comes from God. When Elijah ate the bread of angels, he went on by the strength of that food for forty days (1 Kings 19:8). The supernatural ability that comes into our spirit when it is fed its required diet is the *Blessing of God*.

Just before Israel came out of Egypt, God instructed them to eat the lamb.[3] They were to take one lamb for each family, roast and eat on the night of their deliverance. We see later in the New Testament that the Lamb is a type of the Lord (John 1:29). We see a progressive revelation of His influence as the Lamb increase throughout the timeline of the Bible. It was first a lamb to a household (Exodus 12:1-13), then His influence increased to being the *Lamb of Israel*. We see Him in John as the *Lamb* that that takes away the sin of the whole world. But in the mind of the Father, He had always been the *Lamb* that was slain before the foundation of the world; His impact reaches throughout the universe.

After the Israelites left Egypt, they came to the wilderness. They became hungry and cried to Moses, who in turn cried out to God. God gave them *manna* from heaven (Exodus 16:35). Jesus calls himself the *true bread*; the *Manna* from heaven that the Israelites ate (John 6:41).

After Israel left the wilderness, they crossed over the Jordan and finally reached the Promised Land. The Bible says that they began to feed on the old corn of the land (Joshua 5:11). In the Gospel of John, we note that the Lord refers to Himself as the "grain of corn" (John 12:24). What this discloses to us is that in every season of the Israelites' journey, they had to eat the Lord.

In your wilderness, eat Him. To be established in His Promised Land for you, you must eat Him. He is the spiritual food that imparts spiritual life and energy to us; eat the Lord!

The Blessing Meal

At the meeting of Abraham and the high priest Melchizedek, they shared a meal. The elements of that meal are the same elements of the Holy Communion: bread and wine. Melchizedek brought with him the bread and the wine, and he gave them to Abraham, then Melchizedek spoke a blessing over him.

Just before the Lord fulfilled His *passion*, He instituted the meal that is now called the Holy Communion. The Lord called the drink, the cup of the New Covenant that is in His blood. Both the bread and the wine were received as tokens of the New Covenant.

In Paul's first letter to the Church in Corinth, he called it the "cup of the Blessing" (1 Corinthians 10:16). The *Blessing*, which we have, has been ratified by the New Covenant that was established by the Lord's sacrifice at Calvary. When we eat the Holy Communion, we are being established in the *Blessing*!

Our first father, Adam, entered the curse by wrong eating. We can reverse the curse and live in the *Blessing* by right eating.

> Then Jesus said unto them, Verily, verily, I say unto you, **Except ye eat the flesh of the Son of man, and drink his blood, ye have no life in you**. Whoso eateth my flesh, and drinketh my blood, hath eternal life; and I will raise him up at the last day. For my flesh is meat indeed, and my blood is drink indeed. He that eateth my flesh, and drinketh my blood, dwelleth in me, and I in him. As the living Father hath sent me, and I live by the Father: so he that eateth me, even he shall live by me.
>
> John 6:53-57 (Emphasis mine)

The Lord Himself actually encourages us to eat Him! John 6:57 happens to be one of my favourite Bible verses. It illustrates that we can have the same *Life* that Jesus has. In the New Creation, we have the same Life, positionally; nevertheless, the way to truly enjoy this *Life* we have been given is to partake in the *Flesh* and *Blood* of Jesus.

Jesus said His body is meat and His blood is drink. The Bible says, in Leviticus 17:11 that the life of the flesh is in the blood. We partake of the "flesh" of the Word by reading and studying. But we must go further, to appreciate the full benefit. As we meditate on the *Word*, we are drinking the "blood" of the *Word*, and partaking in the *Life* that is in the *Word*.

Christianity is not just about knowledge, it is also about eating: eating the Lord by *His Word* and expressing the *Divine Life*. Christianity is a feast that began with the Passover meal just before the Passion of Jesus. The feast will culminate at the wedding of the Lord and His Bride. Christ, the Living Word of God, wants to dwell in us, be established in us, and saturate us until we become walking, talking "living words'" of God.

Transformation

Meditation provides us with the ability *to do* God's Word, and the *Blessing* comes from the *doing*. In the Septuagint, the same Greek word *makarios*, transliterated as blessed in Psalms, is used in the Book of James; it is connected with *doing* God's Word.

> For if any be a hearer of the word, and not a doer, he is like unto a man beholding his natural face in a glass: But whoso looketh into the perfect law of liberty, and continueth therein, he being not a forgetful hearer, but a doer of the work, this man shall be **blessed in his deed.**
>
> James 1:23; 25 (Emphasis mine)

The Word of God is described as a mirror. When you look at a mirror, the image that you see is yourself. Get into the *Word*, meditate on the *Word*, and what you will see in the *Word* is an image of yourself. That is your real personality being revealed to you. Let the Word of God change how you think; let the Word of God change how you see yourself.

As we meditate on God's Word, a process of change takes place in our minds. The process of transformation that changes the image we have of ourselves or our worldview is called *mind renewal*. As you engage the Word of God, you are "renewing your mind."

> And be not conformed to this world: but be ye transformed by the renewing of your mind, that ye may prove what is that good, and acceptable, and perfect, will of God.
>
> Romans 12:2

As we continue in the Word of God, by the operation of the Spirit of the Lord, we are changed from one degree of glory to another. *Glory* is the splendour and light that shines from the *Presence of God*.

> But we all, with open face beholding as in a glass the glory of the Lord, are changed into the same image from glory to glory, even as by the Spirit of the Lord
>
> 2 Corinthians 3:18

During the process of meditation, we are allowing the *Light* of the radiance of God's glory to come into our spirits and souls. In the Old Testament, we see how the radiation of glory from God's Presence translates into the *Blessing* in our lives.

> And the LORD spake unto Moses, saying, Speak unto Aaron and unto his sons, saying... The LORD make his face shine upon thee, and be gracious unto thee: The LORD lift up his countenance upon thee, and give thee peace. And they shall put my name upon the children of Israel; and I will bless them.
>
> Numbers 6:22-23; 25-27

The Hebrew word for presence is *paniym*, which means face. The face of God shining upon us means that the light from His presence is on us. This light from God's presence is His glory. It is from His presence that we get His glory. The word *glory* also means *heavy with goodness*, as translated from the Hebrew word *kabod*. It is in the light of His countenance that we receive every good thing that He promised us. The *Light of God's Presence* is heavy with the weight of His goodness.

The *paniym* of God is the source of His *kabod*: "Every good and perfect gift is from above, coming down from the Father of the heavenly lights" (James 1:17). As we meditate on the Word of God, we are involved in a face-to-face or *paniym*-to-*paniym* communion with God. We become recipients of the *Light of His Glory*: "the light that shines in darkness, that is never overcome by darkness but incapacitates, overwhelms and disarms the darkness."

The darkness is the substance of the curse, while the light is the essence of the *Blessing*. By continuing in the *Light of His Presence* that comes from His *Word* we remain in the *Blessing*. God's Word is our spiritual food that communicates spiritual life and energy to us, and as we receive the impartation of spiritual life from God, we are established in the *Blessing* until we come into the fullness of the *Blessing*.

Chapter 11

THE OVERFLOW

At the consummation of all things at the tail end of the Bible narrative in the book of Revelation, we see an imagery that has echoes of the Garden of Eden. This can be described as the restoration of God's original intention in creation:

> And he shewed me a pure river of water of life, clear as crystal, proceeding out of the throne of God and of the Lamb. In the midst of the street of it, and on either side of the river, was there the tree of life, which bare twelve manner of fruits, and yielded her fruit every month: and the leaves of the tree were for the healing of the nations. ***And there shall be no more curse***: but the throne of God and of the Lamb shall be in it; and his servants shall serve him:
>
> Revelation 22:1-3 (Emphasis mine)

This is a depiction of life in the New Heaven and the New Earth. We see the water of life that flows from the Throne of God and the Lamb bringing healing and sanctification to the universe. In this passage of scripture, we see a beautiful illustration of the Triune God as He brings about restoration, overturning the outcome of the fall in Eden. My emphasis, however, is on the first part of verse three, where the curse and everything that is accursed are finally obliterated from God's earth. Every form of adversity is removed, because the power of the *Blessing* has consumed every manifestation of the curse.

While this is a picture of the New Heaven and the New Earth, which is a future reality according to the scriptures, the Bible clearly states that we can partake of the powers of the world to come in this day and age:

And have tasted the good word of God, and the powers of the world to come

Hebrews 6:5

'The powers of the world to come' refer to the powers of heaven. Thank God, we can taste heaven on earth! As the Psalmist says, "Oh taste and see, that the Lord is good (Psalm 34:8). This means that we are empowered to live above the curse by the experience of the power of God in our enjoyment of the *Water of Life*.

The *Water of Life* that issues from the Throne of God and the Lamb is the agent responsible for the complete and final eradication of the curse from God's universe. We see the same *water* in another passage of scripture in the book of John:

In the last day, that great day of the feast, Jesus stood and cried, saying, If any man thirst, let him come unto me, and drink. He that believeth on me, as the scripture hath said, out of his belly shall flow rivers of living water. (But this spake he of the Spirit, which they that believe on him should receive: for the Holy Ghost was not yet given; because that Jesus was not yet glorified.)

John 7:37-39

We see the Lord calling people who are thirsty to come and partake of the *Water of Life*. This *Water of Life* represents the Holy Spirit, according to verse 39. The Holy Spirit is the One by Whom we can live above the curse and enter into the fullness of the *Blessing*.

As we drink of the *Water of Life*, the Holy Spirit, we drink until we become filled with the *Life of God*. As I stated earlier, the *Blessing* is the manifestation of the *Life of God* in Christ. As we are full and overflowing of the Spirit of God, we live above the curse and its effects.

In the Old Testament, we see a portrayal of the water as colliding with our world and, in its wake, destroying everything that is from the curse.

Afterward he brought me again unto the door of the house; and, behold, waters issued out from under the threshold of the house eastward: for the forefront of the house stood toward the east, and the waters came down from under from the right side of the house, at the south side of the altar. Then brought he me out of the way of the gate northward, and led me about the way without unto the utter gate by the way that looketh eastward; and, behold, there ran out waters on the right side. And when the man that had the line in his hand went forth eastward, he measured a thousand cubits, and he brought me through the waters; the waters were to the ankles. Again he measured a thousand, and brought me through the waters; the waters were to the knees. Again he measured a thousand, and brought me through; the waters were to the loins. Afterward he measured a thousand; and it was a river that I could not pass over: for the waters were risen, waters to swim in, a river that could not be passed over. And he said unto me, Son of man, hast thou seen this? Then he brought me, and caused me to return to the brink of the river. Now when I had returned, behold, at the bank of the river were very many trees on the one side and on the other. Then said he unto me, These waters issue out toward the east country, and go down into the desert, and go into the sea: which being brought forth into the sea, the waters shall be healed. And it shall come to pass, that every thing that liveth, which moveth, whithersoever the rivers shall come, shall live: and there shall be a very great multitude of fish, because these waters shall come thither: for they shall be healed; and every thing shall live whither the river cometh.

Ezekiel 47:1-9

We see the increase of the water levels in the temple - from the ankle to the knee, and from the knee to the waist level, till it became a river to swim in. As the water flows from the temple into the streets, it brings life to everything with which it comes into contact. That is what the *Water of Life* does. The *Water of Life* is a manifestation of the anointing. The anointing is the power of the *Blessing*.

Our recreated human spirit is the Throne of God on earth. It is in our spirits that God by His Spirit lives. As we experience the overflow of the Spirit in our lives, we first encounter the *Blessing* and are recipients of its benefits.

For example, the pipe that delivers water from the cistern becomes saturated with water first before the water extends forth to its destination. The *Blessing* that comes with the overflow is so vast that it will affect those around us. Our friends and families will feel its impact; it will also affect our professional colleagues and neighbours.

In the book of Joshua, we see the relationship between the overflow and harvest:

> And as they that bare the ark were come unto Jordan, and the feet of the priests that bare the ark were dipped in the brim of the water, (for Jordan overfloweth all his banks all the time of harvest,)
>
> Joshua 3:15

It is no coincidence that the time of the harvest coincides with the time when the Jordan River overflows its banks. Harvest time is a season of peak fruitfulness. We already defined the *Blessing* as the empowerment to be fruitful; therefore, for us to come to the place of peak fruitfulness, we must be in the overflow. No overflow, no harvest, is the simple equation.

Water is essential to the life and existence of everything living thing. Two levels of water are referenced in the New Testament, and they are synonymous with two different experiences of the Spirit that every believer has.

The first is seen in the Lord's encounter with the woman at the well in the fourth chapter of the Gospel of John. Jesus was on his way to Galilee, but He had to go through Samaria. While waiting by a well, a woman came to fetch water and a conversation ensued between her and Jesus. In the midst of their discussion, Jesus told her:

> But whosoever drinketh of the water that I shall give him shall never thirst; but the water that I shall give him shall be in him a well of water springing up into everlasting life.
>
> John 4:14

The Lord was talking about one particular function of the Holy Spirit: the operation of the Holy Spirit at the new birth. What the believer acquires at the point of salvation is the 'well' of the *Water of Life*. In rural areas, especially in Africa, wells are the primary source of water for daily living. Wells are very important, because they serve either families or certain villages. The 'well' level for the believer, though adequate for himself, is quite limited in service to others. This is one reason for the river.

The other manifestation of the Holy Spirit as the *Water of Life* is revealed as the river. A river can serve more communities than any single well can. Rivers serve towns, cities, and even countries, depending on the length, reach and depth of the river. This is what the early disciples received on the day of Pentecost.

After they received the first encounter of the Spirit of God, when the Lord breathed the Spirit on them that they should receive the Holy Spirit (John 20:22), He asked them to wait for the next experience (Luke 24:29). The Spirit had not been poured out at this time, because the Lord was not yet glorified. The Lord told them that in order to experience a greater level of effectiveness, they must have the second encounter.

> But ye shall receive power, after that the Holy Ghost is come upon you: and ye shall be witnesses unto me both in Jerusalem, and in all Judaea, and in Samaria, and unto the uttermost part of the earth.
>
> Acts 1:8

The well encounter is primarily for the individual, but the river encounter is necessary for effective ministry. For us to walk in the *Fullness of the Blessing*, we must go from the well to the river. This is not a one-time event. We must keep getting filled on a regular basis.

In Acts Chapter 3, the disciples are filled again after the initial river experience. This brings us to the third experience, which is meant to keep both the well and the river in the fullness and, subsequently, the overflow. This experience is the rain.

Without us having the rain in its season, the river could dry up and the wells would lack sufficient water. When there is no rain in a land, the end result is drought. As in the natural, so it is in the spiritual. When we don't encounter the rain of God on a regular basis our lives as believers will become dry and ineffective.

> Until the spirit be poured upon us from on high, and the wilderness be a fruitful field, and the fruitful field be counted for a forest.
>
> Isaiah 32:15

If we don't have the rain of the Spirit, then our lives will be parched lands like the wilderness. Not everything grows in the wilderness. Without the rain in our lives, certain things will not grow; they may even die. However, it is not God's plan that anything should die in our hands. Depreciation is not remotely close to God's idea for the believer. It is God's will that we grow from grace to grace. Our continued fruitfulness and operation in the *Blessing* is only guaranteed when we have the rain of heaven.

When Isaac was blessing Jacob, he said that he would receive rain from heaven. Isaac was very well aware that without the rain from heaven, Jacob could never enter the fullness of the *Blessing*.

> And I will make them and the places round about my hill a blessing; and I will cause the shower to come down in his season; there shall be showers of blessing.
>
> Ezekiel 34:26

Everything we need is in the *Blessing*. Everything around God's holy *hill* is marked by the *Blessing*. The people that surround the hill are transformed into a *Blessing*. God's hill is His secret dwelling-place. This is the place from where we get the rain; the showers of *Blessing*.

Receive Fresh Anointing Daily

For us to experience the overflow, we must be anointed afresh on a daily basis.

> But my horn shalt thou exalt like the horn of an unicorn: I shall be anointed with fresh oil.
>
> Psalms 92:10

We need fresh oil every day of our lives. Yesterday's oil was good for yesterday, but for today we need fresh oil. We must position ourselves to receive fresh oil regularly, because therein lies the strength of the *Blessing*. This is a continuous process of filling. The overflow comes when we are full but never stop consuming. As you stay thirsty and continue drinking, you will keep living in the overflow.

> My glory was fresh in me, and my bow was renewed in my hand
>
> Job 29:20

Job received a fresh anointing each day of his life. As a result, he was successful in his work. God wants us to make a success out of everything we do. It is said of the blessed man that "everything that he does prospers." To prosper in everything, we do, there must be a steady supply of the *Water of His Presence*.

Thou preparest a table before me in the presence of mine enemies: thou anointest my head with oil; my cup runneth over [overflow]. Surely goodness and mercy shall follow me all the days of my life: and I will dwell in the house of the Lord for ever.

Psalms 23:5-6

David said that he lived in the overflow, because he was being constantly anointed by the Shepherd. The word *anointest* is a verb in the present continuous tense. So his walking in the constant overflow was due to his being positioned on a daily basis to receive a fresh anointing. As we receive a fresh anointing, we will stay in the overflow and experience the *fullness of the Blessing*.

If anybody knew about the anointing, it had to be King David; he knew the difference between ordinary and anointed. The outcome of his first contact with the anointing was that he started killing lions, bears and giants! He had to dodge some javelins and survive attacks, though, but the One who anoints, protects the one He anoints. By the anointing David experienced the overflow:

You anoint my head with oil, my cup overflows.

Psalm 23:5b (NIV)

After David entered the overflow, some things changed; goodness and mercy followed him and overtook him. Saying we need overflow could be the gross understatement of the year. We basically cannot do without it. Abundance is in the overflow, copiousness is in the overflow, favour is in the overflow, wealth is in the overflow, and *THE BLESSING* is in the overflow!!!

Prerequisites for the Overflow

The Lord wants us to have the overflow of the *Water of Life*. However, there are key criteria that must be in place for us to live and operate in it. God's part is never the hard part; He is always ready to release the overflow, but our alignment to Him and His Word oftentimes needs work. Let's delve into the principles that must be in place for the overflow.

Repentance

The word, *repentance*, as used in the Greek New Testament, is the word *metanoia*; it means for someone to have a change of mind or purpose. In the New Testament, it is always a change for the better. It chiefly has reference to repentance from sin, and this change of mind involves both a turning from sin and a turning to God.

When the church of Jesus was born, they had an outbreak of the supernatural. In one of his early gospel outreaches, Apostle Peter asserted that the fundamental key to receiving the flow of God's Spirit is repentance.

> Repent ye therefore, and be converted, that your sins may be blotted out, when the times of refreshing shall come from the presence of the Lord;
>
> Acts 3:19

Times of refreshing can only come from the *Presence of God* after there has been genuine repentance. Sin can be a hindrance to us achieving a greater dimension of God's power and presence is our lives.

A great revival of the overflow will be released before the second coming of Jesus. To be a part of the remnant that will usher in His return, we must be a people who have received both the former and the latter rain. In the Jewish calendar, the rain that falls in autumn is known as the former rain. The former rain prepares the ground for the planting season, while the spring rain is the rain that precedes the harvest.

The early church had the former rain, but God will, in these end times, release both the former rain and the latter rain in the same season. What we saw in the Acts of the Apostles will pale in greatness when compared with what God will do in His church in the coming season.

I mentioned in a previous chapter that the Lord spoke to me that, before the coming revival, we will have an outpouring of the *Spirit of the Fear of the Lord*. Holiness is the outward working of the Spirit of the Fear of the Lord; but holiness is preceded by repentance. Our foundation of repentance has to be in place before the release of the times of refreshing.

At one time, when Israel and Judah were about to go to battle with the surrounding nations, Jehoshaphat, King of Judah, asked that a prophet be brought. When the prophet, Elisha, arrived, he gave a brief rebuke and then directed that ditches be dug in the ground of the valley where they were camped.

And he said, Thus saith the LORD, Make this valley full of ditches.

2 Kings 3:16

To make ditches, you must dig out the earth from the ground. The earth is representative of the works of the flesh. So, the prophet was metaphorically instructing them to repent. The result of their digging of ditches was as follows:

For thus saith the LORD, Ye shall not see wind, neither shall ye see rain; yet that valley shall be filled with water, that ye may drink, both ye, and your cattle, and your beasts.

2 Kings 3:17

Though he said that they would see neither wind nor rain, he didn't say that it wasn't going to rain. The result of their digging up ditches was rain from heaven. The result of our living in repentance will be the release of an outpouring of rain under an open heaven.

But unto the Son he saith, Thy throne, O God, is for ever and ever: a sceptre of righteousness is the sceptre of thy kingdom. Thou hast loved righteousness, and hated iniquity; therefore God, even thy God, hath anointed thee with the oil of gladness above thy fellows.

Hebrews 1:8-9

Make no mistake about it: revelation of the goodness and grace of God is what leads us to repentance (Romans 2:4). I've often wondered why people get drunk and hammered every weekend, and wake up with a hangover. There must be something they believe they gain that I obviously don't recognise, which makes them go back for more. God's goodness is better than any type of earthly feeling or high. God's goodness is on such a dimension that it could take an innumerable amount of time for us to fathom the depths of it. When you catch a glimpse of how good God is, your thirst for Him will continually be stirred.

Thirst

> For I will pour water upon him that is thirsty, and floods upon the dry ground: I will pour my spirit upon thy seed, and my blessing upon thine offspring:
>
> Isaiah 44:3

In His John 7:37 declaration, the Lord spoke with a loud voice that He had a special message, but this message was only for the thirsty. You cannot be a partaker of the overflow of the Spirit, if you are not thirsty for it.

> Ho, every one that thirsteth, come ye to the waters, and he that hath no money; come ye, buy, and eat; yea, come, buy wine and milk without money and without price
>
> Isaiah 55:1

In His notable teaching that is now commonly known as The Beatitudes, the Lord said:

> Blessed are those who hunger and thirst after righteousness for they shall be filled
>
> Matthew 5:6

God is saying "I am looking for thirsty people." Are you hungry enough for God? Are you thirsty enough for His rain from Heaven? If you are not hungry for God, there is not much that He can do through you. As the old adage says "you can take a horse to the river, but you can't force it to drink." We can come before the fountain of water, but if we are not thirsty, we will not drink. You can only be filled after you've drunk.

> I stretch forth my hands unto thee: my soul thirsteth after thee, as a thirsty land. Selah.
>
> Psalms 143:6

I cannot overemphasise the fact that God is looking for the thirsty. God cannot cast His pearls before the indifferent. Divine treasures are for the hungry and thirsty. As we desire His *Water of Life*, He will fill us abundantly.

Prayer

The third key to experiencing the overflow is prayer. The answer to prayer is a supply of the Spirit

> Ask ye of the LORD rain in the time of the latter rain; so the LORD shall make bright clouds, and give them showers of rain, to every one grass in the field
>
> Zechariah 10:1

God wants to give us the rain more than we want it, but to receive the rain, we must ask for it. When we become thirsty for the rain, the next step is to ask for it.

> He will also send you rain for the seed you sow in the ground, and the food that comes from the land will be rich and plentiful. In that day your cattle will graze in broad meadows.
>
> Isaiah 30:23

If He sends rain, it is because it was requested. When the rain comes, the seed in the ground will produce. The rain is the key into the increase. The rain is the key to effectiveness. James told the church in his letter that:

> You have not because you ask not
>
> James 4:2b

If we do not ask, we will not have. This is one of the boldest phrases in the Bible, and it is also one of the biggest blank cheques ever written. If you do not have it, it is a direct result of your not asking; therefore, if you want to have, you must ask.

Your receiving is a direct result of your asking in prayer. It is time for our thirst for the Lord to increase, to drive us to our places of prayer to ask for rain. The Lord is willing to release the rain, but the rain is only released in response to prayer.

> And when they had prayed, the place was shaken where they were assembled together; and they were all filled with the Holy Ghost, and they spake the word of God with boldness.
>
> Acts 4:31

The disciples where already filled with the Spirit by this time in the history of the Church, but as they prayed together they were once again filled with the Holy Ghost. One of the most important ways of receiving the overflow is our prayer together in the assembly. When one person prays alone, there is power; but when many Spirit-filled people come together as one, there is such a great outpouring of rain, that the transformational work of the Spirit in our lives is manifested. In the place of corporate prayer, wells are filled and rivers overflow their banks.

There are many reasons for us to be part of a local assembly, but this one is very important. We sometimes do not place as much value on corporate prayer meetings as we ought because we are ignorant of its power. Let us get together and pray together, and have the rain of Heaven released until our water holding places are full and overflowing.

> Elias was a man subject to like passions as we are, and he prayed earnestly that it might not rain: and it rained not on the earth by the space of three years and six months. ***And he prayed again, and the heaven gave rain,*** *and the earth brought forth her fruit.*
>
> James 5:17-18 (Emphasis Mine)

James, the writer of the passage above, starts by saying that Elijah was just a man. Elijah was not an angel. That goes to show that if Elijah could receive answer to his request for rain, so can we. He prayed once for the heavens to be closed, basically activating God's prediction that the heavens over Israel would be closed if they turned their backs on Him. But the Bible says that "he prayed again."

We may have prayed once, but we must pray again. God, in His Word about the *Blessing*, has promised us open heavens. As we pray again about His Word for us, the rain will come. There will be a deluge of the *Blessing* rain.

We enter into the overflow as a result of constant and continuous praying. To stay in the overflow, we must have endless seasons of prayer. In Elijah we observe the effect of the rain: *"the heaven gave rain and the earth produced its fruit."* As we get in the place of prayer by the release of rain from Heaven, our lives, homes, ministries and churches will be fruitful.

It is worthy to note that we seem to be living below our privileges as New Covenant believers. The Lord said of John the Baptist that of every person born by a woman until John, John the Baptist was the greatest. That statement adds Elijah to the people who John was greater than. Moses, Abraham, David and all the other Old Testament greats were not as great as this man by none other than Jesus Himself. Furthermore, He said that:

> …notwithstanding he that is least in the kingdom of heaven is greater than he.
>
> Matthew 11:11b

If the above statement is true (and it is), then it is time for us as New Testament believers to rise and pray *big prayers*. God is bigger than our wildest imagination. God can fill any request for the rain, as long as we have a big enough reservoir to receive it.

> Now unto him that is able to do exceeding abundantly above all that we ask or think, according to the power that worketh in us,
>
> Ephesians 3:20

Praying in the spirit

Praying in the spirit is also known as praying in tongues or speaking in tongues. The term *speaking in tongues* is translated from the Greek word *Glössolalia*. This term is derived from two Greek words: *glössai*, which means *tongues* or *languages*, and *lalien*, which means *to speak*. When a believer is baptised in the Spirit, he speaks in tongues as the initial evidence of this baptism. Usually, a person that is speaking in tongues is typically unable to understand the words that he is saying, but we see in Paul, that we are to pray in our understanding and pray in tongues (1 Corinthians 14:15).

We are to pray in this language we do not understand because the man that speaks in tongues is speaking to God. He is enjoying a deep encounter of fellowship with the *Divine Spirit*. When we pray in tongues, it is our spirits actually doing the praying; this is spirit-to-Spirit fellowship.

This is the human spirit drawing from the *Divine Spirit*. The transmission of *Divine Life* happens in our recreated human spirits by this spirit-to-Spirit communion. This is our deep calling to God's deep, "The Deep to deep calls The Voice to the voice of the waters of your fountains."[1] We draw waters at the fountain of God by our praying with our spirits.

The early church had one secret about prayer that gave them results that we seek in our day. There came a time in the early church when the Hellenists complained against the Hebrews because their widows were being overlooked in the daily distribution of food in the church. It came to the attention of the early apostles, and the apostles said that they could not leave their work, which was their being dedicated to the Word and prayer. They then ordained seven deacons for that service (Acts 6:1-7).

In the original Greek, the word translated *prayer* in the above narration is actually *The Prayer*. There are many types of prayer, but outside of praying in the spirit or praying in tongues, we do not really see any new types of prayer introduced in the New Testament. I am convinced that the apostles meant praying in the Holy Ghost. They were addicted to this spirit-to-Spirit communication. They knew of its benefits; they knew this was the place where they could receive the overflow.

The Apostle Paul said of praying in the Spirit, *"I thank my God I speak with tongues more than ye all"* (1 Corinthians 14:18). If Paul was thanking God that he prayed or spoke in tongues more than the other believers, then this may be one of the reasons for his tremendous success. The purpose of this book is not necessarily to argue at length about the subject of praying in tongues. I intend to illustrate the connection between prayer, especially praying in tongues as associated with the overflow, and walking in the *Fullness of the Blessing*.

> For with stammering lips and another tongue will he speak to this people. To whom he said, This is the rest wherewith ye may cause the weary to rest; and this is the refreshing: yet they would not hear.
>
> Isaiah 28:11-12

Paul refers to Isaiah 28:11 in his first letter to the Corinthian church in his discourse about tongues (1 Corinthians 14:21). It is God's plan that, by speaking in tongues, He will cause us to receive rest and refreshing.

> He maketh me to lie down in green pastures: he leadeth me beside the still waters. He *restoreth* my soul:
>
> Psalm 23:2-3a

Praying in tongues gives us the access to be led by the waters of God, so that our souls can be restored. As we journey through life, our strength, at times, can be depleted and we become weary; but by praying in the Holy Ghost, our weary souls are restored and they enter into the refreshing that can only come by the *Water of Life*.

The words we use while speaking in tongues may be unintelligible to us because of the inability of our minds to understand it (it is spirit language), but the One from Whom the language originates understands us. There are aspects of the overflow that we can only enter by expressing our intercession through the help of the Holy Spirit.

As we pray in tongues, the Eternal Spirit empowers us to pray the mind of the Father for us and for our generation; and causes us to receive His Spirit in fullness until we begin to overflow.

Praying in the Spirit is one way to drink from the *Water of Life*. As we tarry long in that place of praying in tongues, we are guaranteed the overflow in our lives.

> Likewise the Spirit also helpeth our infirmities: for we know not what we should pray for as we ought: but the Spirit itself maketh intercession for us with groanings which cannot be uttered. And he that searcheth the hearts knoweth what is the mind of the Spirit, because he maketh intercession for the saints according to the will of God.
>
> Romans 8:26-27

The word *uttered* in verse 26 can be interpreted as *articulated in intelligible speech*. We must understand that God doesn't necessarily speak our individual languages or local dialects, though that's how we hear Him when He speaks. In trying to express the will of God in prayer, our human language is grossly inadequate to express it. That is why God has given us this new language, sometimes referred to as the tongue of angels.

You can't always pray solely in your understanding and expect the supernatural to reign in the affairs of life by the dominion in the *Blessing*; that is why we have been given the prayer language.

> How forcible are right words.
>
> Job 6:25a

As He was about to ascend into heaven, Jesus told His disciples that they would receive power after that the Holy Ghost had come upon them (Acts 1:8). The word for *power* is the Greek word *dunamis* from where we get the word *dynamo*. One way this power is released is by words; right powerful words. These are the words that are given to us by the Holy Spirit as we pray in tongues. These are words that are *dynamitic* in their result-producing abilities.

As you pray in tongues, your words are dynamite; words that speak to the heart of the matter about the purpose. They are words that speak right to the heart of the matter about the overflow; pure words, *powerful* words. As we pray these words, we are releasing the will of God, "because the Spirit intercedes for the saints according to the will of God." And we know that when we pray according to His will, He hears us and grants us every petition that we ask of Him. The overflow of His *Divine Presence* is His will for us.

New Testament prayer for The Overflow

We have clearly seen that one of the keys to the overflow is prayer. We have many prayers in the Bible, but the prayers in the New Testament, especially the Pauline epistles, are filled with expressions we can adopt in our own prayers.

> For this cause I bow my knees unto the Father of our Lord Jesus Christ, Of whom the whole family in heaven and earth is named, That he would grant you, according to the riches of his glory, to be strengthened with might by his Spirit in the inner man; That Christ may dwell in your hearts by faith; that ye, being rooted and grounded in love, May be able to comprehend with all saints what is the breadth, and length, and depth, and height; And to know the love of Christ, which passeth knowledge, that ye might be filled with all the fulness of God.
>
> Ephesians 3:14-19

Though this was Paul praying for the church in Ephesus, we can also personalise the prayer and pray it for ourselves. The prayer is that we ask God according to the riches of His glory. The riches of His glory refer to the place of His infiniteness, his fountain of limitlessness; to strengthen with might by His Indwelling Spirit.

Strengthened with might in the inner man

What we are praying for here is that we be strengthened with the might of God in our spirits. If you don't strengthen what you have on the inside, you are not going to be able to keep what you have on the outside; you will lose every battle.

> And when he came unto Lehi, the Philistines shouted against him: and the Spirit of the LORD came mightily upon him, and the cords that were upon his arms became as flax that was burnt with fire, and his bands loosed from off his hands.
>
> Judges 15:14

By the power of the Spirit, Samson was released from everything that held Him captive. The fire of God burned up the cords with which he was bound. By the anointing of the Holy Ghost, burdens are lifted and yokes are destroyed. By the anointing, Samson was strengthened to destroy the enemies of Israel.

In the Amplified version, Paul prays that we be *"invigorated with mighty power in our innermost being and personality."* God wants His power to affect our spirits to the point that we get a personality modification. That we move from grumpiness to joy and laughter. That is why the anointing is called *"the oil of gladness."* A man that is constantly filled with the Spirit cannot spend his days in the doldrums of depression. You can't be filled and be constantly depressed. You didn't get a sad Holy Ghost.

The indwelling of Christ.

The word *Christ* means the *Anointed One* and His *Anointing*. He is the One who is resurrected and sitting at the place of authority in heaven. Christ, the resurrected One, can only fully dwell in us to the degree that we are filled with the Spirit. The Holy Spirit is the One who transmits everything that belongs to Christ in us. God is *Life* inherent and immanent.

Christ is the *Life of God* embodied and manifested on earth. The Holy Spirit is the *Life of God* dwelling in us. Christ dwelling, resting, at home, in us, is the power of redemption made real to us, in us and through us. It is by redemption that we have now inherited the *Blessing*.

God is the Father of Glory, Christ is the Lord of Glory, and the Holy Ghost is the Spirit of Glory. The Spirit of Glory manifests in us and through us everything that the Lord of Glory received for us. It's all *Glory*; the full expression of God's goodness. Everything Christ is, the Holy Spirit communicates it to us.

The dwelling of Christ in us is the function of our faith in Him. This faith is the victory by which we live the overcoming life, the victorious life. When we rule in life by the power of the Spirit, Christ is truly dwelling in us; He is at home in us. Christ and sickness cannot coexist. In His full dwelling, sickness, depression, poverty and oppression will become extinct.

Rooted and grounded in Love

The soil in which our lives are planted is the *Love of God*. We are the planting of the Lord, and we are planted in His ground. Christ is the ground on which we are planted. The soil on which seeds are planted is one of the key determining factors of the type of crop and fruit that will be produced. The *Love of God* is fundamentally essential to our producing, as well as what we produce. We must become convinced that we are loved by Him; that we are free to fly and be all that He intends for us to be. The Psalmist said that, "those who are planted in the House of our God, shall flourish in the courts of our God" (Psalm 92:13). As we are planted, grounded and rooted deeply in His love, our lives shall manifest His fruitfulness.

Filled with the Fullness of God

In verse 19, we see the result of this prayer for the Holy Spirit's strengthening of our inner man: The Fullness of God. Fullness is a result of being poured into, and as we keep being poured into, we get the overflow. The *Fullness of God* is the glorious wealth that abides in Christ.

I love the way that the Amplified version renders Ephesians 3:19:

[That you may really come] to know [practically, through experience for yourselves] the love of Christ, which far surpasses mere knowledge [without experience]; *that you may be filled [through all your being] unto all the fullness of God [may have the richest measure of the divine Presence, and become a body wholly filled and flooded with God Himself]!*
Ephesians 3:19 AMP (Emphasis mine)

We are to be completely permeated with the presence and the power of God. God wants us to experience *"the richest measure of the Divine Presence."* It is possible for us to begin to experience and enjoy the abundantly supplied *Presence of God*. The aim is that we be wholly filled and flooded with God Himself.

The place of the overflow is the place where we are thoroughly immersed in God and by God. This was what Jesus had; He had the Spirit without measure. That was why He did what He did. We can be flooded with God.

When we are flooded with God, we are overwhelmed with His presence; which means that we are experiencing the overflow of His *Presence*. I don't know where you stand right now on the issue, but this a good time to begin to ask God to fill you with Himself; to give you the richest measure of His *Presence*, and to cause you to experience the flood of His *Power*. Press in prayer and get in the overflow. The *Fullness of the Blessing* is in the overflow. Step into the waters and be submerged by the flood of His Presence.

In the final analysis, the key to the *Fullness of the Blessing* is the fullness of God. Everything discussed in this book, from *Faith* to walking in *Love*, relates to our maintaining union with God and meditating on the *Word*; and, now, the overflow of the glory of God is to the end that we are filled with all the fullness of God. When we, the church, are filled with the fullness of the God of the *Blessing*, we will have the fullness of the *Blessing*.

Fasting

Fasting is abstinence from food, or limiting of one's food intake, particularly as a voluntary act of sacrifice or as a religious observance. It could also include abstinence from various forms of entertainment and interaction. This is usually done to seek the face of God for direction, or to find a solution in times of need.

Fasting is also one of the primary ways to enter into the overflow. Before the Lord started His earthly ministry, he spent 40 days and nights in the wilderness, fasting (Matthew 4:2). Paul, the Apostle, said that he fasted often. Let me show you a scenario from the gospels that highlight one of the main reasons why we should make habit of fasting.

And the disciples of John and of the Pharisees used to fast: and they come and say unto him, Why do the disciples of John and of the Pharisees fast, but thy disciples fast not? And Jesus said unto them, Can the children of the bridechamber fast, while the bridegroom is with them? as long as they have the bridegroom with them, they cannot fast. But the days will come, when the bridegroom shall be taken away from them, and then shall they fast in those days.

Mark 2:18-20

The Pharisees and the disciples of John saw that, while they fasted, the disciples of Jesus did not. When they asked Jesus why, He told them that as long as the bridegroom is with his friends, they don't fast; but when he is taken away from them, they cannot help but fast. As the Bride of Christ, Jesus is our Bridegroom. When we come to a time in our walk with God when we feel like He is not near, it is a time to fast. When we feel like we are not anointed, then we must go to the place of fasting.

Every effective minister of the gospel that I've come across makes fasting a practice. To get in the overflow, we must fast often. The overflow is a prerequisite to the *Fullness of the Blessing*; therefore, if we must have the *Fullness of the Blessing*, we have no choice but to fast.

> Then shall thy light break forth as the morning, and thine health shall spring forth speedily: and thy righteousness shall go before thee; the glory of the LORD shall be thy rereward. And the LORD shall guide thee continually, *and satisfy thy soul in drought, and make fat thy bones: and thou shalt be like a watered garden, and like a spring of water, whose waters fail not.* And they that shall be of thee shall build the old waste places: thou shalt raise up the foundations of many generations; and thou shalt be called, The repairer of the breach, The restorer of paths to dwell in.
>
> Isaiah 58:8; 11-12 (Emphasis mine)

From the Isaiah 58 account, we see how fasting is connected to the overflow. The Bible here says that, the Lord will *"satisfy"* our souls in drought. This means that where there should have been spiritual dryness, He will flood us with the water of His Presence. All our dry places will become fruitful and all our wildernesses will be filled with abundance.

It goes on to say that by fasting God will make our bones fat, then we shall become *"like a watered garden."* A well-watered garden is always fruitful, no matter the season. One of our definitions for the *Blessing* is an empowerment to be fruitful. As we fast, the *Water of Life* irrigates our fields and whatever we lay our hands to do will prosper.

There is empowerment for fruitfulness in fasting. Fasting is not just a religious activity but a fruitfulness-releasing force. We shall be "like a spring of water, whose waters fail not." Now this just takes it to a "whole 'nother level." We don't only have the overflow, we become like a spring of water.

The word *spring* comes from the Hebrew word *mosa*. It means a fountain, a water-spring, a watercourse. It also means a source of water. If this is not reason enough to fast, I don't know what is. As we spend our time seeking God in fasting and prayer, we become sources of blessing. We shall be called "repairers of the breach."

In the second chapter of this book, I said that the *Blessing* empowers us to become *replenishers*. Now we see how this operates. Let's step into our responsibilities and become city and world changers by the power of the *Blessing*.

Worship and Thanksgiving

> And be not drunk with wine, wherein is excess; but be filled with the Spirit
> Ephesians 5:18

Paul instructs us of what we ought not to be filled with, then he tells us with Whom we ought to be filled. We are commanded to be filled with the Spirit. Smith Wigglesworth said that "being filled with the Spirit is a privilege but it is also a command."[2] We have been commanded to enter into the privilege of enjoying the fullness of the Spirit.

Paul goes on to instruct how to be filled with the Spirit:

> Speaking to yourselves in psalms and hymns and spiritual songs, singing and making melody in your heart to the Lord; Giving thanks always for all things unto God and the Father in the name of our Lord Jesus Christ;
> Ephesians 5:19-20

The third prerequisite that must be in place for us to live in the overflow is worship and thanksgiving. Living a life of thanksgiving to God and making melody in our hearts and before the Lord is a way to be filled with the Spirit. As we joyously thank Him, something begins to well up on the inside of us. I find from my experience that as I begin to thank God and give Him praise, I break out praying in the Holy Ghost. As we make this our daily practice, we enter into the experience of the overflow of the Spirit.

One of the expressions of thanksgiving is *Joy*. You cannot be thankful and not be joyful. Joy and thanksgiving are conjoined. You can't have one without the other.

Be glad then, ye children of Zion, and rejoice in the Lord your God: for he hath given you the former rain moderately, and he will cause to come down for you the rain, the former rain, and the latter rain in the first month. And the floors shall be full of wheat, and the vats shall overflow with wine and oil.

Joel 2:23-24

As we rejoice in the Lord for what He has done; as we rejoice in Him for the measure of anointing that we have, we are setting ourselves up for an even greater dimension of His Presence. If you are not satisfied with the level of power you walk in, I think it's time for you to quit being sad and begin to rejoice for that which the Lord has given you. Your thanksgiving will cause His rain to come on you.

This is the consequence of rejoicing:

And it shall come to pass afterward, that I will pour out my spirit upon all flesh; and your sons and your daughters shall prophesy, your old men shall dream dreams, your young men shall see visions

Joel 2:28

The Order and The Glory

The Lord wants us to be positioned in our place before He sends the rain. When God planted the garden, the Bible says in Genesis 2 that He didn't allow it to rain:

And every plant of the field before it was in the earth, and every herb of the field before it grew: for the LORD God had not caused it to rain upon the earth, and there was not a man to till the ground. But there went up a mist from the earth, and watered the whole face of the ground.

Genesis 2:5-6

God does not waste His resources (John 6:12). Until there was a man in place, there was no rain on the earth. What the earth had was a mist to water the face of the ground. There was no reason for the rain because the rain would cause the plants to overgrow. Without a man in place, God did not deem it fit to send the rain. Until we take our place of assignment, what we will experience is the mist; just enough to get by, but not enough to bring about a change of scenery. May we take our place as a people of God in His end-time move!

God is a God of order. Before the Lord performed the miracle of the multiplication of fives loaves of bread and two fishes to feed five thousand men (not counting the women and children), He told them to sit in groups of fifties (Luke 9:14). This is because the miracle of multiplication will not take place without divine order. As we take our place, we shall see and experience the rain of His Presence.

The Purpose of the Overflow is to Flow

It has been the emphasis of this book that God gives us the *Blessing,* not necessarily for ourselves, but for us to be a blessing. The reason that God wants us to have the overflow is so that we can flow to others.

> In the last day, that great day of the feast, Jesus stood and cried, saying, If any man thirst, let him come unto me, and **drink**. He that believeth on me, as the scripture hath said, out of his belly shall **flow** rivers of living water.
>
> John 7:37-38 (Emphasis mine)

The Lord said on the feast that we must first thirst for this water. After we've thirsted for it we must now drink.

The Drinking Process

> Jesus saith unto them, Fill the waterpots with water. And they filled them up to the brim. And he saith unto them,
>
> John 2:7

The verse above is a scenario from the first miracle that was performed by Jesus in His earthly ministry, which was turning water into wine at a wedding. Jesus was invited to the wedding. They did not wait for the crisis to hit before inviting Him. When we become born again, what we've done is to invite Jesus into our lives to take the centre stage. As people who are now in the family of God, the Bible calls Jesus our elder brother. A brother is born for the day of adversity (Proverbs 17:17). It so happened at this event that they ran out of wine. Mary approached Him to do something about it, but He replied to her that it wasn't His time

The mother of Jesus gave an instruction that I call, "the doctrine of Mary." She told the guys that were there that "whatsoever He tells you to do, do it." As simple as it sounds, it's not always easy for us to do. Sometimes we want to do more than He's asked because it doesn't make sense or sound feasible. God's Word is not meant to make sense; it is meant to produce faith. Obedience should always follow His instructions.

After Mary asked that the people do whatever Jesus told them to do, He instructed them to fill the water pots with water. The Bible describes us as jars of clay; saying that we carry the treasure of God in earthen vessels (2 Corinthians 4:7) Metaphorically, we can be described as water pots.

For us to be solution providers, we must be filled with the *Water of Life*. The filling process is the process of drinking in this *Water*. A water pot does not get filled automatically; it takes a process. We must keep drinking the Spirit with our spirits until we are filled. The drinking process is a continuous activity.

When we've had our fill, then "out of our bellies will flow rivers of Living Water." Notice that the word *"rivers"* is plural and not singular. The flow of the Spirit is not restricted to one kind of activity or demonstration. These are various rivers flowing in the direction of various needs. God pours into us, not for us to become reservoirs and hold the water in, but for us to flow.

After His wilderness experience, Jesus was said to "return in the power of the Spirit." (Luke 4:14). When He got to the synagogue, He read in Isaiah where it was written of Him thus:

> The Spirit of the Lord is upon me, because he hath anointed me to preach the gospel to the poor; he hath sent me to heal the broken hearted, to preach deliverance to the captives, and recovering of sight to the blind, to set at liberty them that are bruised, To preach the acceptable year of the Lord.
>
> Luke 4:18-19

Jesus said the Spirit of the Lord was upon Him, but not without a purpose. The purpose of the Spirit of God coming upon Him was for healing, deliverance and bringing freedom to others. We are to follow His example. As God pours out His Spirit in and on our spirits, we, in turn, pour it out to those in need who we encounter.

In the miracle at Cana, water was turned into wine (John 2:1-13). Wine is also symbolic of the Spirit of God as our joy giver. That is why Paul juxtaposes being drunk with wine and being filled with the Spirit. When someone is drunk with alcoholic beverage, they do not act like normal human beings. They do things that, in their right minds, they would never contemplate. Supernatural eyesight is in the fullness and overflow of the Spirit.

> And it shall come to pass afterward, that I will pour out my spirit upon all flesh; and your sons and your daughters shall prophesy, your old men shall dream dreams, your young men shall see visions:
>
> Joel 2:28

On that day of Pentecost, when the fullness of the Spirit was first released on earth, observers who came to the celebration heard the disciples' utterances and made fun of them that they were drunk with new wine. Then Peter spoke up and said "these are not drunk as you suppose." They are drunk, but not the way you think they are; not with what you think they are drunk with.

So it is with the believer who is filled with the Spirit. As the man who is drunk with wine is led by wine, so must we be filled with the Spirit to be led by Him.

> Draw out now, and bear unto the governor of the feast. And they bare it. When the ruler of the feast had tasted the water that was made wine, and knew not whence it was: (but the servants which drew the water knew;) the governor of the feast called the bridegroom, And saith unto him, Every man at the beginning doth set forth good wine; and when men have well drunk, then that which is worse: but thou hast kept the good wine until now
>
> John 2:8-10

When the wine was given to the governor of the feast, he was amazed at how delicious the wine tasted. This is a picture of what God will do with those who will linger long in His presence; long enough to be drunk in the wine; long enough to be distributors of spiritual wine. We become people who are possessors with the intent to distribute. By the wine of the Spirit, we will fill lives with joy and rebuild the old ruins.

Joy is most often expressed with laughter and rejoicing. Other words defined as joy are great pleasure, happiness, delight, jubilation, triumph, exhilaration, elation, euphoria, bliss, ecstasy, and rapture. Don't we all just love joy? Few years ago, when I saw Christian ministers on television with hysterical laughter in their meetings, it used to make me cringe. It used to be weird and strange to me until I saw that even the Lord loves to laugh.

> He that sitteth in the heavens shall laugh: the Lord shall have them in derision
>
> Psalm 2:4

When my eyes became open to the fact that we sit in the heavenly places with Him in Christ Jesus (Ephesians 2:6). I began to laugh also. But something else about this Holy Ghost laughter is that it carries with it the overflow of the *Water of Life*. I've seen depression depart from people in atmospheres of joy and laughter. I've seen healing take place. Deliverances happen in this atmosphere of the joy of the Lord. Indeed, "The joy of the Lord is our strength."[3]

> Thou will show me the path of Life: In Thy presence is fullness of joy: at Thy right hand there are pleasures ever more
>
> Psalm 16:11

After being filled, it is time for us to release that which we have by faith. We must come to a place where we are convinced that we carry the *Blessing of God* on the inside of us. It is as we release the water by faith that it becomes wine to the drinkers. As we pour out by faith, miracles will happen.

I would like us to place emphasis on the pouring out process. If the servants had not poured out the water, it would never have been turned into wine. The water didn't change to wine inside the water pot; it changed in the pouring out. Often times we say we will pour out the water when "the water has been turned into wine;" but it will never become wine except we pour it out. It was a miracle that was in a sense both performed by Jesus and the servants.

When God used Gideon to defeat the Midianites, the army of Israel cried "the sword of the Lord and of Gideon" (Judges 7:20). It is in the pouring out that we see the supernatural propensities of the *Blessing* that God has deposited on the inside of us. It is as we pour out by faith, the

Blessing that flows in and through our lives, that God's overflow and surplus strike our lives.

> Give, and it shall be given unto you; good measure, pressed down, and shaken together, and running over, shall men give into your bosom. For with the same measure that ye mete withal it shall be measured to you again.
>
> Luke 6:38

As we pour out, God will pour more into us. It will be a virtuous cycle of receiving-giving-receiving. As we stay hungry and faithful to pour out that which we receive from God's presence, we will continually live in the overflow and become a *Blessing* to our world.

The Overflow: Greater Works

> Verily, verily, I say unto you, He that believeth on me, the works that I do shall he do also; *and greater works than these shall he do;* **because I go unto my Father.**
>
> John 14:12 (Emphasis mine)

The Lord promises us that we will perform the same miracles that He did if we believe Him. Then, he said some of the most compelling words about the possibility of the believer: that we will do greater works than He did. The reason for the greater works is because He was going to the Father.

The question you may want to ask is: *What does His being with the Father have to do with it?* The answer is, at this time, He had not completed His passion. After His resurrection, He told His followers to wait for the coming of the Holy Spirit. He told them it was better for Him to go, so that they could have the Spirit. The Holy Spirit's coming was only possible because Jesus was now with the Father.

> Being therefore exalted at the right hand of God, and having received from the Father the promise of the Holy Spirit, he has poured out this that you yourselves are seeing and hearing.
>
> Acts 2:33 (ESV)

The Holy Spirit has been poured out and He can fill us to the degree that we receive Him. In Revelation 22, the Holy Spirit manifests as the *Water of Life*; everything we need for greater works is in the *Water of Life*. As we drink of Him until we are full, and continue until we are overflowing, we will fulfil the Lord's dream for greater works through us. Everything we need for this is found in the *Water of Life*, the anointing of the Holy Spirit.

A Word of Caution

Before we end this chapter, I would like us to observe something that is not commensurate with the overflow in the Ezekiel 47 narrative. Yes, the water had flowed from the temple, but it did not produce the right fruit in certain places, and we will see why.

> But the ***miry places*** thereof and the ***marishes*** thereof shall not be healed; they shall be given to salt.
>
> Ezekiel 47:11 (Emphasis mine)

Two words stand out in the verse above. The *miry* place is a combination of sand and water. The other word, *marish*, is reservoir. The miry place signifies a life that has mixture. In the overflow, a mixture of flesh and spirit is, at best, ineffective. For us to carry the healing, purity and freshness of the *Blessing*, we must be a people of purity, because only "the pure in heart will see God." If the reservoir doesn't give life, it doesn't flow. We can't have the *Blessing* and keep it to ourselves. Growth in this life is reserved for those who will serve in the essence of the *Blessing*.

The end result of the mixture and the reservoir is that they both end up as salt pits. They will not be able to give life. The word *salt* is the Hebrew word *melah* from which the word *melaha* (another word for barrenness) is derived.

If you are not flowing out, then the water that you have will eventually become salt. To help us understand this, the picture of the Dead Sea in Israel is apt. The Dead Sea only receives water, but never gives out; so it is dense with salt. No animal or plant life can survive in it; it is a salt pit.

To stay fresh and useful for Heaven's agenda, we must flow as believers; that is why the Lord is giving us the overflow. If we must stay in the flow of the *Blessing*, we must flow out and stay pure.

And on the banks, on both sides of the river, there will grow all kinds of trees for food. Their leaves will not wither, nor their fruit fail, but they will bear fresh fruit every month, because the water for them flows from the sanctuary. Their fruit will be for food, and their leaves for healing.

Ezekiel 47:12

Bright Clouds

When Zechariah, in his prophecy, instructed Israel to pray for rain in the time of the latter rain, he said that God would send "bright clouds," and then the rain would come (Zechariah 10:1). Before Heaven entirely invades the earth, God is raising a people that increasingly cause the current invasion to expand, which will result in the earth being filled with God's glory until it coincides with the Second Coming of Jesus. These people are known as rain-carriers; they are bright clouds; lightning rods for the *Glory of God*.

A cloud is a large collection of very tiny droplets of water or ice crystals. Jude, the Apostle, talks about certain people who can be described as, "clouds without water" (Jude 1:12). They have the position and visibility without the revelation and ability to bring about the solution.

If the clouds are full, they pour out rain upon the earth (Ecclesiastes 11:3a). There are different intensity levels of rain: light, moderate, heavy and violent. Euphemisms for a heavy or violent rain include gully washer, trash-mover and toad-strangler. In this season, we are not after a drizzle; we are after a downpour of the showers of *Blessing*. The type of rain that will remove all the trash that has stood in the way of our churches thus far, in order for our churches do what God has called them to do.

Water is a type of both the *Word* and the *Spirit* of God. Bright clouds are full, and dare I say overflowing with the *Word* and *Spirit* of the Living God. There are certain ministers in the world today who are described as "bright clouds;" they are climate changers. They enter a local assembly and they release the rain; they change seasons and cause breakthroughs to be witnessed in churches. These are people who have walked softly with the Lord, and have developed their capacity to hold large amounts of rain water (glory) to bring about revival and transformation.

In this season, the Lord wants to raise more people who are clouds full of rain; bright clouds that are lightning rods for His glory. Bright clouds will bring the rain and cause us to experience the fruitfulness that can only be a result of the *Blessing*. You can be a bright cloud. God wants our churches of be full of "Bright Clouds;" rain-carriers who release a deluge of Heaven's Glory. There shall be Showers of the *Blessing*!

Chapter 12

THE ASSEMBLY

It was 1998, in the month of February. As I sat quietly before the Lord after my morning devotion, I heard God speak these words about my local church, Word of Life Bible Church in the City of Warri, Nigeria: "**Word of Life is not a man's idea; Word of Life is not a good idea; Word of Life is a God idea**".

As much as I wasn't surprised, I was quite overwhelmed by the authority, clarity and *Presence* that came with the Voice. As with my local church in Nigeria, every local church where the Lord has put His Name is a God idea.

In the second chapter of this book, we established that *The Blessing* is a *Place*. I can unequivocally say that the local church is a *Blessing Place*. The structure, size and style of worship may differ, but the place where the Lord plants His name is *Blessed*.

The first time the word *church* is used in the Bible, we see Jesus introducing the idea:

> And I say also unto thee, That thou art Peter, and upon this rock I will build my church; and the gates of hell shall not prevail against it.
>
> Matthew 16:18

The concept of the Church is God's idea. It is Jesus building it, but we are the ones who do the actual work. As the Builder of the Church, Jesus doesn't necessarily come down from Heaven to do the job; He uses men and women. Providing direction and strategy, He puts the idea and structure in our hearts, and we flesh out that which He has shown us in the spirit. It is the same as when Moses was allowed to have a peek into Heaven in order to see the pattern of God's temple in Heaven for him to then return from the mountain to build the church that was shown to him. The Lord is the Originator, the Architect, and we carry out the work by the power and enablement of His Spirit under the direction of God's chosen human leadership in the Church.

Let us start by defining what the church is. The word *church* in the New Testament never refers to a building or a place. It always refers to a people: either the total number of believers who have ever lived, or a local group of those believers. For example:

> To the church of God that is in Corinth, to those sanctified in Christ Jesus, called to be saints together with all those who in every place call upon the name of our Lord Jesus Christ, both their Lord and ours:
>
> 1 Corinthians 1:2 (ESV)

From the verse above, we see that Paul's letter was sent to the "church in Corinth." Without discussing other references, we can deduce from this statement that there were other churches that were local to their own individual cities.

> And Saul was consenting unto his death. And at that time there was a great persecution against **the church which was at Jerusalem**, and they were all scattered abroad throughout the regions of Judaea and Samaria, except the apostles
>
> Acts 8:1 (Emphasis mine)

The word *church* is for the Greek term *ecclesia*. It means to be called out of. It was used among the Greeks of a body of citizens gathered to discuss the affairs of State. The word *eccelsia* is also translated as the words *assembly* or *congregation*.[1] So the church is the place where we discuss the affairs of God's kingdom on earth.

In recent times, I have heard people make cringe-worthy statements about the church and the kingdom. Statements like "our priority is no longer the Church; we are now all about the kingdom." Indeed, the Church is not the Kingdom of God; but it is a part of it. God has chosen the Church to be the agency through which the world is reached. Yes, we are part of the Kingdom, but on this side of heaven, the Church is God's priority; therefore, it ought to be ours. The part of the Kingdom that we are engaged with on earth is really the Church.

> For as in one body we have many members, and the members do not all have the same function, so we, though many, are one body in Christ, and individually members one of another.
>
> Romans 12:4-5 (ESV)

On the whole, we have two classifications of Church: the universal Church and the local church. The universal Church is the whole number of the redeemed, both dead and alive, who look to Christ as their life, and the author and finisher of their faith. Though we use the word "churches" as plural, there is only one Church, or "one body" (Ephesians 4:4).

The Local Church

I would define a local church as a group of believers who meet together on a regular basis for the purpose of worshipping God through Jesus Christ; to be exhorted by the Word of God, and to celebrate the sacraments of the Church in a localised setting.

> John to the seven churches that are in Asia: Grace to you and peace from him who is and who was and who is to come, and from the seven spirits who are before his throne,
>
> Revelation 1:4 (ESV)

God has called us to live corporately. Though many, we live as one. In the Bible we see many terms that confirm the fact that the Church life is a corporate life. We are called the sheep of His pasture and regarded as God's flock. We are also called living stones who are put together to build up a spiritual house for a dwelling place for God. As individual believers, and collectively, we are branches in the vine. The Church is called an army, and we are also called members of the *Body of Christ*.

Although we remain individuals, as Christians we are not expected to live for ourselves alone, that is, only for our own interests, activities and goals. On the contrary, God desires that we live a corporate life, conscious of the Body of Christ; looking not every man on his own things, but every man also on the things of others. God wants us to be concerned about the building up of the Church.

We may be from individualistic cultures, or we may just want to live independently; but the idea of believers living independently of the Church is at dissonance with the New Testament concept of Church. Every local church should have this motto: *No individualistic exclusionism allowed here!*

I am sure you must have met someone who told you that they were Christians, but did not "attend church." They served God by themselves alone in their homes.

The epistles were written to the churches and requested to be read in churches, not necessarily to individuals, with the exception of the pastoral books (1 and 2 Timothy and Titus). The epistles written by James and Peter were written to believers in the diaspora that were scattered by persecution. These epistles were written from the perspective that the recipients were still congregating, and deal heavily with their life in the context of the Church.

Throughout the New Testament, the assumption is always the same: that the people of God are faithfully gathering together in a local assembly where the *Word of God* is being disseminated. That unified gathering—not just the invisible worldwide Church, but the local, visible congregation—is at the heart of Christianity.

The Church is the only institution the Lord established and promised to bless. Why would anyone who claims to love the Lord want to keep His people, or family for that matter, from the assembly of the Church?

> *Not forsaking the assembling of ourselves together,* as the manner of some is; but exhorting one another: and so much the more, as ye see the Day approaching.
>
> Hebrews 10:25 (Emphasis mine)

Every believer should be part of a local church. There must be the assembling of ourselves together, especially as the day of the Lord's return approaches. We see the word, "all" many times in the New Testament in reference to the church, emphasising the fact that God's plan is not about individuals, but a group of people, a body: The *Body of Christ.*

Oftentimes, in trying to be independent of the church, we are expressing the desire to be *different*. God doesn't want to reach the world with nonconformists or individualists; His plan is "through the church." We don't have try to be *different*, we are already *different*. It is our responsibility to now live our difference in our world. We are in the world, but we are not of the world. We are not like the world; we are the Church!

This is certainly not a thorough examination of the concept of the Church—local or universal—but a snippet of a discourse about what the Church is and its relationship to the *Blessing*.

The Church as a City

Ye are the light of the world. *A city that is set on an hill* cannot be hid.
Matthew 5:14 (Emphasis mine)

Jesus calls the Church, individually and collectively, a city, and He is the hill on which we've been set on. The word *set* means to stand on or to be established. As the Church, we've been called to stand on and be established on Christ, the *Solid Rock*. "The Gospel church is a city, built on Christ, the foundation; and is full of habitants, true believers…it is pleasantly situated by the river of God's love, and by the still waters of Gospel ordinances; it is governed by wholesome laws, of Christ's enacting, and is under proper officers, of His appointing."[2]

From our exalted position, we shine as beacons of light to a dying world; bringing direction, replacing the dysfunction with order and development wherever we are. There were certain cities in the Bible that were located in Israel that I believe are types of what the Church has been designed to be.

Bethlehem

The word *Bethlehem* means House of Bread.[3] Historically, Jesus was born in Bethlehem. The Church is the place where Christ is born in our hearts and formed in us. Jesus Christ referred to Himself as the *Bread of Life*.

The church is a house of bread; a place where we are fed God's Word. Bread in the Bible is symbolic of the *Word of God*. The Church is a place where we are fed the revelation of God's Word. The teaching of the *Word of God* is one of the most important activities in the local church:

Until I come, give attention to the public reading of Scripture, to exhortation and teaching

1 Timothy 4:13 (NASB)

Part of the emphasis in public worship includes these three things: 1) hearing the Word; 2) being called to obedience and action through exhortation; and, 3) teaching. It is only within the context of the local assembly that these things can most effectively take place. The Bible shows us this example of what the early church did when they met together:

> They were continually devoting themselves to the apostles' teaching and to fellowship, to the breaking of bread and to prayer.
>
> Acts 2:42 (NASB)

These new Christians were taught God's Word and by implication, the benefit of it in their lives. They joined together to carry out various acts of love and service to one another. They commemorated the Lord's death and resurrection through the breaking of bread, and they prayed. Of course, we can do these things on an individual level, but the very nature of these activities require that we do them together. God has called us into His Body, and the local church is the local representation of the universal Body.

As the house of bread, the local church is the place where we meet together to commemorate the Lord's Supper.

Bethesda

> Now there is at Jerusalem by the sheep market a pool, which is called in the Hebrew tongue Bethesda, having five porches.
>
> John 5:2

The name *Bethesda* means *House of Mercy*.[4] This place had five porches and in Biblical numerology, five is the number of the *Grace*; this House is held together by the *Grace of God*. The *House of Mercy* is a place where we encounter God's *Grace*.

From the John 5 account, we are told that in Bethesda there was a seasonal stirring of the waters for people to encounter the healing power of God. The local church is a place where "the waters are stirred" (John 5:4), and we are able to receive healing in every area of our lives: physical, emotional and otherwise.

In a rich man's house, there are many seats. In God's house, there are also many seats, but where He chooses as His own seat is called the *Mercy Seat.* The Bible says that God is rich in mercy. So, in the *House of Mercy*, we encounter God in the richness of mercy that can only come from the One who sits on the Mercy Seat.

Bethel

After Jacob usurped the *Blessing* that should have belonged to Esau according to the natural order of seniority, he had to abruptly depart from his father's house to go live with his uncle, Laban. On his way, he got to a place at night and had to sleep. The following is part of the visual divine encounter that ensued by way of a dream that night:

> And he lighted upon a certain place, and tarried there all night, because the sun was set; and he took of the stones of that place, and put them for his pillows, and lay down in that place to sleep. And he dreamed, and behold a ladder set up on the earth, and the top of it reached to heaven: and behold the angels of God ascending and descending on it… And Jacob awaked out of his sleep, and he said, Surely the LORD is in this place; and I knew it not. And he was afraid, and said, How dreadful is this place! This is none other but **the house of God**, and **this is the gate of heaven.**
>
> Genesis 28:11-12 (Emphasis mine)

In Jacob's encounter with God in Bethel, he saw a ladder that had angels ascending and descending. This is a picture of the church; the gateway of heaven where spiritual activities take place.

A gateway is an opening for a gate or a portal that leads through a wall to go into a city. This place, which is a representation of the church, is the portal through which we access heaven. The church is the place of an open heaven when angels are going back and forth, between heaven and earth. The angels, in their ascension are likely transporting prayers to heaven and in their descent, are returning to earth with answers. It is a continuous cycle of ascending and descending of the mighty spiritual beings on a regular basis.

When Jacob woke up to realise that the vivid and remarkable spectacle he had just witnessed was a dream, he said "God is in this place;" not was, but is. The church is the place of God's abiding presence; a continual habitation, not just a visitation.

On Jacob's return journey back home after the death of his father, Isaac, he had another encounter with angels:

> Now as Jacob went on his way, the angels of God met him. Jacob said when he saw them, "This is God's camp." So he named that place Mahanaim.
>
> Genesis 32:1-2 (NASB)

Though not the name of a particular city, Jacob named a place after his encounter with angels, *Mahanaim*, which means *Two Camps.*[5] These two camps come together in a place, and this is the place where both angels and men fellowship; a place where men and angels interact:

> But ye are come unto mount Sion, and unto the city of the living God, the heavenly Jerusalem, and to an innumerable company of angels, To the general assembly and church of the firstborn, which are written in heaven, and to God the Judge of all, and to the spirits of just men made perfect, And to Jesus the mediator of the new covenant, and to the blood of sprinkling, that speaketh better things than that of Abel.
>
> Hebrews 12: 22-24

The local church is the earthly representation of the heavenly Jerusalem. God is in this place and, wherever the presence of God is, the angels of God love to abide. The Lord is there in His Glory; His blood is speaking great things for us. Little wonder Jacob said "how awesome is this place"! This is the place for the manifest presence of God.

The house of God is not built with mortar or bricks, or whatever your favoured building material is; it is constituted with people - men and women who have been purchased by the blood of Jesus Christ, the Lamb of God.

> **Ye also, as lively stones, are built up a spiritual house, an holy priesthood, to offer up spiritual sacrifices, acceptable to God by Jesus Christ.**
>
> 1 Peter 2:5 (Emphasis mine)

We are the materials (lively stones) by which the house is built and together we are the house Herself. We are a family of priests, and our primary job is to offer up spiritual sacrifices to the Monarch of the universe. A house is a place where a person or people dwell, and God is the One who dwells in this place. His eternal plan is to dwell among us. And as we offer spiritual sacrifices in His house, His presence is attracted to the house, because He dwells in the place where the sacrifice of praise is offered.

May we continue to have the presence of God in our churches, manifest and tangible; so palpable that we could touch it, smell it, and be transformed by it.

Releasing the Activity of Angels

Angels are spiritual beings that we believe to be God's messengers and servants in heaven. They are described as beings that are "mighty in strength, who perform His word, obeying the voice of His word!" (Psalm 103:20). Wherever God's word is honoured, there will be a strong activity of angels.

> The Angel of the Lord encamps around those who fear Him
> Psalm 34:7 (ESV)

The angels of God are assigned to minister to and for those who are heirs of salvation. Being an heir means that you're the recipient of an inheritance; and the assertion of this book has been that, as believers, we have inherited the *Blessing*. It is not something we are trying to obtain; we already have it. This book is about experiencing what we already have and walking in its fullness.

Angels exist to assist us in life; making sure that everything that God has given us for our journey of destiny is released to us. When Daniel fasted and prayed (Daniel 9) for the God's prophetic Word for Israel to manifest, an angel was sent to make sure that God's Word to the nation of Israel came to pass. As you align yourself with God's Will and Word, get ready for an increased activity of angels as you have never experienced.

Over the years, I have increasingly become aware of angelic presence in my life. In the year 2013, while speaking at a three-day church conference in Madrid, I noticed a lady who seemed to just gobble up everything I said. She seemed to receive my ministry better than everyone else. After the event, the pastor told me that as I got up to speak during the first session, God opened this woman's eyes to see that as I stood up to speak, an angel walked with me to the pulpit and stood behind me.

There are certain things that God wants to get to us through His holy angels. We release the workings of these spiritual beings by walking in the fear of the Lord.

There are dimensions of angelic assistance and activity that we may never understand until we get to the other side of eternity. What is more important is that we pay attention to the actions that cause the release of our advancement in the *Blessing* as revealed by His Word.

The Household of God

> I hope to come to you soon, but I am writing these things to you so that, if I delay, you may know how one ought to behave in **the household of God**, which is the church of the living God, a pillar and buttress of the truth.
>
> 1 Timothy 3:15 ESV (Emphasis mine)

In this house of God, we also have the household of God. A household represents the individuals in a family or other group that are living together in one house. In the local church we are part of the family of God in our locality. The church is about the Father and His family.

The household of God is also the pillar of truth. God has made the church responsible for bringing forth the truth of the gospel to the world. We have been called to defend the truth of God's word and His holiness. Also, we have been called to model the lifestyle of truth in a dying world. We are to "be blameless and innocent, children of God without blemish in the midst of a crooked and twisted generation, among whom you shine as lights in the world" (Philippians 2:15, ESV).

Bethshemesh

The name, *Bethshemesh*, means *House of the Sun*:[6]

> But unto you that fear my name shall the ***Sun of righteousness*** arise *with healing in his wings*; and ye shall *go forth*, and *grow up* as calves of the stall.
>
> Malachi 3:2 (Emphasis mine)

Green plants absorb light energy using chlorophyll in their leaves. They use the light to react carbon dioxide with water to make a sugar called glucose. The glucose is used in respiration, or converted into starch and stored. Oxygen is the by-product of this process.

This process is called *photosynthesis*. Temperature, carbon dioxide concentration and light intensity are factors that can limit the rate of photosynthesis. Photosynthesis is the chemical change that happens in the leaves of green plants. It is the first step towards making food; not just for plants, but ultimately every animal on the planet.

The Bible refers to us as *Trees of Righteousness*, the planting of the Lord. The key to our growth as believers is our exposure to the light of the *Sun of Righteousness*. Our growth is a function of the outflow of love, life and light from the throne of God. As we receive His divine energy from His marvellous light, a kind of spiritual photosynthesis takes place; we thereby grow while producing the essence by which we can become a *Blessing* to those in our sphere of interaction.

It is within the context of the church that we grow and mature into the men and women who God has designed us to be.

Those that be planted in the house of the LORD shall flourish in the courts of our God. They shall still bring forth fruit in old age; they shall be fat and flourishing;

Psalm 92:13-14

Bethsaida

The name Bethsaida means a *House of Fish* or *Fishing House*.[7] As Jesus began to preach in Galilee, He met a few men who were intrigued by His message. He then goes on to give them a new assignment:

And Jesus said unto them, Come ye after me, and I will make you to become fishers of men

Mark 1:17

Becoming fishers of men is symbolic for reaching the lost. The church is made up of a people who are followers of Christ; as followers of Christ, our mandate from Christ is to make other people His followers. As a type of Bethsaida, the church is a place where *fish* are caught and cleaned.

The priority of God is still souls. The Bible says that there is ecstatic rejoicing in heaven when one sinner becomes born again and is won for the Kingdom of God [(Luke 15:7). The church is a soul-winning station.

The disciples understood the concept of ecclesia clearly, and they must have received teaching during the 40 days while with the Lord on earth, subsequent to His resurrection.

The church started with 500 members, and then 120 received the Holy Ghost on the day of Pentecost. The very first post-resurrection evangelistic message brought in a harvest of 3,000 souls into the Kingdom. The new converts were added to the church. They might not have had buildings that held more than 8,000 people in one setting, but they were spread across different parts of the town.

We are all called to be fishers of men. The primary role of the church is to bring the lost into the Kingdom of God.

Bethany

Bethany was the abode of the friends of Jesus, Mary, Martha and Lazarus (the one that Jesus Christ raised from the dead). The name Bethany means *House of Affliction*.[8] We don't always like affliction but in every family there has to be some form of discipline.

Before I was afflicted I went astray: but now have I kept thy word.

Psalm 119:67

The writer of Psalm 119 depicts the importance and the result of discipline in his own life. There were times when he went astray, but the discipline of God brought him back to a place of holiness. Because we are children of God, we can expect some form of discipline when we step out of line.

And have you forgotten the exhortation that addresses you as sons? *"My son, do not regard lightly the discipline of the Lord, nor be weary when reproved by him.* **For the Lord disciplines the one he loves, and chastises every son whom he receives.** *"* It is for discipline that you have to endure. God is treating you as sons. For what son is there whom his father does not discipline? *If you are left without discipline, in which all have participated, then you are illegitimate children and not sons.* For the moment all *discipline seems painful rather than pleasant,* **but later it yields the peaceful fruit of righteousness** *to those who have been trained by it.*

Hebrews 12:5-8; 11 ESV (Emphasis mine)

We must understand that God's aim of disciplining His children is to forge His character in them. There was a scenario in the church at Corinth, where one of the church members was sleeping with his father's wife. Paul instructed that the offender be put out of the church and be delivered to satan for the buffeting of his body. The Bible does not explain how the dynamics of being delivered to satan works, but we are told what the effect of the action would be: that his spirit may be saved in the Day of the Lord Jesus. The salient truth revealed in this account is that the church is the only body that has the authority to carry out such a task.

The said offender showed remorse and he was reintegrated back into the fold:

> Now if anyone has caused pain, he has caused it not to me, but in some measure—not to put it too severely—to all of you. For such a one, this punishment by the majority is enough, so you should rather turn to forgive and comfort him, or he may be overwhelmed by excessive sorrow. So I beg you to reaffirm your love for him. For this is why I wrote, that I might test you and know whether you are obedient in everything. ...
>
> 2 Corinthians 2:5-11 (ESV)

The *Love of God* is the bedrock of His correction. Love that doesn't include correction is dangerous. Love can sometimes be stern; that is why we are to speak the truth in love. As the late Christian preacher and author, Jamie Buckingham, used to say, "The truth will set you free, but it will first make you miserable."

We see that some form of punishment was meted by the church to the person who was living disorderly. The church has the power to both correct and discipline errant believers, as well as the authority to reinstate them to their former positions over time. This is one of the duties of the New Testament church that may be lost in the modern-day church. If we must live as legitimate children of God, then we must be willing to subject ourselves to His system of discipline, so that it can yield in us the peaceful fruit of righteousness.

In His teaching about the Vine, Jesus said that the Father prunes every branch that bears fruit, so that it will bear more fruit (John 14:2). Pruning is translated from the Greek word *kathairo*, which means to cleanse of impurity. It also means to prune trees and vines from useless shoots. *Kathairo* finds its origins from the root word *Katharos*. *Katharos* indicates to make clean or pure; to be purified by fire; to be free from every admixture of what is false, so that we can become truly sincere or genuine.

Pruning is a horticultural practice that involves the selective removal of parts of a plant, such as the braches, buds or roots. Reasons to prune plants include removing deadwood, shaping, improving and maintaining health and healthy growth, and increasing the yield and quality of flowers and fruit.

Staying with our allegory of the believer being the planting of the Lord, God prunes us so that we can be healthy fruit-bearing believers. It gives the Father great delight when we increase our level of productivity and fruitfulness; therefore, as a skilled *Husbandman*, God prunes us, cutting things away from our lives that could hinder our spiritual growth and fruit-bearing. We easily understand that the pruning process doesn't always feel good.

The Lord's *pruning* does not necessarily happen because of the presence of sin in the life of the believer; it could simply be as a result of other encumbrances and weights (Hebrews 12:3). But the purpose is always greater fruitfulness.

The *Word of God* is the primary tool for our pruning. Jesus said that we are pruned and made clean by His Word (John 15:3). Moreover, one of the most common ways that God prunes us is to allow affliction and adversity into our lives. Adversity is the fire that removes the dross that could hinder our shining brighter as the Lord's silver. Adversity comes not to kill us, but to make us complete and entire; lacking nothing in any area of our lives (James 1:4).

Jerusalem

Melchizedek, the priest who blessed Abraham, is first introduced to us as the King of Salem, which is an early name for Jerusalem. The name *Melchizedek* also means *King of Righteousness*. Jesus Christ was qualified by God to be our High Priest and His designation as High Priest by God is said to be in the order of Melchizedek (Hebrews 5:9-10). Jesus, our kingly High Priest, was also made into our righteousness (1 Corinthians 1:30).

The name *Jerusalem* in Hebrew is *Y'ru-shah-lah-yim*. It is divided between two root words: *Yarah* and *Shalem*. *Yarah* means a dual (as an allusion to the two main hills on which Jerusalem sits). It also means to shoot, as an arrow; to point out (as if by aiming a finger); to teach. It also means to cast, direct, inform, instruct or show. The word *Shalem* means to be in a covenant of peace, be at peace, complete, safe, full, peaceable, perfect, quiet and whole. It also means to be complete, be finished, make safe, make whole or good, restore, or to make compensation.[9]

Combining *Yarah* and *Shalem* together, as the Hebrew words for Jerusalem, we have a picture of God's intention, His instructions and teaching to mankind. We could say the name Jerusalem means a revelation of our covenant of peace. It means the instruction that guarantees wholeness; that which makes complete; the teaching that restores.

The meaning of the name of Jerusalem reveals the actual nature and character of the *Kingdom of God*. Put all these words together, we see that God's motive or continual intention is for Jerusalem to be the place where He interacts with men in the ways that define its name. As a type of the church, Jerusalem is the place where all those words—within the meanings of its name—are manifested in the church, and in God's interaction with us and our extending the reality of the Kingdom to the rest of the world.

Jerusalem also means the *City of Peace* or the *Abode of Peace*. Paul exemplified that our justification by faith brings us into God's *City of Peace* (Romans 5:1). Being at peace with God means being in alignment with Him.

Jerusalem is described as the City of our God in the Psalms (Psalm 48:1, 8). Jerusalem has seven mountains, and mount Zion is the highest one among them. So the name Zion is often used interchangeably with Jerusalem. God has established His name in this city. Jerusalem and its people are called by the name of the Lord (Daniel 9:19).

Zion is called the *City of God*: "and they shall call you The City of the LORD, Zion of the Holy One of Israel" (Isaiah 60:14). It is where the Lord has chosen to dwell and will dwell again: "for the LORD dwells in Zion" (Joel 3:21). When the temple permanently replaced the tabernacle and was built in Jerusalem, it became the place of God's dwelling; His presence was there, thus named Zion.

In this dispensation, God no longer dwells in temples made out of stones, but in temples of human flesh. As we come together, we are the temple of God, both individually and collectively.

Psalm 46:4 talks about the river whose streams will make glad the *City of God*. The river of the water of life flows freely in this place; fertilising and yielding refreshment to the believers as they experience and enjoy it. This river of the Spirit is the source of our joy. This river flows into the church and through the church to bless the world.

The divine qualities of righteousness, peace and joy are understood to be resident in Jerusalem. Paul said that the Kingdom of God comprises righteousness, peace and joy in the Holy Ghost (Romans 14:17). The church is the place we are a shown how to come into alignment with God and be established in His Kingdom.

The Commanded Blessing

In Psalm 133, we see the concept of God commanding the Blessing on the congregation of Israel as they dwelt together. In the Bible, we see a great correlation between Israel in the Old Testament and the Church in the New Testament:

> Behold, how good and how pleasant it is for brethren to dwell together in unity! It is like the precious ointment upon the head, that ran down upon the beard, even Aaron's beard: that went down to the skirts of his garments; As the dew of Hermon, and as the dew that descended upon the mountains of Zion: **for there the LORD commanded the blessing, even life for evermore.**
>
> Psalms 133 (Emphasis mine)

The word command means to give a directive with specific authority, to give an order, or to ordain by divine act. It can also be defined as a decree issued by a sovereign authority. God is King and sovereign over the universe. He has commanded His Blessing to be somewhere, and "where the word of a king is, there is power; the king's authority is absolute; no one can say to him, 'what are you doing?'" (Ecclesiastes 6:4). When God delivers a command by the reason of the power in His Word, it is established.

According to the thinking in ancient times, gods dwelt in mountains with lush gardens. This was no different in Israel: God dwelt in the mountain of Zion (Joel 3:17). It was the place where God and man would interact. Symbolically, the mountains of Zion, as already stated elsewhere in this chapter, represents a type of the church.

In the same sense, many would think of the Church as the place where you meet God or where God is found. With Israel being a type of the Church, it is my firm belief that God has commanded His Blessing to be with the Church, and the primary way we encounter the commanded Blessing is through the agency of the local church.

The Commanded Blessing is Locational

More often than not, as we study the Bible, we find certain instances where God places His *Blessing* in particular places.

> For **there** the LORD *commanded the blessing*, even life for evermore.
> Psalm 133:6b (Emphasis mine)

God wants every believer to be part of the local church. Because the local church is God-ordained, God commands His Blessing there. You have to be plugged in to a local church. Being a part of a local church is one of the most important things you will do in life.

Finding a local church is not something that should be taken for granted. We must prayerfully consider the local church that we are planted in, as the local church to which one belongs, can, to a significant degree, decide the trajectory of his or her life. Look for your "company" and discover your local church family. There is a local church designed for you.

I know many people who God has spoken to, through dreams and visions, about the local church that they must join. Dreams and visons are not given to us for fun; they are given to us as a means of divine direction, so that we don't make grave destiny mistakes. (Job 33:14-18). One of the main reasons that the Lord will give you dreams and supernatural direction in choosing your local church is because it is the place of the commanded *Blessing*.

The Commanded Blessing is in Relationships

> Behold, how good and how pleasant it is for brethren to **dwell together** in unity!
> Psalm 133:1 (Emphasis mine)

In the local church we are a family. Not just members of the extended universal family of God, but a nuclear family that shares together and does life together. How we dwell together is also important. It is within the context of the church life that God wants us to forge our most important and strategic relationships. As a family, the local church is where we are groomed to be the people that we ought to be as society influencers. It is the place where we are equipped to fulfil individual and collective destinies.

The Lord, in His high priestly prayer in John 17, while praying for the unity of believers, ties this unity to the same type of oneness that He shares with the Father. Believers' relationship with one another has its foundation in the relational dynamics of the *Trinity*. This would mean that every individual in the church is as important as the next person, whether they occupy a more or less conspicuous role within it.

One of the purposes of the church is discipleship, and discipleship can only be effective within the context of relationships. This is why we must have relationships within the context of the church. This may not be a how-to book on church discipleship and relationships, as each church has its culture, but this is to highlight that we must be connected with each other to grow up to the full measure of the image of Christ.

When you buy products, they often come with the instruction, "some assembly required." For us to be effectively put together, some assembly is required. That is why we are not to "forsake the assembly of ourselves together... but exhorting one another..." (Hebrews 10:25).

The illustration conveyed in the scripture from Hebrews is that we may sometimes get discouraged and feel deserted because of life's trials; but the church is a place for us to be exhorted, comforted and reinvigorated by other saints. This will empower us for progress in life, while also inspiring us through the testimony of others. Invariably, we have victory even as we face life's battles.

We possess so much more power when we come together as the church. We need to know how to do relationships. We need to actively plug-in to the local church. We must treat each other with respect. As members of the same family, we must protect each other. Presently, we appear to live in a world that only knows how to relate through a machine; we may need to relearn how to speak to each other, not just through a text message or tweet, but face-to-face.

Paul reveals to us that we can't experience the fullness of all that God has for us apart from other believers (Ephesians 3:18). It is primarily within the local church that we can receive the spiritual substance that each joint supplies. I bring something to the table; the church janitor brings something to the table; the business committee leader brings her own supply as well. If you are not part of a local church, the supply you are supposed to bring for every part to work effectively will be lost. As we connect, we supply what we have and in our flowing, we receive what the other members have.

> From whom the whole body fitly joined together and compacted by that which every joint supplieth, according to the effectual working in the measure of every part, maketh increase of the body unto the edifying of itself in love.
>
> Ephesians 4:16

One of the most understated facts in the church today is what each individual member brings. The reason for poor church attendance can be traced to ignorance about how important a cog in the wheel of each part of the body is. I may be able to cope without my ears, but I would not want to. The church may seem to be coping fine without you, but the church could do so much better with the availability of your supply.

I've often heard people call the church a "bless me club." I used to have a problem with that term, thinking the church shouldn't be about the *Blessing*. However, I've come to the understanding that the church truly **is** a "bless me club." It is not only a "bless me club," it's also an "I bless you club," too. We bless each other in this place. We are a part of the local church to be a blessing to each other.

As earlier emphasised, the *Blessing* is a matter of spiritual growth and can only effectively grow spiritually in the context of relationships.

Discerning the Lord's body

How we treat each other in the Church is of utmost importance to God. After your relationship with the Lord and, subsequently, your spouse and children if applicable, your next most important relationship is your relationship with the church; with people in the body of Christ especially your own local church. Paul said that particular members of the church were weak, sick or even prematurely deceased because they did not discern the Lord's body (1 Corinthians 11:29).

We can look at discerning the Lord's body from two perspectives. Every believer has discerned the Lord's blood; this was how they became "saved"; but, for their healing, they need to discern the Lord's body, because it was in His body that He was bruised for our iniquities (Isaiah 53:5) and by His stripes we were healed (1 Peter 2:24). However, within the context of the text and the church, discerning the Lord's body means treating members of the Body of Christ with utmost respect and love.

How you relate with your church members and fellow Christians is something that has the Lord's attention. He taught that whatever we do to them is done to Him. When we don't realise that the people we relate to in the Church are part of the *Body* and, if treated shabbily, could earn us being cut off from the Divine supply that God has designed to come to us from other members of the Body.

We can walk in the fullness of the *Blessing* by honouring our relationships within the Body of Christ or we can limit our experience of the *Blessing* by our poor attitudes projected towards other believers. The choice is ours.

The Commanded Blessing is in Leadership

Jesus is the Chief Shepherd of the Church, but He has given us people who are graced with the fivefold-ministry gifts (Ephesians 4:8-12) as His representative shepherds. Primarily, the pastor is the one who stands in the Lord's office as the under-shepherd of the sheep.

God promised to give us pastors after His heart and their purpose is to feed us with knowledge and understanding (Jeremiah 3:15). I mentioned about the *Blessing* being a matter of eating, and if the Pastor's job description is to feed you, then there is a part of your walking in the *Fullness of the Blessing* that is connected to your pastor and the leadership of your local assembly.

According to God's divine order, the *Blessing* flows from the head down not the feet up:

> *It is like the precious ointment upon the head, that ran down upon the beard,* even Aaron's beard: that went down to the skirts of his garments;
>
> Psalm 133:2 (Emphasis mine)

The direction of the flow of oil was not from Aaron's skirts to his head, but from his head down to his beards, then to his vest and skirts and everywhere else. God sets men and women in leadership positions in the church, so that the oil will flow from the 'head' down to other 'parts' of the assembly.

In the Bible, an army is used as an analogy for the church. In every army, there is hierarchy and leadership. Instruction is passed from the leader to his fellow subordinate soldiers. In the same way, the local church has constituted authority:

> And he gave some, apostles; and some, prophets; and some, evangelists; and some, pastors and teachers; For the perfecting of the saints, for the work of the ministry, for the edifying of the body of Christ
>
> Ephesians 4:11-12

The constituted authority in the church was established by the Lord Himself. The commanded *Blessing* of the Lord is in His instituted church leadership. It is the Lord who has set ministry gifts in the church.

> Pay careful attention to yourselves and to all the flock, in which the Holy Spirit has made you overseers, to care for the church of God, which he obtained with his own blood.
>
> Acts 20:28 (ESV)

It is God who designates overseers over His flock. He is the One who sets people over congregations (Numbers 27:16). We must come to the realisation of that fact and align ourselves accordingly.

There is so much that God wants to get through to us by means of spiritual authority that he has instituted in the church, but sometimes we make the mistake of seeing them as mere men. People who are more at risk of not receiving the *Blessing* from leaders in church include their spouses, children, family members and friends. They know the person's past or present limitations, so they do not position themselves to receive and come under his authority as the man of God.

A person who obviously understood the concept of coming under authority was the centurion whose servant Jesus healed (Matthew 8:7-10). Jesus called his expression of faith great faith. There are many things that we can say about this passage, but for our purposes, the man referred to himself as one under authority, who knew how the dynamics of authority worked. **We cannot exercise authority in spiritual warfare if we are not a people under spiritual authority.**

The place of subjection to authority is the place of protection. It is the *Blessed* place. The Lord sometimes cannot speak to our situations because we are not under authority.

Because of purpose, God has given gifts to particular individuals in the church, who are dispensers of His blessing as the "better" among us. Since the less is blessed by the better, the *Blessing* that comes from the local church will come on us as we position ourselves aright with constituted authority.

The Commanded Blessing comes by Impartation

As the dew of Hermon, and as the dew that descended upon the mountains of Zion:

Psalm 133:3a

Outside of our devotional life, the local church is the primary place where we are imparted with God's power and anointing to influence our world and reach others for Christ. Let us look at the three primary ways by which we receive impartation in the context of the church.

The Means of Impartation

By Preaching

God has chosen to use the act of preaching as the medium through which He saves us. Jesus said the words that He speaks are spirit and life. As with Jesus, every sent one impacts their hearing audience by the words which they speak. As you worship and receive the word at church, it is not a time for jokes, because serious business is taking place. We can prayerfully receive the blessing impartation every time the word is spoken at our local church.

Job referred to his speech "dropping upon" his hearers like rain "and they opened their mouth wide as for the latter rain" (Job 29:16). It has been my practice for years, every time I am sitting under an anointed word ministry, to open up myself to receive what is being released by praying in the spirit. It is a spirit-to-spirit connection, similar to mouth-to-mouth resuscitation. We ought to metaphorically step up a notch in the *Blessing* after every church service.

I hope your eyes are being opened to see what you may have been overlooking regarding your regular Sunday or weekly visits to fellowship.

This is one reason that a casual attendance to church service will not get the job done.

> My doctrine shall drop as the rain, my speech shall distil as the dew, as the small rain upon the tender herb, and as the showers upon the grass
>
> Deuteronomy 32:2

In the above verse, Moses, the man of God, said that when he opened his mouth to speak, his doctrine poured down as rain upon his hearers. Putting this into context, rain comes down to the earth to water it, so that new life may grow and old life is sustained and enabled to thrive. The anointed teaching and preaching of the Word drops like dew and rain, and without these, a land becomes affected by drought; it will become parched and dry, yielding no growth. The significance, and indeed the importance, of preaching the anointed *Word of God* cannot be overstated.

> While Peter yet spake these words, the Holy Ghost fell on all them which heard the word.
>
> Acts 10:44

Though this wasn't a local church setting, we see the same principle at work. The Holy Ghost fell on them as Peter was preaching. When the *Word of God* is preached at church, the spirit of life is ministered unto us. A distribution of the *Life of God* takes place by His Spirit as an operation of God.

Something happens when God speaks through a man of God. When an anointed man of God releases words from God's heart, he is releasing the same power that emerges from where the word originated; thus, the water flows from the Throne of Grace. Words from the throne carry the *Water of Life*. This is one reason why it is vital to pray for the man of God to receive utterance (Ephesians 6:19). Utterance comes from the Spirit of God, as well as through God's word, in the mouth of the spirit-filled believer, or in this case, the mouth of the man of God.

> For as the rain cometh down, and the snow from heaven, and returneth not thither, but watereth the earth, and maketh it bring forth and bud, that it may give seed to the sower, and bread to the eater: So shall my word be that goeth forth out of my mouth: it shall not return unto me void, but it

shall accomplish that which I please, and it shall prosper in the thing whereto I sent it.

Isaiah 55:10-11

As God's *Word* from His mouth drops down like rain, so shall the *Word* from the mouth of His servant. It is like the release of rain and it goes out to fulfil its purpose. The end result of the release of the *Word of God* on Sundays or whenever believers are assembled is not just for us to get a "feel-good" preach, but for us to be empowered by the *Blessing* and make an impact in our world.

By the Laying on of Hands

Another way that the *Blessing* is released is by the *laying on of hands*. The laying on of hands is one of the foundational doctrines of the church:

Therefore leaving the principles of the doctrine of Christ, let us go on unto perfection; not laying again the foundation of repentance from dead works, and of faith toward God, Of the doctrine of baptisms, and of laying on of hands...

Hebrews 6:1-2

But beyond being a foundational doctrine of the church, it is one of the ways that the *Blessing* is released within the context of the church.

One day some parents brought their little children **to Jesus so he could touch and bless them**. But when the disciples saw this, they scolded the parents for bothering him

Luke 18:15 NLT (Emphasis mine)

The parents knew the power of laying on of hands to release a blessing, so they brought their children to Jesus that He might touch them and *Bless* them. We received the *Blessing*, especially in the context of the local church by the laying on of hands by the pastors and elders.

And Joshua the son of Nun was full of the spirit of wisdom; for Moses had laid his hands upon him: and the children of Israel hearkened unto him, and did as the Lord commanded Moses.

Deuteronomy 34:9

Joshua received an impartation of wisdom from Moses by the laying on of hands. The laying on of hands is not limited to church ordination services, or for ministering to the sick; it is one of the primary ways by which the *Blessing* is released from the leadership of the local church.

By Declaration

Words spoken over the congregation are not constrained to those said in prayer. In the Old Testament, God instructed Moses to tell Aaron to speak a *Blessing* over the children of Israel. This is an example of the commanded *Blessing* being invoked over a people from the set man in a local assembly:

> And the LORD spake unto Moses, saying, Speak unto Aaron and unto his sons, saying, On this wise *ye shall bless the children of Israel, saying unto them*, The LORD bless thee, and keep thee: The LORD lift up his countenance upon thee, and give thee peace. And they shall put my name upon the children of Israel; and I will bless them.
>
> Numbers 6:22-27 (Emphasis mine)

We see God's pattern of establishing the *Blessing* on His chosen people by His constituted spiritual leadership speaking the *Blessing* on them. If we employ the Hebrew concrete thinking to elucidate the Aaronic Blessing, we see something very beautiful. Like we've already seen, the Hebrew word for *bless* is *barak*, which literally means "to kneel." A *berakah* is a *blessing*, which is the bringing of a gift to another "on bended knee." A good church leader is one who will wholeheartedly serve his people by the Word and Spirit to the effect that they will be established in the *Blessing*.

The illustration of the *Blessing* that God commanded Aaron to speak over the children of Israel, and by default, believers, is that, "The Lord will kneel before you presenting the gift of His Presence to you and by His glorious Light He will illuminate the fullness of his being toward you bringing order and he will beautify you." The word for peace means unhewn, uncut, which means that "by His Light, He will look upon you with His favour and cause you to be whole and complete." By declaring words of *Blessing* over a people, God's name is being placed on them and they will be established in the *Blessing*.

251

Through the Church

In this dispensation, God only has one plan with which He wants to transform the world: the church. With no alternative, we must get it line with what he is doing and that plan. The local church is the last bastion of hope for the world. Outside of the church, God doesn't have another avenue to reach the world.

It is through the local church that God wants to touch our communities

> [The purpose is] that through the church the complicated, many-sided wisdom of God in all its infinite variety and innumerable aspects might now be made known to the angelic rulers and authorities (principalities and powers) in the heavenly sphere.
>
> Ephesians 3:10 (AMP)

The purpose of the church is to manifest God's glory by declaring His multifaceted wisdom to the universe. This is in line with His eternal purpose! God's plan for the church is the great secret hidden, revealed by the Apostle Paul. This lifespan of this plan began before the foundation of the world; it is an eternal plan. The church is primarily the place on earth where, and through, God designed to ultimately reveal and give the world full disclosure of Himself.

As we individually bring our supply, collectively as the local church, we will flow into our communities and cities. When each locality produces their supply, then our nations will be drenched by what flows from our churches. This is what the prophet Joel meant when he spoke God's mind saying:

> And it shall come to pass afterward, that I will pour out my spirit upon all flesh:
>
> Joel 2:28a

We've been poured into, so that we can pour out. In church, we seem to have made it a habit of asking God for an outpouring. What God desires us to be hooked up to heaven's invisible supply of *Living Water* from the Spirit of God to our spirits. It is this pouring out from the *Throne of God*, from which we've received from the *Presence of God*, will be poured out on all flesh; this is the outpouring spoken of by Prophet Joel. At the birth of the church, in Acts of the Apostles, Peter said "this is the beginning of that which was spoken by the Prophet Joel." That which began in 29AD, will reach its crescendo just before the Lord returns.

All flesh means all flesh. The world will experience a global outpouring as each local church pours out what God has given them in their localities. As much as I celebrate individual ministries, God's desire is that through the local church, the world will come to know and experience His *Blessing*.

For as the waters fill the sea, the earth will be filled with an awareness of the glory of the LORD.

Habakkuk 2:14 (NLT)

The earth will be covered by the overflow of glory from the flow of the local churches around the world. The essence of the *Blessing*, is the *Glory* of the Lord. **Let's let it flow.**

Walking in Unity

If we must see change in our cities, we cannot work in isolation with each other. Whilst every local church should have their defining vision, we all have one uniting vision, and the vision is to see our cities transformed by the *Power of God* in our generation.

I usually joke that there is only one denomination that was mentioned in the Bible and that is the Baptist; John, he was Baptist. But on a serious note, there is only one Church. The one bought by Jesus' blood and birthed on Calvary by blood and by water. There must come a time when we put our own programmes aside and come together under one umbrella to fulfil God's agenda. We must ignore the non-essentials that divide us, and bring ourselves into line with what unites us. We all agree on one thing: that Jesus is the only way of salvation.

There is a scenario in the Book of Judges where Samson wanted to burn a large farmland that belonged to the Philistines. He caught 300 Foxes and had their tails tied together in pairs, then he fastened a torch between their tails.

And when he had set the brands on fire, he let them go into the standing corn of the Philistines, and burnt up both the shocks, and also the standing corn, with the vineyards and olives.

Judges 15:5

There are things that the enemy has set up that just one local church may not be able destroy. It will take a massive united front as the Body of Christ in our various cities to come under that one banner, where we all declare that Jesus is Lord. One fox could run away, but when they were tied together, they all ran united in the same direction. They had to have the same vision, which was to take the fire into the bush. As our tails are tied together and we spend time together praying, we will experience genuine revival.

In closing, staying with our water analogy, each local church has a part to play in releasing their river. As we all operate in the *Fullness of the Blessing*, the river of God will flow from our individual churches. As these rivers begin to flow from all directions into our cities from our various locations, there will be a deluge of revival in our nations that cannot be contained. As our cities become submerged in the River of God's Love; this deluge of revival will push back the forces of evil, and our cities will become transformed by the *Power of the Blessing*.

EPILOGUE

When you turn your television on or browse the Internet for the latest news, a casual observation reveals so much disaster and pain in the world. Many people are hurting and communities are in crisis. We often, in Christian circles, organise prayer meetings to call on the Lord to step into the situation and bring about miraculous change and transformation to our cities and nations. We are in perplexing and bewildering times; and, yes, we need to seek the face of God for His intervention. But more than that, we need to take action. As the old Quakers used to say, "when you pray, move your feet."

This reminds me of the account where Jesus fed the multitude—about 5000 men, not counting the women and children—by the miracle of multiplying five loaves of bread and two fish. When the disciples approached him in the wilderness because the people had been there for three days and were now very hungry, Jesus instructed the disciples to "give them something to eat." While they were "praying to Him" to do something about the situation—the disciples would have preferred Jesus to send the crowd away—He differed with them on the solution. He expected them to quit trying to get Him to do something and take action themselves.[1] It is high time that we realise that we've been given the Power of Attorney, as vice-regents for the Lord on the earth, to provide answers to the questions in our world.

Blessed to be a Blessing

In our initial introduction to God in the Book of Genesis, we see a *Person* who is the *Creator*. Not only that, we are also introduced to the *Problem Solver*. As people who bear His DNA, we have become co-creators with Him on our planet and have also been made *problem solvers*.

When Abraham encountered the Lord, part of the *Blessing Declaration* that he received was that he would be *Blessed* to be a *Blessing*. The word *Blessing* referenced in that encounter comes the Hebrew root word that means *gift*. God has made us gifts to our generation. You should look at yourself in the mirror every morning and say that you are a gift to your generation; a blessing going somewhere to happen and a problem solver.

The Lord, in one of his usual pronouncements against the Pharisees, highlighted the importance of *Justice* and *Mercy*. Jesus called *Justice* and *Mercy*, along with *Faith*, the weightier matters of the Law.[2] Yes, God has called us to go into the world and preach the gospel to every creature and make disciples. He has also called us to carry out projects of justice, actions of mercy, and advocacy for faith-filled transactions to occur within our societies.

We live in a world that is bent out of shape, and we have been given the accountability to reshape it. In Psalm 82:5, the children of the Most High were described as gods on the earth. The word *god*, when viewed in this context, means *judge*. A judge is someone who ensures that justice is established on the earth. As *gods* on the earth, we've been called to establish justice in places where chaos and lawlessness prevail. There are many issues bedevilling our planet today, from child pornography, sex tourism and child trafficking, to modern slavery, racism, and poverty, just to name a few. Someone has to be a voice to the voiceless; a help to the ones whose lives and communities would remain in disaster otherwise.

As I write, I am reminded of one of the heroines of Christianity in Nigeria, Mary Slessor. From what I learnt in my Social Studies class in year four, she stopped the killing of twins in the City of Calabar, in the South-eastern Delta of Nigeria in the 19th Century; or, William Wilberforce, whose work as a Christian parliamentarian in the British Parliament led to the abolition of slavery in the 18th Century.

I am very aware that there are many justice and mercy projects in implementation throughout the world today that are sponsored by churches, non-governmental organisations, and individuals; but we need to do more and give more to these projects because truth be told, that is why we are in the *Kingdom*. We are the ones with the solution to bring God's Kingdom on earth and cause "His will to be done on earth as it is in Heaven."

While the government does its job, we will have to find ways to collaborate on repairing broken educational systems, mental health care, and to assist people living with disabilities. If you see something that riles you up enough to make you lose sleep and forget to eat dinner, you may just have been called to change it. In several places where we live and in the various sectors of life, we have been positioned as change agents for our kingdom.

We need more Christians in parliament, business, education, and civil and social services to invade and influence the world with the power of the *Blessing*. We may not be able solve all the problems in the world, but we can contribute to make the difference in the assignments for which we've been tasked. If we all contributed our quota, there would be less to complain about.

When Peter and John met the man at the gate called Beautiful, they told him to focus on them. Their popular statement, "such as I have, give I unto you" was an indication that they were without an iota of doubt that they possessed the solution to his plight.[3] My desire and prayer is that we become fully persuaded that we are the ones with the solution to the crises in the world. We carry the substance of Heaven with which we will bring God's solutions to man's plight wherever we are. You are a problem solver; it is now your call. Let us give our lives to that for which we were given life. Go in this thy might: the might of **The Blessing!**

NOTES

Chapter 1: The Blessing of the Lord

1. Millard J Erickson; Christian Theology: 2nd Edition. (Baker Academic, Grand Rapids), 1998.
2. Ibid.
3. Ben Witherington; Revelation: The New Cambridge Bible Commentary (Cambridge University Press, New York), 2002.
4. Terry Crist; The Image Maker (Creation House, Lake Mary), 2000.

Chapter 2: Blessed

1. The Septuagint from the Latin word septuaginta (meaning seventy), is a translation of the Hebrew Bible and some related texts into Koine Greek. The title and its Roman numeral acronym LXX refer to the legendary seventy Jewish scholars who solely translated the Five Books of Moses as early as the 3rd century BCE.

Chapter 3: The Anatomy of the Blessing

1. Roberts Liardon; God's Generals: Why They Succeeded And Why Some Failed (Whitaker House, New Kensington), 1996.
2. James Strong; Strong's Exhaustive Concordance of the Bible; (Hendrickson Publishers Marketing LLC, Peabody), 2007.

Chapter 4: Curses and Causes

1. Merriam-Webster Dictionary.
2. Tokunboh Adeyemo, Is Africa Cursed? A vision for the Radical Transformation of an Ailing Continent, Nairobi, WordAlive, 2009.
3. James Strong; Strong's Exhaustive Concordance of the Bible; (Hendrickson Publishers Marketing LLC, Peabody), 2007.
4. W E Vine; Vine's Expository Dictionary of New Testament words; (Thomas Nelson Inc., Nashville, Tennessee), 1997.
5. Ecclesiastes 10:8b.

Chapter 5: Breaking Barreness

1. James Strong; Strong's Exhaustive Concordance of the Bible; (Hendrickson Publishers Marketing LLC, Peabody), 2007.
2. Ibid.
3. Ibid.
4. Ibid.
5. Ibid.
6. W E Vine; Vine's Expository Dictionary of New Testament words; (Thomas Nelson Inc., Nashville, Tennessee), 1997.
7. Ibid.
8. Ibid.

Chapter 6: Maintain the Union

1. Romans 8:17.
2. W E Vine; Vine's Expository Dictionary of New Testament words; (Thomas Nelson Inc., Nashville, Tennessee), 1997.

Chapter 7: Faith in the Blessing

1. W E Vine; Vine's Expository Dictionary of New Testament words; (Thomas Nelson Inc., Nashville, Tennessee), 1997.
2. Priscilla Jane Owens and William James Kirkpatrick; "Will Your Anchor Hold"; Church Hymnary, 4th Ed. (Canterbury Press, Norwich UK), 2005.
3. W E Vine; Vine's Expository Dictionary of New Testament words; (Thomas Nelson Inc., Nashville, Tennessee), 1997.
4. Collins English Dictionary - Complete & Unabridged 2012 Digital Edition.
5. James Strong; Strong's Exhaustive Concordance of the Bible; (Hendrickson Publishers Marketing LLC, Peabody), 2007.
6. Ibid.

7. James Strong; Strong's Exhaustive Concordance of the Bible; (Hendrickson Publishers Marketing LLC, Peabody), 2007.
8. Watchman Nee; Sit, Walk, Stand; CLC Publications.
9. James Strong; Strong's Exhaustive Concordance of the Bible; (Hendrickson Publishers Marketing LLC, Peabody), 2007.
10. The original Greek rendition of the phrase "have faith in God" from Mark 11:22.
11. James Strong; Strong's Exhaustive Concordance of the Bible; (Hendrickson Publishers Marketing LLC, Peabody), 2007.

Chapter 8: The Commandment
1. W E Vine; Vine's Expository Dictionary of New Testament words; (Thomas Nelson Inc., Nashville, Tennessee), 1997.
2. Ibid.
3. http://edition.cnn.com/2011/HEALTH/08/17/bitter.resentful.ep/
4. James Strong; Strong's Exhaustive Concordance of the Bible; (Hendrickson Publishers Marketing LLC, Peabody), 2007.

Chapter 9: The Honour Principle
1. Ruth Paxson; Life on the Highest Plane; (Moody Bible Institute, Chicago), 1928.
2. Millard J Erickson; Christian Theology: 2nd Edition. (Baker Academic, Grand Rapids), 1998
3. James Strong; Strong's Exhaustive Concordance of the Bible; (Hendrickson Publishers Marketing LLC, Peabody), 2007.
4. Ibid.
5. Ibid.
6. Ibid.
7. N T Wright; Virtue Reborn; (Society for Promoting Christian Knowledge Publishing, London), 2010.
8. Joseph S. Exell and Henry Donald Maurice Spence-Jones; The Pulpit Commentary; (Nabu Press), 2011.
9. W E Vine; Vine's Expository Dictionary of New Testament words; (Thomas Nelson Inc., Nashville, Tennessee), 1997.
10. James Strong; Strong's Exhaustive Concordance of the Bible; (Hendrickson Publishers Marketing LLC, Peabody), 2007.
11. Collins English Dictionary - Complete & Unabridged 2012 Digital Edition© William Collins Sons & Co. Ltd. 1979, 1986 © HarperCollins.

Chapter 10: Spirit Food
1. Campbell McAlpine; The Practice of Biblical meditation; Sovereign World; 2002.
2. James Strong; Strong's Exhaustive Concordance of the Bible; (Hendrickson Publishers Marketing. LLC, Peabody), 2007.
3. Exodus 12:1-13.

Chapter 11: The Overflow
1. Psalm 42:7; Aramaic Bible in Plain English.
2. Ever Increasing Faith; Smith Wigglesworth.
3. Nehemiah 8:10.

Chapter 12: The Assembly
1. E Vine; Vine's Expository Dictionary of New Testament words; (Thomas Nelson Inc., Nashville, Tennessee), 1997.
2. John Gill; John Gill's Exposition of the Entire Bible; (Amazon Digital Services, Inc).
3. Ibid.
4. Ibid.
5. James Strong; Strong's Exhaustive Concordance of the Bible; (Hendrickson Publishers Marketing LLC, Peabody), 2007.
6. Ibid.
7. Ibid.
8. Ibid.
9. James Strong; Strong's Exhaustive Concordance of the Bible; (Hendrickson Publishers Marketing LLC, Peabody), 2007.

Epilogue
1. Matthew 14:13-21.
2. Matthew 23:23.
3. Acts 3:1-10.

ABOUT THE AUTHOR

Rotimi Kaleb is an inspirational Bible teacher and revivalist. He holds a master's degree from the University of Buckingham in the United Kingdom, and he also studied for an M.A. in Christian Faith and Practice at Spurgeons Evangelical Christian Theological College in London, England. He has a mandate to take the message and the spirit of faith, and share the truth about who the Believer is in Christ, across the world. He has traveled to many nations sharing God's Word, praying for the sick and taking the Power of the Holy Spirit. He is married and resides in London, England with his family.

rotimikaleb.com